THE ESSENTIAL DIGITAL VIDEO HANDBOOK

A COMPREHENSIVE GUIDE TO MAKING VIDEOS THAT MAKE MONEY

PETE MAY

First published in the United States of America by
Rockport Publishers, Inc.
33 Commercial Street
Gloucester, Massachusetts 01930-5089
Telephone: (978) 282-9590
Fax: (978) 283-2742
www.rockpub.com

ISBN 1-59253-024-9

First published in the UK by
RotoVision SA
Route Suisse 9
CH-1295 Mies
Switzerland

RotoVision SA
Sales, Editorial, and Production Office
Sheridan House
112–116a Western Road
Hove BN3 1DD, UK
Telephone: +44 (0) 1273 72 72 68
Facsimile: +44 (0)1273 72 72 69
Email: sales@rotovision.com
Website: www.rotovision.com

10 9 8 7 6 5 4 3 2 1

Design: Jerrod Janakus
Production Design: *tabula rasa* graphic design
Cover image: Pete May
Copy editor: Charlie White
Proofreader: Ron Hampton

Printed in China

THE ESSENTIAL DIGITAL VIDEO HANDBOOK

RotoVision

This book is dedicated to my wife Ruthie, who has been in the business for as long as I have, loved me all those years, and helped keep this book on track through some very difficult times, even to the extent of authoring four topics herself. Thank you.

To my parents, Mary and Pete May, who are everything to me parents can and should be, including fun.

To my mother-in-law, Athleen Haas, who has shown me how to live gently and intently.

To my circle of friends.

I'm very lucky.

Contents

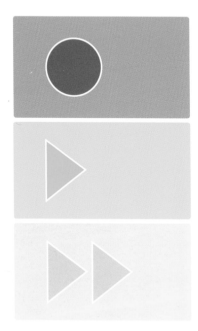

Introduction

Dr. Philo T. Farnsworth

In 1957, *I've Got a Secret* host Gary Moore called the game short when he realized his panel of celebrities was way off the mark. He decided to reveal his guest's secret. The gentleman sitting next to him, Philo T. Farnsworth had, at age 14, invented "electronic television."

Remember that: Philo T. Farnsworth, age 14. It's good TV trivia.

After the applause and I-should-have-guessed-it nods from the panel, the host asked Dr. Farnsworth what he saw in television's future. On that show in '57 Dr. Farnsworth spoke of flat panel displays and forecast the coming of high-definition television. A half-century later, we've got flat panels and high-definition standards (though not as refined as Farnsworth predicted). However, something Dr. Farnsworth hadn't imagined has happened as well. The tools required to make television programs have fallen into the hands of the audience!

Not too long ago, television professionals divided video into two domains, broadcast quality and everything else. Broadcast quality took money—hundreds of thousands, even millions of dollars! Broadcast called for big, expensive cameras on Volkswagen-sized pedestals rolling around cavernous, brilliantly lit studios. Even when video broke out of the studios and became mobile, the cameras were simply scaled down versions of their studio-city parents, smaller but hardly less expensive.

The shrine of broadcast quality was first assaulted by shows such as *America's Funniest Home Videos*. Broadcast engineers scoffed, but within a decade reality shows of all kinds elbowed into the listings. Their success proved people would forgive technical imperfection as long as the content was engaging and the walls came tumbling down...but the engineers still scoffed.

Finally, the gap has closed. Thanks to the introduction of a handful of digital video formats, the average person can afford a broadcast-quality camera and edit package. That's what brings you and me together here today. You can access the equipment to do broadcast-quality work in the technical sense of the word. I have the information you need to help you do broadcast-quality work in the aesthetic sense of the word, no matter who your audience is—family or clients.

At the age of 14, Philo T. Farnsworth invented the electronic television.

Having worked in the business of TV through the better part of the portable revolution and now the digital revolution, I want to share with you the wonder and excitement I feel today. There has never been a better time to be in this business. Say it just that way to many of my colleagues and you'll get this argument: Advertising dollars haven't expanded at pace with the number of advertising venues. Where once the three dominant TV networks and six national magazines gobbled a lion's share of the national advertising pie, it's now being split between broadcast networks, cable networks, Web advertisers, and special-interest magazines and the poor content producers are getting fed smaller and smaller pieces of an all too tiny pie! That's just plain shortsighted. It's true there won't be as many million-dollar production houses working multimillion-dollar accounts, but there will be something better. There will be opportunities-a-plenty for the media producers who have the skills—planning, scripting, shooting, and editing—to do it all. The reason is that, just as the means of production have fallen into the hands of the audience, so has the means of distribution. Today, mom and pop software developers can market, sell, and deliver their products over the Web. Video programming is tomorrow's software. For the first time in video history, programs won't be required to appeal to everyone to justify their production. It is now possible for producers to serve narrowly defined audiences. In this age of narrowcasting and video on demand, both field hockey enthusiasts and Barbie collectors will be able to indulge their particular interests through highly targeted programming. Given this level of demographic targeting, advertisers with their wallets at the ready won't be far behind. Read this book. Learn the skills—planning, scripting, shooting, and editing—and you'll be well on your way to profiting from the next wave of the revolution.

In Praise of the Accomplished Amateur

In 1947, Kenny's dad was the engineer on a Burlington Northern run between the port of Milwaukee and northern Illinois mining country. He often took Kenny and his brother along for the ride. I never met Kenny's brother. I don't know his name. I do know he shot 16 mm film with a windup Bell & Howell left over from World War II. That particular model was about as point-and-shoot as you can get, but in the hands of an operator with a good eye, it was magic. More than a half-century later, Kenny's dad was long gone and Kenny's brother was about to follow. Kenny lived next door to us and, knowing I worked in TV, figured I might be able to get some of his brother's old films transferred to home video. He gave me $40 to cover the transfer and as a thank-you. I never told him it cost me $400. There in our darkened living room, sixty years after that bright winter afternoon, Kenny's dad rode again. The footage was brilliant, the hulking train cutting black shadows from the cold blue sky. Now, I'll grant that Kenny might have been just as emotional if the pictures had been shaky or blurred or overexposed. I am equally convinced I wouldn't have been so affected if Kenny's brother hadn't told the story so well.

I saw a lot of old footage that day. His brother had spent a decade knocking around the Pacific Northwest, the old Bell & Howell always at his side. For years after he returned, he entertained family and friends talking over reel after reel of documentary stock—Klinket Indians drying seal pelts, crews wrestling the Alaska highway from stubborn forests, and of course, many, many passing trains.

I left the lights out even after the transfer finished to give Kenny some time to recover. Between staccato breaths, he stated the obvious. "My brother sure could shoot."

From that afternoon I took this away: Documenting the lives and travels of family and friends is a noble tribute to our time on this stage, a meaningful gift to all generations, worth doing and doing well.

Turning Professional

Shoot a little video and you're immediately inviting comparison to the best in the business. Exposed to network TV daily, even the most casual viewer recognizes the difference between home movies and professional production. The bar is set high but it's not out of reach. My goal is to boost you up and over. I want to turn, "Good for a home video," into "Good, period." I want to help hobbyists achieve professional results. I want to help

With a scripted single-camera shoot, you have more control over what happens and when.

With an unscripted single-camera shoot, you'll have to go with the flow.

aspiring professionals get into the business and young professionals get better. All these aspirations, yours and mine, are within reach.

The subject of video production is worthy of many more pages and considerably more depth than this book will allow. In deciding what made it in and what didn't, I was forced to make assumptions. I figure as long as you know what I'm assuming, we'll do fine. First, I assume that you've read all your manuals. I'll get into the finer points of setting exposures, but if I say, "turn the auto iris off," I expect you to figure out how. I also assume you're excited enough about the subject of video production to practice.

I'm assuming when I talk about DV you understand that DV simply means "digital video." Ninety-nine percent of the principles I express will carry over, whether you're planning on shooting Digital8, DVCAM, DVCPRO 25, or DVCPRO 50, all of which are digital video formats. Personally, I like basic DV. I like the resolution, the compression, the cassette size, and the fact that most consumer/prosumer cameras sold today are DV.

I'm going to cover two common categories of production. First, here's the scripted single-camera shoot. A writer pens, "EXT, evening, JOGGER witnesses accident, calls PARAMEDICS, helps VICTIMS." Someone finds a location, rounds up an ambulance, actors learn their lines, lights are set, the camera and microphones are placed, the director yells, "Action!" and the scene is recorded. Movies mostly fit this mold, many industrial projects do as well. Since we're talking about video production, this style is sometimes called single camera EFP or electronic field production.

The second category is the unscripted single-camera shoot. TV news, sometimes called ENG or electronic news gathering, can be described this way. A reporter and photographer are given a location and some contact names. Interviews and cover footage are shot. Nothing is scripted until after the story elements are gathered. Documentaries fit this mold. In the category of documentaries, I would include home video. There is little difference in approach between a news organization covering a protest, a documentarian examining vanishing wetlands, and a home video enthusiast at a niece's birthday party. Event coverage such as small weddings and business meetings, family reunions, and speeches might also fit the unscripted single-camera category.

As I begin to lay out the basics of shooting and editing I'm not going to excuse the documentarians or aspiring movie directors from one section or another. For example, don't skip the section on scriptwriting because you don't intend to write a script. In the final analysis, it doesn't matter whether you're going to write in a climax or find one in your footage. Either way, you need to understand story structure.

Now, I'm no Spielberg. I'm just a guy who made a conscious decision one day to bail out of my former career and get into television. My old work was fun. I did mechanical design for a small studio where we invented products and hand-built prototypes. How cool was that? But it wasn't enough. I wanted more variety, I wanted *more* fun, I wanted to travel, have adventures, and make a lot of money! Well, four out of five ain't bad. Precisely *because* working in television is full of travel, adventure, and variety, everyone wants to do it—and it doesn't have to pay well! You'll be paid eventually for your experience and creativity, even though it can be difficult in the beginning.

I don't regret my days at the drafting table. My scientific mind has served me well in TV. My first job was working local news, doing "live shots." It involved long hours lugging heavy equipment for an ungrateful station while still qualifying for food stamps. Still, I was smitten with the industry. I immediately learned the live truck well enough to write a standard operating procedure. Over the years, I've done a bit of everything in this industry and, by nature, gathered my experiences into a pretty solid set of video production SOPs. Take my rules, add your creativity, and there's an excellent chance you'll get good at this. Practice and you could get *great* at this.

Chapter 1:
Choosing Your Equipment

Five-Step Foolproof Checklist for Finding *Your* Ideal DV Camera

There are a lot of reasons why I can't tell you what camera to buy. I don't know how much money you have to spend. I don't know what features would make you happy. And I know that half the model numbers will change by the time you read this book. But, don't despair. I can tell you what's important and what's not. I can tell you what works and what doesn't. I can help you read the specifications and help you decipher all the talk about lux, lumens, lines, and lenses, so you'll feel confident when you've found a model that meets your needs.

Features

Unless you have more money than time, don't rush through the camera comparison process. It's not fast and it's not easy and the camera manufacturers don't help. The sales and marketing of consumer and prosumer video cameras is a high-stakes race that doesn't always go to the top competitor. You must navigate an obstacle course of hype, rumor, publicity, and half-truths. Frequently, examining the strengths of its competitors will reveal the weaknesses of a camera. If one company advertises, "low battery consumption keeps you shooting longer!" they may see power draw as their competitor's Achilles' heel. A company that *doesn't* crow about low-light capabilities might have something to hide

---

What Is DV?

Technically speaking, DV, or digital video, is a specific video standard, though the initials have come to imply any digital video, from desktop Webcams to cameras that use MiniDV cassettes to high-end high-definition digital video. In this book, we use the term DV to refer to equipment adhering to the true DV standard.

DV specs

+ In 1994 Sony, Panasonic, JVC, Thomson, Philips, Hitachi, Toshiba, Sharp, Mitsubishi, Sanyo, and 45 other companies finalized the format known as DV or digital video.

+ DV is a true component video format, recorded at an 8-bit depth with four channels of 12-bit 32 kHz or two channels of 16-bit, 48 kHz (better than CD-quality) audio. You'll hear the video elitists talk down on DV because it's sampling rate of 4:1:1 (4:2:0 in some PAL versions) is less accurate than the high-end broadcast and production samples of 4:2:2 or even 4:4:4. Without getting too technical, the 4 in 4:1:1, the luminance value, has to do with the brightness and, ultimately, the resolution. The two 1's have to do with the color, or as the engineers call it, chrominance. DV has all the resolution of the highest quality professional formats though the chrominance sampling (governing color reproduction) is done at a reduced rate.

+ DV is based on a 5:1 compression codec accomplished by a chip set in the camera. A codec (a shortened way of saying "*compression* and *dec*ompression" altogether in one word) is what makes DV so accessible to mere mortals. If all the video were sent out of the camera and onto tape without being compressed, it would be much more difficult to work with, taking up too much room on the tape and making it very hard

to edit on your computer, too. So with a 5:1 codec, the video is five times smaller than it would have been had it not been compressed at all.

+ The DV format has built-in error correction eliminating drop-out, unsightly white speckles, and dashes found in old analog recordings.

+ Taken from the camera digitally, over FireWire, a dub to another digital cassette is a no-loss clone of the original DV information. Taken into a computer equipped to handle native DV and again, there is no loss at all unless effects are added or until the footage is converted to analog for broadcast or viewing in the old NTSC standard. In an all-digital environment (theoretically) loss of signal quality, what you've noticed in an analog dub of a dub, is a thing of the past.

+ There are two other DV formats important to note: Sony's DVCAM and Panasonic's DVCPRO, both created in response to a professional migration toward the attractive cost-to-performance delivery of the original generation of DV Camcorders. DVCAM and DVCPRO machines will usually be downwardly compatible, playing back DV tapes, both full-size and MiniDV. DV machines, both camera and decks, will not play back DVCAM or DVCPRO.

+ MiniDV is a tape size, not a format. While MiniDV cassettes are approximately the size of a DAT, 65 × 49 × 12.2 mm (approx 2.6" × 2"), full size DV cassettes are larger, 125 × 78 × 14.6 mm (approx. 3" × 5"). Recording lengths vary by format due to differing tape speeds. DV sacrifices some degree of high-frequency quality (seen in the reproduction of fine detail) to DVCAM and DVCPRO, gaining additional recording time. All DV tapes are 6.35 mm (0.25") wide.

Key Features	Canon GL2 Mini DV Camcorder	JVC GY-DV300 Mini DV Camcorder	Sony DCR-VX2000 Mini DV Camcorder	JVC GR-HD1 Mini DV Camcorder	Panasonic AG-DVX100 Mini DV Camcorder
	at 49 stores	at 25 stores	at 38 stores	at 41 stores	at 28 stores
	remove	remove	remove	remove	remove
Key Features					
Format	Mini DV	Mini DV	Mini DV	Mini DV	Mini DV
Number of CCD	3	3	3	1	3
CCD Pixels	410K pixels	410K pixels	380K pixels	1180K pixels	410K pixels
Recording System	NTSC	NTSC	NTSC	NTSC	NTSC
Optical Zoom	20x	14x	12x	10x	10x
LCD Panel Size	2.5 in.	2.5 in.	2.5 in.	3.5 in.	3.5 in.
Audio Format	12/16 Bit PCM Digital Stereo Audio	12/16 Bit PCM Digital Stereo Audio	12/16 Bit PCM Digital Stereo/Audio Dub		
Lens					
Optical Zoom	20x	14x	12x	10x	10x
Digital Zoom	100x		48x	200x	
Lens Size	4.2 - 84 mm	5.7 - 79.8 mm	6 - 72 mm	5.2 - 52 mm	32.5 - 325 mm
Viewing					
LCD Display	Yes	Yes	Yes	Yes	Yes
LCD Panel Size	2.5 in.	2.5 in.	2.5 in.	3.5 in.	3.5 in.
Color Viewfinder	Yes	Yes	Yes	Yes	
Advanced Features					
Image Stabilizer	With Image Stabilizer	With Image Stabilizer	With Image Stabilizer	With Image Stabilizer	
Digital Still Shot Mode	With Still Shot Capability		With Still Shot Capability	With Still Shot Capability	
Multimedia Card	Yes		Yes	Yes	
Low Lux	6 Lux	2.65 Lux	2 Lux		3 Lux
Recommended Illumination	100 Lux				
Recording Speed	LP/SP	LP/SP	LP/SP	LP/SP	
MPEG Movie Mode	No	Yes	No	Yes	
Max Still Image Size	1488 x 1128		640 x 480	1280 x 960	
Connectors					
Outputs				A/V, S-Video, Fire-Wire	
Video In Out	Out	Out	In/Out	In/Out	In/Out
Audio In Out	Out	Out	In/Out	In/Out	In/Out
DV Terminal	Yes	Yes	Yes	Yes	Yes
Interface Type	USB	Serial		USB	
Power Supply					
Battery Life		2 hrs.	1.25 hrs.	2.25 hrs.	
Battery Type	Lithium-ion Battery Pack (BP-915), Lithium-ion BP-930/945 Battery Pack (optional)	Rechargeable Lithium-ion Battery (BN-V428U-P)	InfoLithium Battery Pack (NP-F330), InfoLithium NP-F530/F550/F730/F750/F930/F950/F960 Batteries (optional)	Lithium-ion Battery Pack (BN-V428U), BN-V416U Battery (optional)	
General Features					
Warranty	1 Year parts and labor		1 Year parts, 90 days labor		
Dimension					
Weight	2.47 lb.	3.1 lb.	3.06 lb.	2.8 lb.	4.4 lb.
Depth	12 in.	14.06 in.	13.5 in.	10.75 in.	
Height	5.38 in.	6.31 in.	5.75 in.	3.94 in.	
Width	4.63 in.	5.13 in.	4.63 in.	4.56 in.	

Digital Media Net (www.DigitalMedia-Net.com) is a United States–based site that serves as a hub to their 40-plus sites worldwide. These sites are communities—one-stop destinations where digital media enthusiasts can find the tools and information they need to get their jobs done. This includes news, tutorials, features, research, reviews, profiles of industry leaders, and extensive user forums through their affiliation with the Worldwide Users Groups.

Five-Step Foolproof Checklist for Finding *Your* Ideal DV Camera

There are a lot of reasons why I can't tell you what camera to buy. I don't know how much money you have to spend. I don't know what features would make you happy. And I know that half the model numbers will change by the time you read this book. But, don't despair. I can tell you what's important and what's not. I can tell you what works and what doesn't. I can help you read the specifications and help you decipher all the talk about lux, lumens, lines, and lenses, so you'll feel confident when you've found a model that meets your needs.

Features

Unless you have more money than time, don't rush through the camera comparison process. It's not fast and it's not easy and the camera manufacturers don't help. The sales and marketing of consumer and prosumer video cameras is a high-stakes race that doesn't always go to the top competitor. You must navigate an obstacle course of hype, rumor, publicity, and half-truths. Frequently, examining the strengths of its competitors will reveal the weaknesses of a camera. If one company advertises, "low battery consumption keeps you shooting longer!" they may see power draw as their competitor's Achilles' heel. A company that *doesn't* crow about low-light capabilities might have something to hide but I guarantee you this, you won't be able to tell from their published specification. Low light is a good place to start.

Camera manufacturers express their low-light capabilities in terms of how little illumination is needed to produce an acceptable picture. Footcandles and lux (the metric equivalent) are both units of measure of light intensity; lumens are a measure of how many footcandles or lux illuminate a measured surface. Here are four points to recall when you see those impressively low numbers posted under "low-light response" in a spec sheet. First, there is no stringent, consistent test procedure everyone follows, so results vary. Second, the number is based on a subjective measure of an "acceptable picture." Third, some cameras assist themselves in low light situations by pumping up the gain, artificially brightening

the scene, and fourth, these companies are grading themselves! It's like the fox guarding the henhouse—consider how tempting it is to grade on a curve. If you're still going to compare numbers regarding footcandles, lumens, and lux, the smaller the number the better. If you see signal-to-noise ratios, higher is better. Comparing weight, be sure they're weighing the camera with a battery installed. Batteries are relatively heavy. Also, be suspicious of battery life claims. A camera might be able to stay powered up for eight hours, but it may not be able to record for eight hours. Look to wattage, a truer representation of energy used.

A chart of similarly priced and equipped cameras, with all their features and specifications laid side by side, would certainly be a valuable tool for comparison shopping (see page 13). Unfortunately, it would take hours of research and compilation to construct such a table...if it weren't for the folks who run DigitalMediaNet.com's Digital Media Shopper. DMN has unified and brought structure to the often difficult-to-decipher lists of equipment features and specifications supplied by manufacturers. This allows DMN to generate reasonably complete, apples-to-apples comparisons between cameras, editing software, or several dozen other products.

When comparing cameras, look first to the chips. CCDs (charge coupled devices) are the "film" of a video camera, responsible for registering the image that will ultimately be stored as data on your tape. Unless you're really trying to work on the cheap, buy a camera with three CCDs, where with the help of a prism behind the lens, the responsibility of recording luminance and chrominance are split between the three (red, green, and blue) pickups. The result is better detail, better color, and better low-light performance.

In CCDs, there's no argument—size matters. You'll see two measurements of size. One is physical size (¼," ⅓," or ½") and the other is pixel density (usually expressed in thousands of pixels). Buy the biggest CCDs with the greatest pixel density you can afford.

Another "bigger is better" feature—the viewfinder. Go for the big LCD. Go for the brightest LCD you can find as well. In sunlight, most LCDs become difficult to see. On that sunny day, you'll need to rely on your eyepiece viewfinder instead. That's why it's important to test the eyepiece for range of motion. Can you use the eyepiece if the camera is down on the ground or up above your head?

Audio is often overlooked on a video camera. On the low end of the price scale there won't be many options. As you spend more and more, look for audio metering in the viewfinder and adjustable input levels so you won't have to rely solely on the easily fooled automatic gain circuits (AGC). Also, it's critical to have the option of using an external microphone with the camera. Be sure there's an input. Also, be sure the camera has 16-bit audio recording capability.

> **Tip:** Digital stabilization involves processing the image, electronically scanning for obvious points, and pinning them in place. Processing degrades your image.
>
> Optical stabilization is accomplished in the lens and doesn't hurt the picture a bit. It eats up a little extra battery, but I leave it on all the time because steady is a big part of "well shot!"

Here, you see a wide shot, the full extent of the optical zoom, and the full extent of the digital zoom (note the loss of focus).

Keeping focus on an object moving toward you is a difficult thing to do. Like holding a shot steady, it takes lots of practice. Auto focus does it automatically. However, auto focus is stupid. It might accidentally acquire an object in the foreground and throw your subject out of focus, so it's nice to be able to suspend its effect. Auto iris, by virtue of the fact it is extremely active, is especially prone to error.

Don't buy a camera, new or used, without FireWire. FireWire, called iLink by Sony or IEEE1394, or simply 1394 by techies, is a high-speed serial data transfer standard chosen by the many manufacturers of digital camcorders as the preferred pipeline for pumping video in and out of computers and other peripheral devices. FireWire has become the industry standard for consumers and professionals alike, and it's how you'll get your footage out of your camera or record deck and onto a hard drive for editing. If there isn't a FireWire cable included with your camera, be sure to buy one before you leave the store.

A feature offered on most new DV cameras nowadays is called image stabilization. It's amazing. When I was a news shooter,

one skill that was highly valued was the ability to hold a long telephoto shot steady. It's not easy. You may think you're standing still, but until you've tried to lock down a hand-held telephoto shot you don't realize that even when you're standing still, your swaying slightly and even if you can pretty much prop yourself up to limit the swaying, your heartbeat will continue to shake the camera noticeably. I have decades of practice steadying shots, but the day you engage optical image stabilization, you are my equal. Make sure it's on your camera. Be aware that there are two different ways to accomplish image stabilization: optical image stabilization and digital image stabilization. You want optical.

"Digital zoom" is a digital swindle. You'll see it silk-screened on than TV cameras. As a result, if you shoot a computer monitor with a television camera "hum bars" or "scan bars" are revealed. The bright white or dark bars seen drifting up the screen can often be lessened or eliminated by adjusting the shutter. One word of caution: not all electronic shutters can correct for scan errors. Shutter speeds have to be fractionally adjustable to be entirely effective. If the camera you're looking at is capable, the manufacturer will advertise this feature.

Be careful when assigning value to various features. Manufacturers are constantly inventing new features with snappy, must-have names, but what it all comes down to is whether the camera feels good in your hand, takes good pictures, is convenient to operate, offers you the features you need, and allows you manual control of those features when you need it.

Ergonomics

My first DV camera came as an unknown entity, acquired unexpectedly in barter rather than at the end of a careful, coordinated search. It was a good camera, highly rated and a good value, but it wasn't the right camera for me. Two main reasons: First, the designers had placed the still image button less than a finger's width from the zoom control. I can't tell you how many times my big finger slipped from the zoom and captured a still. Second, I don't know my own strength. The aperture control was a combo affair with a push/push action. I don't think I ever reached to iris up without turning the auto iris on. I have a friend with the same camera, but he experiences neither of these problems. The moral of the story is, do not buy a camera until you've held it in your hand and seen it work.

There are controls you'll touch all the time. You'll actively focus, tweak your iris, and ride your audio levels. It's important to rise to a skill level where you can make all these adjustments without looking. You'll just know where they are. Make sure, as you hold a new camera for the first time, you find each of these controls and decide whether, with experience, you'll get used to their positioning and feel. If, for example, the buttons are too close together for *your* big fingers, you may never feel comfortable reaching without looking.

Consider how you'll use the camera. Will it be on a tripod or mostly handheld? If you think you'll use your camera on a tripod, get a tripod and try to find all those same controls again. Be sure none are blocked.

Understand that your battery will always die at the most inopportune moment. It should be easy to change and should lock crisply into place.

Longer shutter settings can blur action for stylized effects.

Where a shot of a car whipping through the frame might be nothing but a blur, a shorter shutter setting can capture the object sharply.

"Hum bars" on a computer monitor can be lessened by adjusting the shutter.

In an effort to be attractive to shooters, camera manufacturers often offer a range of electronic features. Some are valuable, some are fun, some are useless. In the hands of a skilled operator, the manual overrides of a camera's auto functions often give better quality results. Others, you wouldn't want to bother with them. I wouldn't eliminate a camera from consideration for lack of any of these features. I might if it lacked all of them.

☺ Shooting Modes

Shooting modes make the photographer's job easier in special situations. **Shutter Priority** and **Aperture Priority** modes fix one, adjusting exposure by automatically fiddling with the other. Another common shooting mode is **Backlight.** In a situation where the subject is lit brightly from behind, creating a silhouette, the backlight mode will attempt to compensate. In **Spotlight** mode, the camera compensates for the fact that the real center of visual attention, the person in the spotlight, could be lit many hundreds of times brighter than the rest of the stage. Finally, the **Sand and Snow** mode, where the camera attenuates the exposure a bit to compensate for bright scenes with limited contrast.

☹ Digital Effects

Cameras today can fade in and fade out, they can produce color effects, and they can add freezes, strobes, and stutters. Those features are aimed at people who aren't on the same path as you and I. You and I will own edit systems and I can't think of a single digital feature that can't be done cleaner and with more control in the edit.

☺ Zebra Pattern

Zebra pattern is perhaps the most important feature in this list. When turned on, a pattern of obvious black-and-white diagonal lines is superimposed on areas of the screen where brightness peaks above a predetermined threshold. The threshold is often adjustable but is usually set at either 100 percent to indicate overexposure or sometimes 70 percent, the textbook exposure level for faces. The pattern is only seen in the viewfinder, never recorded to tape. I keep my zebra turned on all the time.

☹ Still Mode

Many digital cameras are capable of recording still pictures. I would ask, "Why?" The quality of these stills, in both resolution and color, tends to be inferior to even moderately priced digital still cameras.

☹ Wide Screen

Wide screen (16:9) mode on most DV cameras is nothing but the standard aspect ratio (4:3) cropped. I see no value to this function. If you need to match shots to, say 35 mm stock shots you're using, shoot for the crop then crop them in the edit.

☺ Inputs and Outputs

Though it's critical to have a FireWire I/O, it's nice to have other options as well. Analog video and audio inputs and outputs allow you to gather video from other sources (tuner, DVD player, VCR) and to feed other sources (monitor, VCR, DAT).

☺ Time Lapse

Time lapse is potentially useful if your hope is to let the camera run for hours. Just speeding a two-minute shot up to 15 seconds can be accomplished easily within most edit systems.

☺ Gain

Gain, sometimes called boost, relies on amplification of the video signal to increase low-light capabilities. Expressed in decibels, you'll see numbers like +3 dB, +6 dB, +12 dB, +18 dB or higher. Unfortunately, amplifying a video signal amplifies background noise as well (this is where good signal-to-noise ratios pay off) and results in obvious graininess.

☹ Time/Date Stamp

Few things look more amateurish than a time/date stamp on footage. It's better to simply be devout about labeling your tapes, noting the time and date if it's important to you.

+ Gator

The first shooting style I call the "gator." The gator lies in ambush, just part of the scenery until an opportunity arises and it strikes. If this is the way you see yourself working, choose a small camera with long battery life because you'll want to have it always at the ready. It helps if the camera has a low-consumption standby mode and that it'll awaken quickly from this state. Use this method when you're dealing with friendly, cooperative subjects, unlikely to object and comfortable with their appearance—family perhaps? Be aware that whipping out a camera takes you from the background right to the foreground and that's not conducive to candid shots. The camera becomes a player in the scene, begging people to mug and pose.

+ Invisible Man

Another way to go is the "invisible man." This method takes you out of the action and resigns you to the fringes. Done well, you blend in enough for people to forget you're there, never sure if you're rolling. This style is the most common documentary method but is less than ideal in family situations. If you're going to be the invisible man, look for a camera that's moderately small, energy efficient, and boasts a pretty substantial zoom to keep you in the action even when you're across the room. Be sure the camera mic has a good range or replace it with a better mic.

+ Shooter

The final approach I call the "shooter." The trick with being a shooter is to get to the point where people comment if you don't have a camera. The advantage is that ultimately no one pays any attention to you, it's just Buddy with his camera again. If you're going to be the shooter, anything goes. Choose as obvious and intrusive a camera as you'd like. It'll be easy to carry a big camera bag with spare tapes, batteries, filters, and another lens. Buy a good camera; people are going to expect quality from someone who takes videography as seriously as the shooter.

Try this; it will open your eyes. Grab a soup can out of the pantry and a stopwatch. Hold the soup can shoulder height at arm's length in front of you and start the watch. How long do you think you can hold it? Five minutes? Ten minutes? I think you'll be disappointed. I'm going to guess that after one minute, you'll be looking for an excuse to end this little test. Now consider the camera you're about to buy. You might not have to hold it at arm's length, but I guarantee you you'll find yourself in awkward positions from time to time.

Look over the camera body. Find all the connections you might use while you're shooting. Find out where you plug in external microphones and your headset. Find out where you'd attach a video cable for an external monitor. Be sure that if you're using an external monitor or external microphone that you can still comfortably hold the camera and continue to reach all the important buttons.

If there's a handle, verify that it is sturdy and firmly attached to the camera body. Molded-in is best. Assess, generally, the camera's sturdiness. It will get knocked around from time to time.

Be sure your hand fits in the hand strap and while it's there, make sure you can easily reach the Record Start/Stop button, usually with the thumb of your right hand.

Examine the LCD viewfinder. It should be sturdy and adjustable. Be sure the viewfinder has a diopter. The diopter is a lens mounted in line with the LCD screen of the viewfinder. The diopter can be adjusted to compensate for problems with your eyesight. I have terrible vision and find the diopter not just handy but critical.

How long can you hold a soup can at arm's length? Think about that when you're considering your camera's weight.

A telephoto lens can flatten your image and aid in creating focus effects.

Add-on adapters can result in vignetting.

Tip: Zoom Lens Basics

Lenses are normally classified as wide angle, telephoto, and standard angle. A standard angle lens is thought to roughly simulate the viewing angle and spatial relationships seen by the human eye. While 50 mm is widely recognized as standard in 35 mm still cameras, standard in a DV camera varies by the size of the pickup CCDs. For a $\frac{1}{4}$-inch (.05 cm) CCD, the standard focal length is 5.2 mm. For a $\frac{1}{3}$-inch (0.8 cm) CCD, it's 6.9 mm, and for a $\frac{2}{3}$-inch (1.6 cm) CCD it's 13.8 mm. So, for instance, numbers below 6.9 mm on a camera with a $\frac{1}{3}$-inch (0.8 cm) CCD would be wide angle, greater than 6.9 mm telephoto. In actuality, the wide-angle look wouldn't become obvious until you get below 5 mm, or telephoto greater than 20 mm. So if that $\frac{1}{3}$-inch (0.8 cm) CCD camera had a lens that could zoom from 4.5 mm at its widest to 63 mm at full telephoto, it would be said to have a zoom ratio of 14:1. The zoom ratio (often spoken as "14 times" or "14 by") is a measure of magnification. Zoom all the way in with a 14× lens and, at the telephoto end, the screen will be filled with one-fourteenth the original image.

Zoom lenses are also rated for speed, measured in f-stops. The lower the f-stop rating of a lens, the faster it is. Fast is good because a fast lens allows more light to pass through to the CCD pick-ups. Two f-stop numbers listed for a lens indicates the f-stop at full wide compared to the f-stop at full telephoto. The fact is, long lenses eat up f-stops. It makes sense. Imagine how much light is admitted to a lens when the viewing angle is wide compared to how much light is allowed in when you're seeing a narrow, fractional view of the original scene. That's one of the reasons longer is not always better in the world of lenses.

Optics

I had to see it to believe it. I produced a project where we rolled two cameras on every interview. The camera bodies were identical. Only the lenses differed. One lens was factory issue, the other a relatively expensive TV zoom lens. Reviewing the footage, it was never difficult to tell which was which. The camera with the nice piece of glass always looked better. Noticeably better. Bottom line: buy a good lens. How will you know? Read "The Test" (page 20).

In reality, both telephoto and wide-angle lenses have their advantages and disadvantages. Telephoto shots are more difficult to steady than wide shots. Telephoto shots distort spatial relationships, flattening your image and accentuating movement. On the other hand, telephoto lenses can allow you to emphasize objects in the frame by focusing selectively while wide-angle lenses are more forgiving of both movement and focus.

It may be tempting to try to buy one lens and get more mileage out of it by adding a wide-angle adapter or a telephoto extender. Be careful! If the adapters are optically true, they can be very expensive. If they're third party add-ons, they can cause problems like vignetting, or in the case of extenders, prevent the lens from focusing consistently over the range of the zoom.

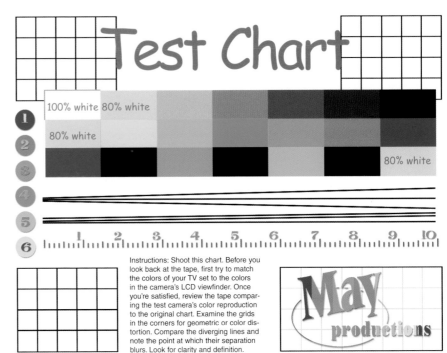

Instructions: Shoot this chart. Before you look back at the tape, first try to match the colors of your TV set to the colors in the camera's LCD viewfinder. Once you're satisfied, review the tape comparing the test camera's color reproduction to the original chart. Examine the grids in the corners for geometric or color distortion. Compare the diverging lines and note the point at which their separation blurs. Look for clarity and definition.

Grab a piece of cardboard (A4 or U.S. letter size). Paste a picture on one side. Choose a big picture, something with both light and dark areas and some detail in both. On the other side, paste a chart of your own making. Copy the example above in black marker onto a piece of white paper or create the image in a computer paint program. If you can't find a suitable picture or you're dangerous with markers, both of these images are available on my website at www.petemay.com.

The Test

You've thought it through—what kind of shooter you want to be, and what kind of equipment you can afford. You've picked apart the specs, assessed your options, and you've flat run out of reasons not to buy a camera.

Here's what I want you to do: put together a camera testing kit. Start by grabbing a bag and tossing in a MiniDV tape, a pair of full muff headphones, a small tape measure, and a small but bright flashlight.

Next, rent a MiniDV camcorder. It's not particularly important which one, as long as it has outputs and cables that will allow you to play the tape you're going to record on your home TV. Finally, enlist the help of an assistant. Be sure your assistant wears a shirt or blouse with a detailed print (avoid pinstripes or a tight check patterns). Also, be sure your helper has a watch with a second-hand. Now, get to a store that sells camcorders, someplace where you can actually pick them up and play with them, because that's just what I want you to do. You don't need to take that camcorder you rented with you, either—you'll be using that later.

Once you get to the store, try to avoid being ushered out by first alerting the salesperson of your intentions. With the carrot of a sale hanging there, he or she might be willing to answer some of your critical questions like, "How do I turn this thing on?"

You're going to run a series of nine tests on each camera under consideration. When you've finished with the test on one camera, eject your tape, put it in the next camera and run the same tests in the same order again. Don't roll any more than fifteen seconds of footage per test. Ideally, at the end of the tests, you'd be able to see shots from the different cameras in a split screen for direct comparison. If you have a home edit system, that's exactly what you should do. Assuming you don't have an edit system yet, you're going to have to watch each test and try to remember your impression as you cue to the same test on the next camera. That's why it's best to limit the length of the shots and keep them close together. The more you have to fast forward and rewind, the less clear you'll be on the differences between cameras.

To prepare for the test, give your assistant the art card and flashlight. Have him or her find a spot about 8 feet (2.5 meters) away, and hold the card with both hands, as steady and level as possible. Be sure it's well lit but doesn't show any glare. Have your aide number the test by pointing to the number on the edge of

the card. Load the DV tape in your first test camera. Be sure the camera is in the full automatic mode with auto focus and optical image stabilization turned on. Plug in your headphones and you're ready to begin. Each time you roll, say the name and model of the camera out loud to help ID the shots later.

Once you've finished the test, take the tape home, sit down, and watch it critically. After several viewings, you'll start to get a feeling for the relative merits of the various units. Taking the tape home for review also provides a perfectly legitimate excuse to escape the clutches of that impatient salesperson who couldn't understand why you didn't just pick a camera like normal people do.

▷ Tip: A Nine-Point Camera Test

1. **Resolution.**
Shoot 15 seconds of the test pattern side of your card nearly full frame. It's not necessary to hold the shot rock-steady, but hold it as still as possible. When you review this shot later, you'll be looking at the camera's ability to resolve the lines we've drawn and looking for undesirable artifacts like stair-stepping on your horizontal lines. You'll also be measuring where the converging lines become indistinct. The closer they get without appearing to merge, the better. Watch for distortion of the lines around the edge of the picture. Sometimes lens defects will make them curve or change color.

2. **Color Reproduction and Detail.**
Have your helper turn the card to the picture side and shoot another 15 seconds. Later, when reviewing the tape, you'll have to make some subjective judgments about color reproduction. You'll also examine the picture for detail in the dark and light areas.

3. **Banding, Streaking, and Smearing.**
Have your assistant shine the flashlight at the lens. Widen your shot and roll for a few seconds. You're watching for banding, a strong vertical smear line at the point of the bright light. Also be aware of streaking, the same phenomenon in the horizontal plane. Banding, streaking, and smearing are CCD problems.

4. **Sound.**
Have your assistant stand approximately 1 yard (1 meter) directly in front of the lens and recite the short poem below in a normal speaking voice. You may substitute your own verse if necessary. If your assistant is game, have them nearly shout out the last line! Keeping the camera pointed straight ahead, have your aide arc to the left or right, still the same distance from the camera and repeat the verse again.

> There once was a racer named Dwight
> Whose Porsche was faster than light
> He sped off one day,
> In a relative way,
> And returned on the previous night.

When reviewing, you'll be listening for the clarity of the audio, whether it's distinct from the background noise and whether the AGC clips the sudden, loud, last sentence. If any of the audio track is sparse enough, listen for the unwanted sound of the camera itself.

5. **Auto Iris.**
Set a shot of the store and pass your hand through the shot, a short distance in front of the lens. Watch the auto iris react. If it's too touchy you may have a problem with it constantly overcompensating for natural movement. If it seems to react too slowly, you may see overexposed or dark shots linger longer than you'd like.

6. **Auto Focus.**
Have your assistant walk about 30 feet away from you. Signal the person to walk toward you as you frame a head-and-shoulders shot of the approach. Zoom out slowly to keep the shot size constant. Watch the auto focus. It should keep the shot crisp.

7. **Zoom.**
Again set a shot of the store at the widest angle the camera allows. Zoom all the way into something a distance away. Hold the shot for ten seconds. With each subsequent camera you're testing, start with the same wide shot and zoom to the same point and hold it. This will give you a concrete visual representation of the lens' zoom ratio and the effectiveness of the optical image stabilization.

8. **Auto White Balance.**
If the store has a window to the outside, try panning from an interior shot to a shot out the window. Note how quickly the auto white balance compensates and its accuracy in color representation.

9. **Low Light.**
Look around. Is there a dark corner, an area under a display, anyplace that appears dark to the camera? Shoot it with attention to the camera's ability to pull detail out of the darkness. Inspect the dark areas for graininess and noise.

Options

Don't be fooled by the list price of that camera you like. Keep your mind (and your wallet) open until we finish talking options.

In today's world of digital cameras, there's not much need for UV filters. So why buy one? When a tree branch snaps back or a pebble pops up, it'll scratch the cheap UV filter rather than that very, very expensive lens. We'll take a closer look at my reasons in the section called Film Look (page 163), but for now let me suggest you consider a neutral density or ND filter kit (0.3, 0.6, and 0.9).

When weighing all the options, consider the expensive but very dramatic effect of a polarizing filter. Polarizing filters take advantage of a characteristic of bounced light to reduce or even eliminate reflection. It'll allow you to see below the surface of the water or the driver through the windshield of the car. But best of all, polarizing filters add a stunning, almost surreal deep blue to the average clear sky.

When you buy a camera they'll usually include one battery and a charger that doubles as the AC power unit. That's fine to start, but by the end of the first week, you'll realize you need at least one more battery. Consider buying bigger batteries than the one that came in the box. Batteries are rated in amp-hours. The higher the amp-hour rating, the more recording time you get on a single charge. With that in mind, you might be tempted to just buy the biggest batteries you can get. Before you do, remember the soup can. Typically, the battery charger that comes with a camera is a stripped down trickle charger. If you want to be able the charge more than one battery at a time or charge more quickly, you're probably going to need to spend extra on a better charger.

Protect your camera investment by buying either a soft-sided or hard-sided camera bag. If there's a chance you'll ever check your camera gear as baggage, go for the hard-sided case. If you're going to lash the camera case to the roof of the Jeep or drag it up the side of a mountain, again, choose the hard-sided case. If your camera is always going to be a carry-on, soft-sided should suffice.

The salesman will try to sell you more batteries, more filters, straps, satchels, headphones, and lights. I'm not going to tell you, "Don't buy them." I will tell you it's smarter to wait until you've had the camera for a while and taken stock of your shooting style before you pull out your wallet.

Reduce reflections in water or enrich the sky's blue color with a polarizing filter. It's like a pair of sunglasses for your camera.

Having a tripod when you need one is the mark of a professional.

There's one last option we should talk about: the tripod. Tripods make your shots look more professional. They take away the constant drift of hand-held shots. But they're not cheap. A moderate prosumer tripod and head can cost between $600 and $1,600. As tripods become more expensive, the motion of the tripod heads become smoother and more adjustable.

If you think you'll never set the camera in a shooting position and walk away, you may never need a tripod. If you think you'll never shoot anything telephoto for an extended period of time—a play, a bird, or a stakeout—you might be able to skip the tripod. If you think you'll never do long, steady pans across the horizon or dynamic tilts to the top of a skyscraper, you might not need a tripod. With optical image stabilization and some practice, you can be nearly as steady as you would be on a tripod but you'll never be perfect (like you can be with a tripod). Personally, I wouldn't be without one. It's a professional tool and I'm a professional.

This isn't a big consideration if you're shooting professionally, but if you're planning on maintaining your amateur status, you might want to be more than the one who's shot all this great video—you might want to get into the shots yourself, and that requires a tripod as well.

Shotgun mics

Moving Pictures Need Moving Audio

Top-rated local news broadcasts earn enough to support high-priced consultants with ideas about how to stay the top-rated local news broadcast. We'd see them wandering around the station saying things like, "People want news they can use," "Ask the widow how she feels," and "Try opening the top button on your blouse." One smart thing I remember them saying is "Audio is half the picture." OK, you know what they meant. Well, all these years later, TV people still don't fully exploit the power of audio and if you don't believe in the power of audio, watch a Kodak spot with the sound off and see if it still moves you. So, this'll save you the cost of a high-priced consultant: Pay more attention to audio. Were going to learn how later in this book but for now let me say this, if you're going to make better use of your audio, you need to record the best audio possible and that's a function of placing the right equipment in the right place. We'll start with "the right microphone."

Microphones and audio accessories

A young shooter and his reporter were out on a story, being shadowed that day by two undergrads hoping to learn about the business. The reporter offered the earnest young male student the opportunity to conduct an interview that the reporter would observe and then critique. As the interview went on, the shooter became aware of whispers and giggles behind him. The reporter was not observing the interview but enjoying the playful nature of the female student. Later, at the station, the shooter was horrified to find he'd never swapped mic inputs. The reporter's mic had been open, recording every bit of his witty banter and none of the male student's incisive interview. There was much explaining to be done, including *why the shooter wasn't monitoring audio with a headset.* It is a tale lacking sound, full of fury, suggesting

this: buy a light, comfortable set of double-muff headphones and wear them when you work. When shooting scenics or b-roll, ear buds or "listen-through" headsets might do, but interviews require great attention to both foreground and background audio.

Now, take those new headphones with you when you go to buy the rest of your audio equipment. You see, most cameras do indeed come equipped with a microphone, and some of those mics are very good for picking up general ambient sound. But if you are planning on doing interviews or shooting in anything but studio-quiet settings, you'll need more. We'll go into a more in-depth discussion of microphones later, but for now, take my word for it—you'll want at least two more mics.

First, get your shotgun. A shotgun mic is a long, thin tubular microphone. They're highly directional and a good one (not just one that *looks* like a shotgun), will exclude most sounds coming from the sides while offering a clear, noticeably exclusive rendering of the sound source you target. They're perfect for noisy environs and can double as a stick mic, that ubiquitous ice cream cone reporters shove under politicians' noses every night on the news. Again, we'll get into specific characteristics later but for now, look for a mic with a narrow focus, low handling noise, and a good frequency response.

The other mic you'll want is a lavaliere. Sometimes called "peanut mics" or "lavs," they're omnidirectional but small enough to sneak right up under the speaker's mouth. You often see lavalieres clipped to lapels or pinned to ties worn by guests on talk shows. Look for the same characteristics in lavs that you did in your shotgun. They should sound clean and pleasing, offer a full dynamic range, and have as little handling noise as possible. Of course, people don't actually "handle" lavs but the mics are usually pinned to their clothing. Trust me, there are few audio problems more vexing than a lav that picks up every little movement of its cord, every rustle of the subject's clothing. Isolating lavalieres for clean audio is a true art.

If you can afford it, even though it's a bit of an extravagance, buy a wireless transmitter and receiver for use with your shotgun and your lav. Wireless is a great way to go, allowing you to mic one position and shoot from another, unencumbered by cords. On the lower end of the wireless price scale, lavalieres are often sold hardwired into the transmitter. In areas where there's lots of radio frequency (RF) interference, or where extra batteries aren't available, you'll wish you had a corded mic. Be sure that the transmitter you choose can be used with either the shotgun or the lav. If the transmitter is hardwired to the lav, you lose the versatility you'll need to use either one wirelessly.

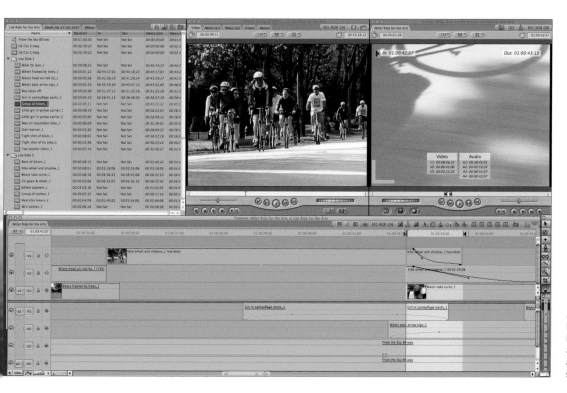

Apple's Final Cut Pro is a popular non-linear editing (NLE) program. The layout is typical with a browser that lists shots, a play window where shots are viewed, a record window where the assembled shots are reviewed, and a timeline.

The Cutter's Toolkit

Nonlinear video editing programs

In 1989, Avid introduced one of the first and certainly the most successful nonlinear editing (NLE) systems. That premiere product, Avid Media Composer, was destined to change the world of video editing. At the time, underpowered computer processors and the small capacities and slow speed of digital storage made the more-convenient nonlinear editing, unable to match the picture quality of established tape-to-tape linear editing. With the advances in processing speed and storage enjoyed in the computer industry since those early days, nonlinear edit systems have not only achieved (at the highest levels) parity regarding quality, they've managed to break out of the exclusive, expensive world of the professional edit suite and found their way onto desktops around the world. Welcome to the revolution.

These days, most NLEs look similar. There's a browser of sorts, with lists of shots or representative picture icons (picons). The shots are opened in a viewer window for examination. A section of the shot is identified for inclusion by setting an incue and an outcue. A graphic representation of the shot is then transferred

to the timeline and becomes visible in the record window. The shots may be trimmed or lengthened to fit. Transitions such as dissolves and wipes may be added *between the shots*. Effects like slo-mo or color tints may be added *to the shots*. That's the way, shot by shot, audio clip by audio clip, commercials, documentaries, news stories, wedding videos, and home videos alike are assembled.

A few years back, I wrote an article comparing two very popular NLEs: Avid's XpressDV and Apple's Final Cut Pro. Both support native DV. Both offered all the basic cutting tools. In addition, both supported sophisticated video production capabilities including scores of transitions, digital effects, titling, and color correction. Neither was particularly difficult to learn if one was devoted to the task. It was a close call. When the article was published, I got a lot of nice comments from many professional editors who were trying to decide which program to buy. I also got a letter from an editor working on network news and magazine shows in New York. He and his fellow cutters had found "every *typical* piece cut for the morning and/or evening national news could easily have been done using iMovie." Apple's free nonlinear editor, iMovie truly works like "a word processor for

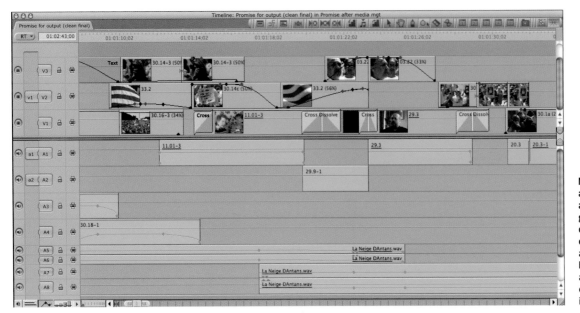

Nonlinear edit systems are built around timelines composed of video and audio tracks upon which your program is assembled. Sometimes the difference between low-end and high-end edit systems is how many tracks are offered. One difference between high-end edit systems is often the amount of flexibility you have—how easy it is to trim, slip, and slide media in the timeline.

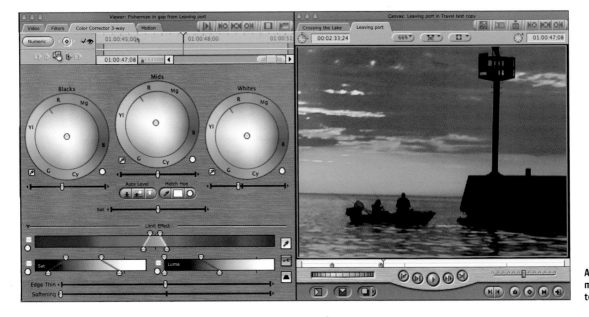

Advanced color correction lets you manipulate colors in the shadows, midtones, and highlights of video footage.

Most of your projects will be enhanced by adding text and titles. Some NLEs have deep and capable titling tools where others' are simple. Some rely on stand-alone titling apps and many are friendly to paint programs like Photoshop and Studio Artist.

media. It will make you laugh—it's that simple—yet iMovie is much "deeper" than 9 out of 10 people think. Final Cut Pro may be less expensive than Avid XpressDV, but iMovie is free!"

You can't beat that price. And, if network producers in New York don't need some of the bells and whistles, do you? iMovie is just one of a handful of free video editing applications out there, easily found on the Web. Besides iMovie, there's Avid Free DV and Windows Movie Maker. I located a half dozen others that are available free on a trial basis—usually 30 days—but that should be plenty long enough to figure out a new piece of software. I encourage you to start with some free software and practice until you understand the value of the various functions, and then you'll be able to identify features you must have.

Maybe you'll never spend a cent on editing software, but if you change your mind and decide to invest in an NLE, these are the kinds of enhanced benefits you can expect.

- **Audio and video tracks** are usually needed for creating layered effects, sometimes even simple dissolves. Some free or low cost systems only offer two audio tracks and two video tracks. It's especially easy to run out of audio tracks. Narration, natural sound, and stereo music will gobble up four tracks easily. If music cross-fades or sound effects are layered in, you're at eight tracks before you know it. Professional systems will offer many more, 99 or even 999 tracks. I seldom use more than eight video and fourteen audio tracks, but I almost always use four video and eight audio tracks.

- **Added transitions** will allow more than the most basic of dissolves and wipes that are included in most free programs. Some of the free programs do support plug-ins, which are third-party subprograms that add effect and transition capabilities.

- **Trimming tools** can be found on every video edit system, but higher-end systems offer more versatile trimming modes, making it easier to trim up one side of a video edit or work more effectively with music.

- **Real time effects** allow transitions and special effects to be previewed without rendering. This is often a function of processor speed rather than limitations of the software. Without a dedicated accelerator card, most effects will require rendering when you send them back to DV tape.

- **Monitor preview** allows effects, real time or otherwise, to be seen on an external video monitor in addition to being seen on the edit computer's screen. Again, this is often a function of your system capabilities and is most advantageous if you intend to have clients watching you edit.

- **Enhanced color correction** capabilities offer you the opportunity to create a "look" using color effects or simply "correct" footage improperly shot. Simple tools that allow changing hue, saturation, and brightness will not repair a bad white balance. You might be able to bring one color around to its correct value, but others will appear incorrect.

- **Interface customization** involves the ability to put buttons and commands where they suit you. In the highly competitive NLE market, companies hope to minimize one objection to switching by assuring editors they can rearrange their new system to match their old.

- **Time remapping** or **speed ramping** is the ability to both alter the frame rate of your footage, say from normal speed to slow motion to fast motion and back to normal, with smooth transitions between speeds.

- **Levels of undo** are important for backtracking and in more expensive systems the user is often allowed to choose levels of undo, frequently up to 99.

- **Enhanced titling** allows the editor more flexibility in the creation of graphics. Where an inexpensive system might offer limited choices of font sizes and styles, an enhanced graphic program will allow the editor to mix font styles and sizes, to add shadows, extrusions, and even movement such as crawls and scrolls or rolls (like in movie credits).

- **EDL, or edit decision lists,** allow communication with linear edit systems. This is only important if you intend to take projects into a professional edit suite for finishing or if you might move your projects from one edit system to another edit system of a different make.

- **Autosave** functions as a dynamic backup system taking a snapshot of your edit at user-definable intervals just in case the system crashes.

- **Enhanced media management** is critical when dealing with hours of footage needed to create documentaries, most of which routinely shoot a minimum of 15 times the footage that will actually be used in the final product. Media management allows you to categorize various shots in ways that make them easier to sort through while working with hundreds of clips in a large project.

- **Audio mixing** capabilities vary from program to program, but on the high end they can be quite spectacular, some offering real time mixing, effects, and the ability to compose musical scores built right in.

Let's talk chicken and egg for a moment. Depending on which comes first—your software purchase or your computer purchase—you may have to adjust your ideas for one based on the other. If you're buying software for a computer you already own, check

A Cut Above

Here are the big names in nonlinear editing. They've been around for a while, so it's fair to expect they'll still be around tomorrow. Most are Microsoft Windows–based except where noted.

+ Final Cut Pro (Mac only)
+ Avid Xpress, Avid Xpress DV (Mac and Windows)
+ Adobe Premiere Pro
+ Sony Vegas
+ Pinnacle Liquid Edition
+ Media 100 (Mac and Windows)
+ Ulead Media Studio Pro
+ NewTek Toaster
+ Pinnacle Moviebox DV
+ Movie 3 (Mac only)
+ iMovie (Mac only)
+ Windows Movie Maker

the literature for recommended processor speed and RAM requirements...then double them. Video editing isn't easy for a computer. It taxes the system and requires everything, from hard drives to RAM to busses, to work together flawlessly. If they don't, you'll see crashes, dropped frames, unacceptable render times, and all manners of pops, clicks, and flashes. Your projects won't look good and you'll be unhappy. Today's NLEs depend heavily on the capabilities of the computer hardware so if you're buying new, buy all the processing speed you can afford and all the RAM the box will accept.

Since the computer has to talk to the camera in order to capture footage, check the Web, call, or examine the product literature to be sure one supports the other. You want your computer to recognize and take control of the camera first time, every time.

Factor in support costs when you buy your software. There's usually a short grace period after purchase, but a year from now you might have to fork over a substantial fee for expert insight. Online chat rooms and bulletin boards have always served me well. Check them out before you buy for two reasons: first, to determine how active and helpful they might be and second, to see what kinds of problems other owners are having. Don't automatically be put off by an active board fielding lots of issues. Remember, most people don't hang around the forums *unless* they have problems and besides, all that activity indicates there's a good-sized user base, and that's a good thing.

So there's no confusion, I'm talking DV editing here. If you intend to edit any other formats, analog or digital, you'll need to either transfer the footage to DV first or buy an NLE that supports other compression schemes as well. A problem with other formats is they lack the elegant and effective compression scheme that has helped make DV so popular. For example, while DV footage nibbles a mere 3.6 MB per second, full resolution uncompressed video devours 20.2 MB per second. That's five and a half times more data on the move per second and five and a half times more storage space required, bringing us to our final NLE issue.

A rate of 3.6 MB per second works out to 13 GB per hour. Not bad. Even though most NLEs warn you against having the program and your media on the same drive, it wouldn't be too outrageous to have 15 or 20, even 40 hours' worth of internal storage available in your system. That may sound like a lot, unless you think in terms of long form documentary work or trying to keep all your home movies available all the time. If you were to start coming up short, it's easy to add supplemental external storage using FireWire drives. If you do, be sure the drive speed is a minimum of 7,200 rpm and, to avoid data bottlenecks, you've found the highest sustained data transfer rate available.

Ultimately, the only way you can go wrong buying a nonlinear edit program is if you buy one that is incompatible with your computer, unfriendly to your camera, or inconsistent with your short-term edit ambitions.

Supplemental software for special effects, audio, cleaning, and compression

My advice on shopping for special effects, audio, cleaning, or compression software is wait and see what you need. The problem is, the reason you might need *expensive* supplemental software is that you decided to go with *inexpensive* nonlinear editing software. It's not so much a Catch-22 as a Goldilocks paradox. You need to find the combination of software that's *just right for you*. I stand by my earlier advice to try working with free or very cheap edit software as you start out. Once you get a feel for editing, you'll be in a better position to choose an editing product knowing also, the higher you climb that NLE ladder, the more you'll find the capabilities of these standalone programs included. I'm not saying the effects and compression functions built into moderately priced NLE software packages equal the capabilities of the best high-end professional products. They don't. But color correction, keying, titling, layering, and compression necessary

> **Tip: Read ahead!**
>
> Before buying any supplemental software for cleaning, compressing, or coding, read the sections "Distributing on DVD" (page 174) and "Web Streaming" (page 176) in our final chapter "The Finished Product." Understanding what's involved in getting your edited project out of your computer and into a distribution format will help you choose the software that's right for you.

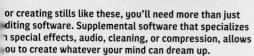
or creating stills like these, you'll need more than just diting software. Supplemental software that specializes n special effects, audio, cleaning, or compression, allows ou to create whatever your mind can dream up.

for building DVDs and accomplishing Web streaming—all functions you might have had to buy separately—are currently available in many moderately priced NLE packages. If you intend to rocket into the stratosphere of production you might need the added boost of some high-end equipment, but if you're simply concerned with executing everyday edits or being sure your final product will land safely on a DVD or Web server, I'd wait to spend the extra money.

There are exceptions, like paint and animation. Few edit programs offer more than the most rudimentary paint capabilities. If you expect to do a great deal of work with still pictures, especially still pictures that might require alteration, an investment in Adobe Photoshop or Synthetik Software's Studio Artist might be in order. If you want to do any true 3-D animation, you won't find that capability built into any edit programs that costs less than a two-week Caribbean cruise (promenade deck).

If you're coming at video editing from the audio world you might have a heightened sense of what you're missing in most video editing packages—things like extreme equalization, pitch shifting, and the ability to take in and feed out 8-, 12-, or even 24-track mixes. If the lack of these advanced capabilities might cramp your musical style, consider buying a stand-alone audio program. Most recognize imports and offer exports in the majority of popular audio transfer formats, but if you've already chosen your video editing software, take the time to confirm complete compatibility.

There is a category of software you might want to get to know right away—plug-ins. Plug-ins are usually inexpensive yet often amazingly effective subprograms that extend the capabilities of your software. Sometimes plug-ins add special effects, other times they simply enhance existing capabilities. I own plug-ins that can create romantic diffusion, particle explosions, and even a convincing film look, complete with errant hairs in the gate. Plug-ins also exist for the audio portions of video editing programs allowing you to add anything from a "telephone" effect to complex reverb schemes designed to mimic the acoustics of various sized rooms. Plug-ins are written for specific programs with little crossover compatibility, so be sure to check before buying.

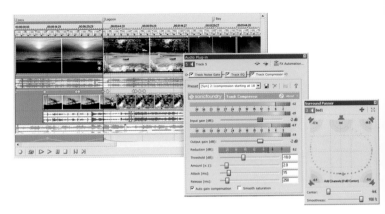

Sony's Vegas Video NLE started life as audio editing software, giving it a unique pedigree in the world of video editing. With its history there's no wonder its audio editing and sweetening abilities outstrip those of most NLEs.

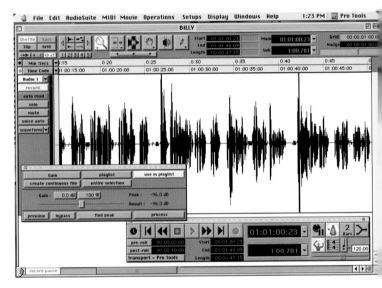

Though NLEs continue to improve their audio capabilities, if you intend to do more audio editing than video editing there is still an argument to be made for owning a stand-alone audio editing program such as the venerable Pro Tools.

Plug-ins give your video a world's worth of effects and enhancements.

Diffusion

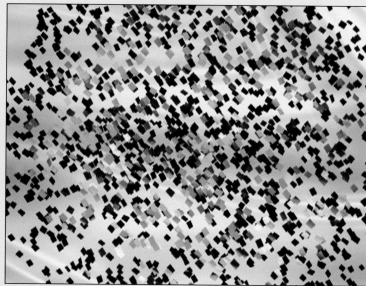

Explosion

Best FX

Here are the names of some of the most popular and enduring special-effects software packages:

+ Adobe After Effects
+ Apple Shake
+ Boris Red, Boris Motion Graphics, Boris Continuum
+ discreet combustion
+ discreet flame, flint, and inferno
+ Eyeon Digital Fusion

Codecs, Cleaning, and Compression

To code your final cut for inclusion on a DVD, CD-ROM, or for streaming or downloading from the Web, it's often necessary to transpose to a specific codec. Here are a few common names in the world of compression and cleaning:

+ Canopus ProCoder
+ discreet cleaner XL
+ Sorenson Video, Sorenson Squeeze
+ Main Concept

Chapter 2:

Finding Work

The last time I went into business for myself, I did so on the strength of a relationship with one good, solid client—a major U.S. corporation. I'd done a series of high-profile projects for them over the years, and every one had been a rousing success. However, leaving my situation would be a big step so, just to set my mind at ease, I took the video manager out to lunch and told her what I was thinking. I knew she couldn't *promise* anything, but I wanted to know if she foresaw any change in the level or number of videos her department would produce. She assured me that, if anything, the numbers would rise! Within a month I was printing business cards and letterhead and, with my eyes trained on my bright, busy future, never saw the pendulum swing. In that same month, a middle manager at the firm said, "Why are we spending all this money on independent producer/directors? Let's get someone in-house!" It was five years before I heard from that client again. That was two decades ago and since then that same pendulum has traced that same arc several times. The experience provided me with a bit of wisdom I often share: *You will never have the same clients two years in a row.* Over the years, I've been right more often than not and even if I am wrong, you're well advised to assume I'm going to be right and get some eggs into some other baskets. The first thing we're going to do is find you some baskets and point out some eggs.

Where to Look

I was sitting in the marina clubhouse early Saturday, catching a few hours of work before we shoved off, when he lumbered in and took over the far corner of the room. He spread out the morning paper and snapped the lid off a fresh cup of coffee and the room went quiet again. He was grey-haired, big as a bear with a booming voice that surprised me when he called out. "Nice laptop! Whadaya use it for?" "Writing and editing video," I shot back loudly, mostly for having been startled. "Hey, me too!" he said as he stood and galumphed toward me with his hand ready to shake. "Coach," he said. I introduced myself and was treated to a short biography. His resume ended with an interesting application of DV equipment.

He'd retired from coaching high school football a year earlier. They'd had the whole football season taped by a couple of kids from the multimedia club. He wanted to edit together the highlights of his last, very successful season as coach so he bought an

edit program and taught himself how to use it. Once he'd edited the highlights of the season together, he discovered there was a built-in, easy-to-reach market for the DVD. He started selling them for $100 bucks a piece, not an exorbitant sum to the new generation of proud parents, willing to pay $900 for senior pictures. "You do the math," he added and I did. Coach had called a few other coaches in the area and worked out a similar deal with each of them. "So much for being retired!" OK, there's one idea. Here are a few more. Starting out, trust me, you'll need more than one.

Boaters love their boats. The harbormaster at one marina, in addition to selling T-shirts of his own design, shoots videos from his little runabout of proud captains under way. He adds lots of music and slo-mo.

Though it's not the easiest field arena for beginners to enter, the field of law offers various opportunities. One is taping depositions. As far as production technique, this is easy work but it is evidence and can't be taken lightly. Know and adhere to rules of legal procedure in your state. You may need a license and you certainly need the good sense to make your portrayal neutral—no zooms or moves, no lights if you can avoid them.

Another support service for lawyers, even harder to break into but both lucrative and fulfilling, is video settlement brochures. VSBs are minidocumentaries designed to lay out a plaintiff's case, with all the interviews, photos, experts, and emotion, in an effort to convince the defendants of the wisdom of settling out of court.

Stations with very big viewing areas and very small staffs sometimes contract videographers called "stringers" who'll cover the outskirts of the area where their staff shooters have neither the time nor the inclination to go. Then, when they need 30 seconds of footage, say, 50 miles south, the stringer shoots it, saving the station the time and expense of dispatching a crew.

A news shooter at one of the TV stations where I once worked started working part-time shooting curbs, driveways, and gutters from a slow moving vehicle. "Why?" I asked. So when the home owner comes back to them after a street project and says, "Hey, had curbs all along here and a driveway skirt," they can review the tapes and say, "No, you didn't."

Wherever there are people who are passionate about something, whether it be their children or their boats, you will find opportunities for video work.

Not-for-profit organizations produce frequent videos but never have much to spend. On the bright side, many big agencies see nonprofit and pro bono jobs as an opportunity to stretch their creative muscles without risking the big paycheck. This could also be your chance to show what you can do.

More religious organizations than ever before are using video, not only to record sermons but as a preaching tool within the service. Could your place of worship use some visual support?

Local cable companies often offer advertising packages that rival radio rates. Watch for local businesses that seem to be doing well and offer them packages—production and a media buy all rolled into one. If you pull it off a couple of times, you might be able to get a preferred insert rate from the cable company, further increasing your profit margin.

People who have expensive collections want documentation for vanity as well as insurance reasons. Examine still life paintings for clues to good "tabletop" work. You'll notice the ubiquitous eye-centering glow on the backdrop and soft, flattering key lights in the foreground. Exploit the formula well. People won't stand for unflattering portrayals of their prized assemblages.

A friend of mine takes a page from Coach's playbook and tapes his daughter's annual class play. He shoots three performances from different positions and edits it together. He works against a guaranteed minimum number of sales established with the school. Think of how many events might attract enough buyers from the ranks of the attendees to make two days of work worth it:

- Children's parties
- Community events and pageants
- Auto rallies
- Sporting competitions
- Hobby shows
- Horse shows
- Garden shows

Weddings are especially difficult jobs, not made easier by the locations, level of emotion, and the fact you don't get a "Take two!" Still, it's an amazingly large, lucrative market. That's why

How's shooting livestock portraits as an opportunity for work?

we deal with shooting weddings in some depth in Chapter 3. While shooting the ceremony might be a tough sell for the beginner, consider marketing the production of the increasingly popular "love story" video. They're usually constructed out of still photos, home movies, and interviews with parents, best friends, and the couple themselves. Add slow dissolves and lush strings and there won't be a dry eye in the house.

A variation on the love story is the life story. Also constructed out of still photos, home movies, and interviews, these documentary chronicles are popular and manifestly personal birthday and anniversary gifts. It's a tough market to contact but, once you understand the demographic (upscale, mature) a few well-placed ads will do the trick.

To get bookings nowadays, most bands need a music video. This isn't the high-flash, big-cash video destined for music television; this is the cleanly shot, well-mixed example of the band's sound and stage presence. Start with your friends and count on good word of mouth.

Real estate walk-throughs aren't cost-effective for tiny suburban ranches, but are well within the marketing budgets of developers raising palatial country homes on tracts outside big cities. You'll need a wide-angle lens for shooting spacious-looking interiors. A firm in one city was able to make the numbers work for a weekly home-tour show, broadcast Sunday mornings.

Video on demand (VOD) is offering a new generation of independent producers the opportunity to reach smaller and smaller market segments efficiently and cost effectively. With broadband delivery eliminating many traditional distribution costs and Internet promotion lowering marketing costs, the numbers begin to work for highly targeted, special-interest videos on everything from napkin folding to metal casting.

I've heard of a gentleman who spends his Saturday mornings, teamed with the course pro, taping golfers' swings.

This probably won't fly in major metropolitan areas, but in rural areas there are people doing a great business shooting livestock portraits. It's tricky to get a Holstein looking her level best. There's makeup, posing and, I wouldn't kid about this, a goat involved.

Video production is an appealing industry full of interesting people and amazing opportunities. There are more specialty areas than you could ever imagine. As you begin your life as a professional, your time must be evenly split between finding work and working on your skills. As you advance and begin to have a body of work to show, your opportunities increase in number. There's even more commercial, business-to-business work to be done than the business-to-consumer opportunities we've already examined. Then there's entertainment, those myriad cable and satellite channels dancing with images 24/7. It all lies ahead.

Making It Pay

Starting a freelance video business is like starting any other business. It's a difficult balancing act requiring not only creativity and sales ability, but time- and money-management skills.

Tips: Freelancing

+ Give every production the attention it deserves, no more and no less. OK, not *much* more at least. The more unbillable hours you work on any production, the less you're being paid per hour.

+ Stick to your budgets.

+ Be professional. Arrive on time, and be prepared, polite, and considerate of everyone's feelings, interests, and agendas.

+ Dress the part, #1. If pressed, I could name at least four people I know who've lost gigs for dressing inappropriately. Dark, plain clothes are best in most situations for two reasons. First, you don't stand out and second, you don't reflect. Think about it.

+ Dress the part, #2. I know what I just said about wardrobe, and that's good advice when you're in production. When you're in the early stages of wearing your writer/director creative hat, you might want to consider the fact that there are certain expectations people have when they hire "creative types." Don't disappoint. Leave the beret at home and wear a jacket and tie if that's the kind of place you're visiting, but don't miss the little chances to prove, subtly, that you're one of a kind. Use your better judgment.

+ Be careful about being held to a fixed price. Clients often cite the need to predict and limit costs, but be sure it's not done at your expense. Don't offer fixed bids to first time clients unless there is a clear understanding about everything including:

    Approval points and process. Determine who must approve, set an approval schedule, and don't step back past earlier approval points.

    Resource commitments. Spell out what crew and equipment will be used and for how long.

    Responsibilities. If there are other tapes or stills to be acquired, who is responsible? If there's insurance needed or shooting permits required, who is responsible?

Contingencies. If it rains the day exteriors are scheduled, who bears the cost?

Quality levels. Achieving perfection costs money.

Delivery dates. Know when the finished product is expected and stick to the agreement. Delivering earlier or later can cost money and opportunity.

Revisions. Revisions should be reasonable in timing, extent, and number or you should be paid extra.

Payment schedule. It's common to receive one-third to one-half up front and another payment after shooting is completed.

Build in an overrun plan. Try to get an agreement that if the project goes more than 25 percent over the allotted time, through no fault of yours, there will be a renegotiation. Alert the client when you're coming near and when you've reached the point of running over.

+ Respect confidentiality. Whether Uncle Jim has agreed to tell you his war stories or a client has allowed you a preview of the new product rollout, prove you deserve their trust.

+ Respect paperwork. Keep it up to date and turn it in as required. It may be important to your client and you as well. It'd be a shame to miss a reimbursement because you didn't get an expense report in on time.

+ Keep track of your hours. Whether you're being paid by the hour or not, it's helpful to know how close you've come to your estimate.

+ Don't stop selling while you're producing or you're in for some dry times.

+ Don't ever forget the 7 P's (Chapter 3).

Chapter 3:
The Seven P's

Overview

Remember these 7 P's: Proper Prior Planning Prevents Piss-Poor Production.

I've heard it said a half dozen ways with a variety of P's but the meaning persists; planning is paramount! If you don't believe it, scare up some horror stories. Everyone in the industry has some. You'll hear about the live report from the swim meet that is drowned out by the previously unnoticed loudspeaker above. You'll hear about the crew turned away from a critical shoot in the Middle East because women are required to wear skirts, not shorts! You'll hear of luggage lost, actors sauced, and wires crossed. Whose fault is it? Who cares?! The fact is, recorders jam, clients change scripts, grooms get cold feet, and it rains, sometimes for days on end. All a video maker can do is hope for the best, plan for the worst, and try to find the bright side. Tell the client the rain will make the shot "edgy."

Tips: Planning Checklist

+ Know your audience, where they'll watch, and why they'll watch
+ Work within your abilities. Adding unreasonable levels of difficulty to a production points you down the road to failure.
+ If you're using a script, be sure it's the best it can be. Ten rewrites are cheaper than one reshoot.
+ Scout your locations for shots, sound, and light.
+ Have all clearances and permits necessary on hand.
+ Have all props, enough charged batteries, whatever special equipment might be necessary, some lens tissue, and plenty of gaffer's tape.
+ Know your storyboard, if you're using one, shot for shot.
+ Know your schedule, shot by shot. Everything takes longer than you think.
+ Be sure everyone knows call times, dress code, and parking regulations.
+ Be sure the talent understands wardrobe and has the latest copy of the script.
+ Be sure you have talent releases on hand, ready to sign.

An intimate message might not play well in a public place. A soft sell might have a hard time in a noisy mall. Consider what distractions may compete for your viewer's attention.

Will your scene engage your intended audience? Outsiders may not see the humor in an inside joke. Poking fun at administrators might not be funny to a room full of administrators.

Without the advantage of family or familiarity, a piece must stand on its own production merit.

The theme here was "Superheroes," but rather than cast big, strapping body builders, we used employees. To someone outside the corporation, these might appear to be unlikely superheroes but that was the point. To their coworkers, they are superheroes!

Audience

Begin planning by discovering the *who, where,* and *why* of your audience.

Who they are—how old, how liberal, how educated, and how rowdy—will inform your choice of music, humor, jargon, and attitude.

Where the audience will be watching is critical. Will the viewer be comfortable and focused or standing in a line, bombarded by competing messages? Shorter is better if the audience is strolling around a trade show, but if you're going to ask them to line up, file in, take a seat, and wait for the lights to dim, the production should be long enough to satisfy expectations.

Why is the audience watching? A half hour into your niece's first birthday party tape and you're still smiling because the images conjure memories. Five minutes into your *neighbor's* niece's first birthday party tape and you're ready to fake a stroke to get out of the room. It's not that people can't enjoy watching other folk's home movies. People are fascinated by other people. Who doesn't enjoy passing time in the airport "people watching?" Then why won't they sit for hours and watch your home movies? I believe it comes down to the fact that in the airport the "viewers" get to choose what they'll view. They have a broad field of vision and are able to constantly change the focus of their viewing. They seldom pick out one person and simply stare them down. That's not people watching, that's staring and that's impolite.

If you're hired to tell a story, you'll be told why the audience will watch. For example, they might be required to watch as a condition of employment or circumstance. There may be something to gain from watching: a reward, like making more money, advice on getting Junior into college, or solving a persistent problem. In either case, the audience will tolerate a more limited production budget. The level of difficulty spikes when your job is to *entice* an audience to watch, a challenge just like every big-time television network faces everyday, constantly competing for "eyes." If the audience isn't challenged, shocked, delighted, or otherwise engaged, viewership suffers.

> **Tip:** Don't ever disregard the value of letting people see themselves. In many corporate projects, in lots of car commercials, and in all weddings and home video productions, the "spoonful of sugar" is the fact that the actors are well known to the audience.

A common mistake is to assume a video can be made to serve several audiences. The message for the potential customer is, "This product will solve all your problems." The message for the salesperson charged with selling the product might be, "Challenge the customer to list her problems and show how this product will solve each problem." Maybe the pictures and music will serve both messages but the script sure won't.

Trying to combine the how-to-sell and why-to-buy projects in one production will potentially confuse the two different audiences and risk missing the mark with both.

Maybe you've heard the old TV saw, "Content is king." Believe it. Live by it. Know people will watch fuzzy black-and-white surveillance camera footage if there's a heart stopping robbery, a fistfight, or a pratfall involved. Understand also that people will tire of even the most beautiful footage if, ultimately, nothing happens in the frame.

> **Tip:** If you get a chance to show your work, watch your audience. Sitting in the living room with the family or in a viewing room with your audience, pay attention, listen for deep breaths, and look for wandering eyes. Try to pinpoint where you have them and where you've lost them.

Ability, audacity, and reality

There is a genre of films that skips gaily along the line between documentary and comedy known as mockumentaries. *This Is Spinal Tap, Best in Show, A Mighty Wind,* and *Real Life* all fit this category. One of my favorites was a mockumentary called (with apologies to the Band) *The Last Polka.* The story about two polka-playing brothers from a fictitious land called Leutonia, "a flat treeless land on the dark side of the Balkans." Late in their careers, the Schmenge Brothers, played by Eugene Levy and John Candy, are attempting a comeback. They've rented a huge stadium and in what looks like a candid conversation with their stage manager, they tell him of their idea to do a "big laser show" and pullout a couple of fake *Star Wars* light sabers, obviously plastic tubes with flashlight handles. I warn you, right here, right now, don't promise your clients a big laser show if you can't deliver. Don't count on anyone in the audience cutting you any slack, either. Nothing looks more foolish than earnest efforts at special effects that just don't pass the test. That's not to say you can't decide to do something cheesy for the comic value. Just be sure it's very clear the audience knows that you know the effect looks cheesy.

You owe it to your clients to be realistic about your abilities and what can be done within your budget. There are times to stretch and times to be conservative and it's not too hard to figure out which is which. Clients don't hire producers to explore their limits. They hire producers because they have a message that needs to be dispersed, a story that needs to be told. As a professional,

Shows featuring funny clips sent in by viewers, police car cameras, and security cameras prove quality of image takes a back seat to quality of action.

If you intend to make people fly or bend steel in their bare hands, you'd better be able to pull it off convincingly.

your job is to do that as efficiently and cost effectively as possible and not stray into the dangerous territory where you remove the audience's focus from the message and place it on your production. Videos that have committed this sin sometimes win awards but they don't win return customers. Save the big stretch for the times when you're working on your own projects, when you have no one to please but yourself, and even then, don't fool yourself into believing awards mean you've done the best job possible of communicating your message to the audience.

Be wary of comedy. It's not impossible but darned near. Remember that networks, with all their resources and all the writers, are seldom successful. In any given season there are no more than a half-dozen consistently funny and widely enjoyed comedy programs. Remember that the quality of your video production will always be tied to and emblematic of the quality of your client's product.

A friend of mine always says, "To you it's a video, to them it's their career." Videos are expensive. In a small firm or small department of a large firm, the video in this year's budget could be the single largest line item. If the project is a big success, people will notice. If the project is a big failure, people will notice. Be sure you and your client are noticed for the right reason.

Do yourself a favor; underpromise and overdeliver.

Studying the masters

I bought *Star Wars, Episode II: Attack of the Clones* not for any abiding love of the saga but for one word I saw on the back of the box—previsualization. Previsualization, or pre-viz, is a form of 3-D computer storyboarding employed by George Lucas and his team and closely examined in a disc-two documentary entitled *State of the Art: The Previsualization of Episode II*. It didn't disappoint, delivering interesting inside looks at the process of working out the action sequences of *Episode II*. But the section of the documentary that stuck with me was actually a reference back to the original *Star Wars* film. Lucas, in an interview, talks about how he's always had to use visual devices to get a feeling for motion within scenes. He talks of how he chose to use examples from World War II films to fashion a battle scene in the first episode. As he speaks, we're seeing footage from an old black-and-white film comprising dramatic shots intercut with actual World War II documentary footage of dogfights over Europe. Below the box showing this film is a second box showing a *Star Wars* battle clip. Amazingly, the shots matched exactly, frame for frame, edit for edit. Zero deviation. Lucas, a master in his own right, was not above reaching into the past for inspiration and instruction. The point here is, if you need inspiration or even a shot-for-shot template, look to the masters. Dissect your favorite commercials and study the dialogue patterns of your favorite comedians. Look to the great cinematographers, directors, and scriptwriters for framing, pacing, and story structure. Like the man said, "... all of life's riddles are answered in the movies."

Scripting

The primary planning device in any videomaker's toolkit is the script. Though scripting family gatherings might get you dropped from the will, all other situations demand it. Whether you intend to shoot a dramatic scene of your own invention or tape an actual event, the script tells others (and reminds you) of your plan. Though there are times they run parallel and times they diverge, we're going to follow the topic of scripting down three different roads.

Dramatic scripts

Aristotle, pupil of Plato and tutor of Alexander the Great, dissected the plot of *Animal House* in the fourth century BC. He worked out *High Plains Drifter, 8 Mile,* and *Rocky,* too. Thousands of stories share a basic structure. We meet a character or a group of characters that face adversity and overcome it. It is a simple rising and falling of action. Aristotle also specified there should be a beginning, middle, and end comprising a continuous, unified action, in other words, a plot driven by cause and effect. In the beginning, characters are introduced and the situation and location are set. In the middle, we find out what the characters want, and who or what is standing in the way. In the end, the actions of the characters resolve their situations and the story ends. It sounds simple but there are countless examples of productions that ignore this time-honored formula. They're called "flops."

Tell the audience about your characters through images and actions. This character spends a lot of time arranging things. Watching her arrange even little shampoo bottles speak volumes about her character's personality.

 Plot versus Story

+ A story reveals actions and incidents as a sequence of events. A plot reveals actions and incidents selectively, in order to build drama, sustain interest and establish conflict.

+ A story is constructed of certainties. A plot contains ambiguities and innuendo.

+ A story may not have a natural dramatic structure, a plot must.

+ A story depends on impartial facts and logic. A plot is driven by the character's perceptions of facts and their own subjective logic.

Write characters people will care about. The easiest way to make a video that viewers won't like is to populate the piece with characters who are unlikable. Viewers want to sympathize with movie characters and find commonalities.

Characters are defined by what they say *and* how they react to other characters. Facial expressions, glances, or telling close shots often fill in the blanks. Does one character always look to another for approval? Does one character avoid eye contact with another? Much is implied.

Tips: Keeping Your Characters Real

+ If characters must advance the plot through dialogue, give them "business," something physical to do while they talk. They'll not only seem more real, the action will add another layer of information. While the dialogue might reveal a "plan," watching the two employees might reveal one of them is too impatient or nervous to execute the plan properly.

+ Visual cues, sound effects, and music create rich layers of information that needn't be repeated in dialogue. If we see a character fidgeting nervously, we don't need to hear the character say, "I'm nervous."

+ When writing dialogue, it's important to relax your standards of grammar and sentence structure. People don't talk in complete sentences and dialogue written too precisely can seem stilted. Before you begin to write conversations, record a few, transcribe them, and see for yourself.

+ Character-driven screenplays frequently involve stories of the mind rather than stories of the body. Stories of the body are often plot-driven, full of conflict, contests, and action. Stories of the mind are stories of love, deceit, suspense, mystery, comedy, hope, ambition, and comeuppance.

Tips: True to Form

+ There are accepted formats for scripts. Unless you're working alone, others will need to read and understand your script and you'll need to follow the rules. Keep in mind the accepted script format became the accepted script format because it works. Aspiring writers can find everything from screenwriting software to how-to guides at www.writersstore.com. If you're going to take screenwriting seriously, buy anything by legendary screenwriting coach John Truby or go to the guru Syd Field and his classic how-to *Screenplay: The Foundations of Screenwriting*. When you find yourself taking it too seriously, read legendary screenwriter William Goldman's *Adventures in the Screen Trade*.

+ For every dramatic script that follows the Aristotelian model I'm selling, you'll be able to find examples of other successful, moving, memorable, even Academy Award–winning works that don't. However, you'll find few, if any, that were written by beginners. Before attempting to break new ground in storytelling, learn to execute the tried-and-true format successfully. Picasso became an accomplished draughtsman before he developed his abstract style.

Tip: As you draw your characters, find the good and the bad in each. Only in fairy tales are characters pure evil or perfectly good.

Tip: Motivate your characters. Actions and reactions should be just as logical in character-driven productions as in plot-driven productions.

If you've ever read a movie script, you'll recognize the format. For a complete nuts-and-bolts guide to professional formatting try *The Screenwriter's Bible: A Complete Guide to Writing, Formatting, and Selling Your Script* by David Trottier. Studio readers will dismiss a submitted script unread if it doesn't follow the proper format.

Characters often experience self-realization, finally examining their own lives, loves, beliefs, and attitudes. Audiences expect the main characters to be reshaped by the events of the screenplay, changed by their experiences.

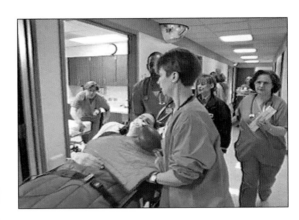

In plot-driven films, we don't require main characters to change. Instead, we often see them change the lives of other characters, solving problems, righting wrongs, then moving on.

Overview

Remember these 7 P's: Proper Prior Planning Prevents Piss-Poor Production.

I've heard it said a half dozen ways with a variety of P's but the meaning persists; planning is paramount! If you don't believe it, scare up some horror stories. Everyone in the industry has some. You'll hear about the live report from the swim meet that is drowned out by the previously unnoticed loudspeaker above. You'll hear about the crew turned away from a critical shoot in the Middle East because women are required to wear skirts, not shorts! You'll hear of luggage lost, actors sauced, and wires crossed. Whose fault is it? Who cares?! The fact is, recorders jam, clients change scripts, grooms get cold feet, and it rains, sometimes for days on end. All a video maker can do is hope for the best, plan for the worst, and try to find the bright side. Tell the client the rain will make the shot "edgy."

Audience

Begin planning by discovering the *who, where,* and *why* of your audience.

Who they are—how old, how liberal, how educated, and how rowdy—will inform your choice of music, humor, jargon, and attitude.

Where the audience will be watching is critical. Will the viewer be comfortable and focused or standing in a line, bombarded by competing messages? Shorter is better if the audience is strolling around a trade show, but if you're going to ask them to line up, file in, take a seat, and wait for the lights to dim, the production should be long enough to satisfy expectations.

Why is the audience watching? A half hour into your niece's first birthday party tape and you're still smiling because the images conjure memories. Five minutes into your *neighbor's* niece's first birthday party tape and you're ready to fake a stroke to get out of the room. It's not that people can't enjoy watching other folk's home movies. People are fascinated by other people. Who

doesn't enjoy passing time in the airport "people watching?" Then why won't they sit for hours and watch your home movies? I believe it comes down to the fact that in the airport the "viewers" get to choose what they'll view. They have a broad field of vision and are able to constantly change the focus of their viewing. They seldom pick out one person and simply stare them down. That's not people watching, that's staring and that's impolite.

If you're hired to tell a story, you'll be told why the audience will watch. For example, they might be required to watch as a condition of employment or circumstance. There may be something to gain from watching: a reward, like making more money, advice on getting Junior into college, or solving a persistent problem. In either case, the audience will tolerate a more limited production budget. The level of difficulty spikes when your job is to *entice* an audience to watch, a challenge just like every big-time television network faces everyday, constantly competing for "eyes." If the audience isn't challenged, shocked, delighted, or otherwise engaged, viewership suffers.

Just as in dramatic scriptwriting, it's best to give your subjects some business. Rather than interviewing the chef at a table, talk to her while she works.

Even when documenting your family, look for some business. Have your aunt thumb through a photo album, have the kids make chocolate milk or carve a pumpkin. Save waving at the camera for stills!

Metaphors can be useful devices for illustrating complex ideas. Here, the videographer shows how the DNA code that controls the replication of human genes is similar to the chanting that guides the replication of traditional patterns in Persian rugs.

Is this a mob or a crowd? Are these protesters or activists? It is vital for you to always make your meaning clear through the use of dialogue that defines what the viewer is seeing.

 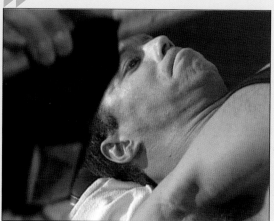

Footage of weightlifters would seem an inappropriate cover for a discussion of genetics, if not for the fact that it has been set up properly in the script. While the narration centers on cutting-edge scientific advances in high-tech labs, the story is told without shots of bubbling test tubes or researchers in white lab coats.

n historical documentaries, footage may be scant, or far in the past, or nonexistent. In other cases appropriate images might be difficult to gather or not engaging enough to sustain the viewer's interest. What's a documentarian to do? Often the answer is found in illustration and analogy.

n a documentary about genetics, there's a great deal to say but little to shoot. Standard laboratory footage can get old fast. The scriptwriter's challenge becomes finding other ways to tell the story. The answer is visual analogy. For instance, the question is asked "How many times have you heard it said, 'Sure, that bodybuilder looks great now, but all that muscle will turn to fat?'" The mention of bodybuilding sets up the gym footage. The gym footage covers narration discussing the fact that muscle cells can't turn to fat but, scientists *have* found a way, using gene therapies, to reprogram other cells to turn into heart muscle cells.

It's important when writing to consider the weight of words and how the marriage of pictures and words challenges viewers to extract meaning. One famous court case favored a woman who filed suit against a station after she was shown simply waiting for a bus in her neighborhood as the narrator talked about prostitution problems. The combination of picture and word left an unintended connection.

If your goal is to present a balanced look at a subject, you're faced with the difficult task of choosing neutral words to describe events. Bias may be impossible to squeeze out of a script entirely, but letting it slip by unaware is an invitation to criticism. An obvious example is the distinction between a mob and a crowd. Less obvious is the fact that words like *protester* or *demonstrator* are slightly more negative than *activist* or *marcher*.

The documentary script format, though not as rigid as the movie script format, has evolved to suit the needs of documentarians. Typically, each script page is divided in two vertical columns. The right side contains audio information while the left side of the script calls out the visuals. The documentary layout allows for easy timing, something less important in comparatively open-ended productions. It's also easier to read than a dramatic script, especially for people interested in narration only or shot descriptions only. Music, sound bites, narration, graphics, and special effects are easier to see and separate. This format also offers space for laying out supporting graphics, common in fact-heavy documentaries and in our third script type, industrial scripts.

Industrial scripts

"Industrials" has become a generic, catch-all term for business productions. A fund-raiser for a nonprofit, a corporate training video, a business-to-business (B2B) image piece, a municipal marketing video—they're all "industrials." All the methods, tricks, and conventions we've laid out for dramatic and documentary scripts apply to industrial scripts as well.

Where industrial scripts differ from the previous two types is in the laserlike focus necessary to make a project successful. Industrials tend to have a well-defined purpose and a firm budget. The success of an industrial project is measurable and the producer is held accountable.

Art and *business* conflict in the world of industrial video. On one hand, business clients consider producers to be vendors and expect the same high level of customer service, cost consciousness, and professionalism they'd receive from a vendor. On the other hand, clients understand video production is a creative enterprise, and success might hinge on invention and inspiration—both difficult to specify in a contract. Video producers must strike a conscious balance between attention to the message and free-flowing creativity.

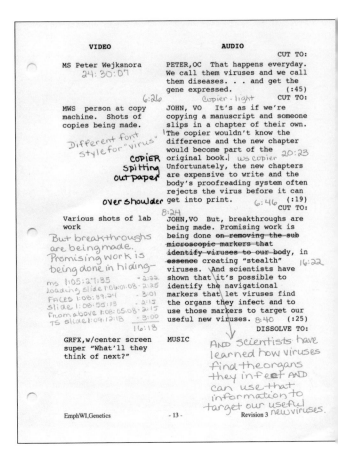

Actual documentary script page

Instead of gathering various shots of an exasperated manager struggling through a workday, the juggling analogy had more impact, staying power, and visual appeal.

DOLLAR SIGNS

Americans who say their
parents taught them to...

comparison shop   85%
donate money   80%
save and invest   75%
balance a checkbook 58%

USA Today

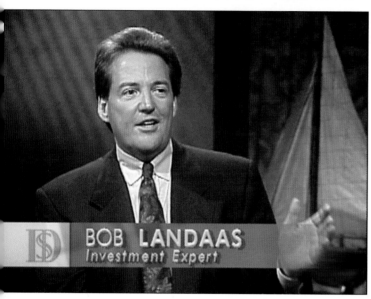

BOB LANDAAS
Investment Expert

Here's a simple, indisputable fact: People can't listen and read at the same time unless they're hearing and reading the same thing. If you're feeding information with graphics on the screen, don't make the mistake of simultaneously feeding dissimilar information in the narration. One or the other will be lost. One exception is "attribution." We've been trained to read a speaker's name and job title even as they speak.

It's also critical to remember, though you may work on half a dozen industrials each year, your client will likely preside over just this one and they're hoping you'll put together a kudos-all-around career builder.

Often, once a client realizes the script is on the right side of the page, that's all they'll read. Don't allow it—remind them to also carefully study the video information on the left. First, the video offers additional information and support for the script. Second, there could be unintended issues created by the combination of certain text and certain pictures. Finally, it's vital for the client to understand what you intend to shoot, because the client may be able to point out issues you, as an outsider, could miss. For instance, approaching a conference table, some firms prefer sales reps to sit across a corner from, rather than opposite the client. Shooting it the wrong way could make the footage unusable.

> ## Tips: Clarity and Comprehension
>
> + An overriding goal in writing an industrial script is clarity. Don't use long sentences or awkward sentence constructions. Viewers can't go back and "re-listen." Understood or misunderstood, the piece rolls on.
>
> + Don't ask viewers to drink from a fire hose. Pumping out too much information makes gathering any of it difficult. Faced with incomprehension, viewers will simply shut down.

 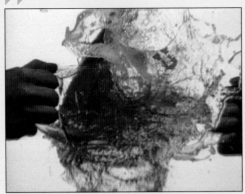 

Keep things simple. In this public service announcement for the National Transportation Safety Board, a series of beer mugs comes together in slow motion to the sound of automobiles skidding and crashing. Before the final "accident," a friend intervenes, stopping the others from driving drunk. It's a simple concept, inexpensive to shoot, and exceptionally memorable.

Overview

Remember these 7 P's: Proper Prior Planning Prevents Piss-Poor Production.

I've heard it said a half dozen ways with a variety of P's but the meaning persists; planning is paramount! If you don't believe it, scare up some horror stories. Everyone in the industry has some. You'll hear about the live report from the swim meet that is drowned out by the previously unnoticed loudspeaker above. You'll hear about the crew turned away from a critical shoot in the Middle East because women are required to wear skirts, not shorts! You'll hear of luggage lost, actors sauced, and wires crossed. Whose fault is it? Who cares?! The fact is, recorders jam, clients change scripts, grooms get cold feet, and it rains, sometimes for days on end. All a video maker can do is hope for the best, plan for the worst, and try to find the bright side. Tell the

VIDEO	AUDIO
1.7 MS Ped up and widen on a picket fence.	VO NARRATOR There were picket fences...
DISSOLVE TO:	(:02)
1.8 MS Camera dollies along looking straight down on the **FIELDSTONE WALK.**	VO NARRATOR ...and fieldstone walks...
CUT TO:	(:02)
1.9 MWS Extreme wide angle, extremely close to a **GARDEN GNOME.**	VO NARRATOR ....multitudes of lawn ornaments.
CUT TO:	(:04)
1.10 WS **OVERGROWN LAWN** shot from the near ground with **HANDLEBARS** of missing tricycle seen above grass.	VO NARRATOR And where there was lawn it grew - sometimes long as wheat and thick as 60's shag.
CUT TO:	(:07)
2.1 MWS The camera peds up on **A SQUAD OF HOME-OWNERS** with **LAWNMOWERS** and various **ICONS OF LAWN CARE.**	VO NARRATOR And the people gathered, anxious to trim the wild lawns and get on with the weekend.
CUT TO:	(:06)
2.2 EWS Homeowner checks his **WATCH.**	SND FX SND FULL Ticking of watch (:02)
2.3 MWS Low angle, looking up at an **"ANCIENT ONE,"** and impressive silhouetted figure with his hand and arm raised like a traffic cop's stop signal.	MUSIC SND UNDR Music resumes with ominous horns
CUT TO:	VO NARRATOR But the ancient keepers of the lawns stood in their way...
2.4 MS Homeowners in the BG as their spokesperson steps slowly to the foreground mouthing the words, "Just say the word. JUST SAY 'MOW.'"	(:04)
	VO NARRATOR And the people implored, desperate to go forth into the yards and get it over with. They begged the ancients, "Just say the word. JUST-SAY-'MOW.'"
CUT TO:	(:10)
2.5 MWS Wide angle, looking at the "ANCIENT ONE" from behind.	VO NARRATOR But the ancient ones mocked them saying...
FAST 180° **DOLLY TO:**	(:03)
2.6 MWS Wide angle, still looking up. The ancient one flips a **"SEED CAP"** onto his head as the light changes and he is revealed to be a crotchety curmudgeon -a "neighborhood ancient one," now known simply as **"OLD GUY."**	OC ANCIENT ONE Mow? Mow! You can't mow. Don't you know the rules? (as he's revealed his voice changes from "Charlton Heston" to "Ross Perot")
	OC OLD GUY This grass is soaking wet! You can't mow wet grass! It'll clump...
CUT TO:	(:08)

Here's the format for an industrial script. Make sure your client reads both sides of it.

Location Work

Location scouting is a time consuming and difficult enough task that there are people in the film and video businesses who do nothing but scout locations, looking for that spot that combines the best of scenery and convenience. Of course there are times when you have no control and you just have to make do with the location you've been given. The most important examples would be:

Weddings

As of this printing, the average U.S. wedding costs around $22,000, a cost borne by 2.3 million American couples and their families, making weddings a $54 billion per year business. Wedding photography and videography corners an average of 6.6 percent of that total or $3.6 billion per year. Typical prices for these services range between $500 and $10,000. There's a lot of opportunity there, but there's danger as well. At weddings, emotion and video production dance together without the advantage of one important video production benefit: They lack a "Take two!" Weddings have to be done right the first time! Here's how.

Before the event

Attend the rehearsal. If you're going to have to move the camera around during the ceremony, use the time at the rehearsal to figure your angles, routes, and positions. Keep the 180° rule (see sidebar) in mind as you choose your positions. You're always looking for the closest, most direct shot of the action.

When at the rehearsal, keep in mind that weddings of different religions and different cultures will flow differently. Couples will often personalize the ceremony and configuration further. Don't take anything for granted. Ask. It's critical to understand the flow of the ceremony, anticipate movements, and prepare for contingencies. Find out what everyone will be wearing. Anticipate contrast issues. If faced with the choice, expose for the attendees and let the background go dark or blow out. That rehearsal will also be a good time to find out if the bride or groom has a surprise planned for the other. Be discreet.

The day of the event

On the day of the blessed event, arrive early, leaving a great deal of time for setup and checking your equipment. Be sure nothing has changed, no flowers have been placed that might block your camera position. This would be a good time to determine where the main characters will be before the ceremony. Preparation shots might play nicely into the video.

It's also a good time to keep an eye out for prewedding activities, whether they are planned or not. Follow the action. The limo that's late, the mix-up with the flowers, Uncle Louie ending up across town—all these (if not painful and better forgotten) may be memorable moments in the course of their day. Little things that seem unimportant to you may hold great significance for the wedding couple.

Make sure there's a wireless mic on the groom. If you have two senders and receivers, put the house audio feed on the other. That feed might be line level so be sure you have an audio pad available. Don't try to set up lights. Most venues are just too large to light evenly and effectively. Creating a contrast problem between the bride and groom and the rest of the surroundings doesn't help anyone either. Use fresh tapes every time. Bring enough to roll all cameras all the time. Agree upon how long the raw footage will be kept.

Use your newest, freshest batteries for every ceremony. Use new batteries in your wireless mics as well. Know the location of AC outlets just in case. And as a final technical assurance, check and double-check all connections, battery levels, and audio levels before the ceremony begins. Tape down cables that run down hallways or across doorways.

Be sure to use a tripod during the ceremony. Handheld is nice when you're close enough to be smooth and steady. If it's a single-camera shoot, change positions crisply and quietly.

Work out a cue with someone who knows what's going on, perhaps the wedding planner, so you'll be ready to roll when the ceremony starts. While you're waiting for that all-important cue, shoot cutaways of guests. Here's where you'll be glad if you asked the bride and groom in advance of the ceremony how important it is to capture every face. With that information in your bag of tricks, you'll know who the special people are, the people whose absence would be a serious mark against your success.

There will be shots you're *expected* to get. Don't take a chance; talk it over with the couple.

In the edit
Determine the length and scope of the edit beforehand. While some people will want a condensed "highlight" version of the ceremony, others will expect the tape to run nearly real time. Cross-cutting between the bride preparing, the groom preparing, and the preparations at the church or hall can be an effective method for getting close-ups of the entire wedding party into the video as well as a method of building anticipation.

If you're looking to enhance the impact of your presentation, don't fall into that beginner's trap: excessive effects. They may be cool today but leave people cold next year. Dissolves and half dissolves never go out of style. However, it's a good idea to use music to amplify the emotion of the day. There are many libraries of beautiful music available either on a per use or buyout basis. Be careful of rights and clearances. As the producer/editor, you will be held responsible for the illegal use of copyrighted music, regardless of who supplies the CD and regardless of whether the client signs a document releasing you from responsibility. Finally, work efficiently, but it's not necessary to deliver a finished tape overnight. A one-month turnaround, from wedding day to delivery, is common and competitive.

Once you understand the principles and procedures I've laid out here, you're going to have to shoot a few weddings in order to build a reel. You won't get jobs if you don't have a reel. Your best bet will be to shoot the weddings of friends and family (for the cost of the tape). For your very first shoot, do the wedding of someone in your immediate family. They're more likely to forgive you someday.

Tip: Mandatory Shots

+ The bride entering
+ The father giving the bride away
+ Wide shots of the wedding party
+ The readings
+ Exchange of vows
+ Breaking of the glass (Jewish tradition)
+ Reaction shots of the immediate family
+ Honored guests
+ The couple exiting
+ The receiving line (not common in Jewish weddings)
+ Getting in the limo
+ The gift table
+ The cake
+ Cutting the cake
+ The toasts
+ The first dance
+ The tossing of the bouquet and garter

Tips: Making Weddings Your Business

+ When buying your equipment, you might want to consider a purchasing a second, smaller camera and tripod good for a second angle lockdown shot. Choose a camera with a remote control and a tally light to tell you it's rolling.
+ You'll need to advertise and take a booth at bridal fairs to drum up business until word of mouth starts working for you. Promotion is a cost of doing business. Factor it into your price structure. Work out a price structure based on options before, during, and after the wedding. Be sure you offer packages for any budget.
+ If you're serious about this career path, join the Wedding and Event Videographer's Association (www.WEVA.com) where you have access to sample videos done by some of the best. You'll always benefit from advice from the experts.

In the wedding video business there's no "Take two!" so be sure to arrive early, double check everything before the wedding begins, and when possible, have more than one camera set for multiple-angle shots.

Location scouting, stealing shots

In shooting, just as in real estate, location is everything. It's not that you can't make many locations suffice; it's just that every power line or cruddy corner that needs cropping out limits your shot angles and reduces your options. On the other hand, by aggressively cropping and choosing shot lengths and angles, you can coax a shot out of almost any location. In the middle of an urban setting, a low angle shot with a touch of blue sky framed by a few leaves could provide enough visual coin to sell the idea your subject is hiking through an open meadow.

I never go location scouting without a compass, a notebook, and a digital still camera. I recently shot a script that called for kids playing ring-around-the-rosy in a field. The money shot was a high angle overhead, so the grass was key. It couldn't look like a freshly mown lawn, but the grass couldn't be as high as a real field or we'd lose them. I spent two days driving around looking at fields. In addition, since I was working with lots of children, parents, and a large crew, I needed to be sure the location was accessible, close to the city, and had all the toilets I might need. Short grass, tall grass, trees in the background, wide-open spaces, I saw it and shot stills of it all. For each still I shot, I made a note of where I stood and added the compass direction. I'm absolutely certain that without the shots and all those notes I might have found the location, but I'd never find it again!

Are you finding it difficult to locate an interior that works *and* can be freed up for shooting? Try renting a model home. They're mostly empty during the week and come fully furnished. Add a few props for that "lived in" look. Consider using industrial parks as street locations. They're private property so you'll need per-

For this ring-around-the-rosy shot, I spent two days looking for just the right grassy field. Scouting out your location well ahead of the shoot will give you the best chance at achieving just the look you want.

Tip: Location Checklist

+ Are you on private property? Who owns it? If you're unsure, check the city's register of deeds for the owner's name. You'll need permission, and it's best to get it in writing. There's a typical location release form available on my website at www.petemay.com. It's also a good idea to have production insurance just in case you crush someone's prize dahlias or set the place on fire.

+ Is there sufficient parking for you and your crew? Is there going to be a lighting truck or just personal vehicles?

+ Is the location accessible? Most heavy gear is on wheels. A third floor walkup without an elevator will wreak havoc on your production schedule.

+ Is there some place for talent and crew to relax when they're not needed on set? Be sure they can't be heard while you're shooting.

+ Is there someplace to feed the crew?

+ Have you thought about bathrooms? How about a place for actors to change and makeup to be applied?

+ Is the location right at the right time of the day? Always visit a location you intend to use, on a sunny day and at the time of day you intend to shoot to get an idea of the sun's position and judge how shadows and reflections might affect your schedule.

+ Is the location quiet enough for your shoot? Is the location on a bus line or a flight path? Is the room next to the very noisy old elevator? Many noises are intrusive enough to ruin shots and needlessly lengthen your shoot. Remember that the rest of the world operates on a schedule developed without you in mind. For example, you might find the perfect factory interior only to learn later the bottling lines run every morning from nine to noon, eliminating any chance of getting good sound.

+ Are there permits needed? Shooting on most city streets requires a permit issued by that city's film office. If the area isn't large enough or organized enough to have its own film office, check with the department of public works or the mayor's office for direction. Some areas require a permit fee paid up front.

Renting a model home gives you all the cozy domestic locations you'll need, and they're furnished, too.

Do you really need to shoot interiors and exteriors in the same building? People are very forgiving of *minor* errors in continuity. The interiors here are shot in a studio, the exteriors on location.

mission but they're mostly empty weekends and evenings. Houses for sale and offices for rent are also likely locations. There are short-term furniture rental companies who normally cater to the temporarily assigned corporate client. Some stores will rent furniture and props out of their inventory for roughly 10 percent of the items' retail cost.

Don't be afraid to approach cities and parks for location permits or other assistance. It's often no more difficult than making a phone call to get parking reserved or traffic blocked from a street for a few hours. Enlightened municipalities understand being friendly to the film and video community brings good will and welcome revenue to the area. There might be a permit fee based on the city services you require. If you need police to reroute traffic, you'll have to pay for it.

For the more daring directors, there is another alternative—stealing shots. Many low- and no-budget films count on being able to jump out and get the shots they need before the cops arrive and put them out of business. It's a harrowing way to work and can incur a city's wrath if the cast and crew aren't mobile enough to scatter at the first sign of trouble.

Tip: International Voltages (V)

+ U.S.–110V
+ U.K.–230V
+ European Union–230V
+ Japan–110V
+ Australia–240V

Is there sufficient electrical power adequately dispersed? Though most of the equipment we use on shoots is pretty easy on the energy, lights are the exception. It may be necessary to find a couple of outlets far enough apart so they are likely on different circuits. If there's any doubt as to whether you're in danger of popping a breaker, calculate your draw this way. Lighting instruments are rated in watts. You need to estimate total wattage by adding up all the lights you might use. Maybe you're planning on using two 650 W lamps and a 1,000 W. That's 2,300 watts total. Divide that number by the voltage (110 in the U.S., see table for others) and you get, round number, 21 amps. Wattage divided by voltage equals amperage. That's a little more than the average 20-amp circuit breaker will tolerate. You ought to consider splitting up the load, putting some of the lights on another circuit. Make sure you know where the circuit breakers are just in case you're not too good with math.

REMEMBER: Wattage divided by voltage equals amperage

In this shot, we had the fire department hose down the streets for that great shine. Since it was below zero the night we shot, the sanitation department had to come in just after and salt the area...free of charge. Enlightened municipalities understand that being friendly to the film and video community brings good will and welcome revenue to the area. Never assume anything: always be diligent about calling the right people to confirm so there are no expensive surprises.

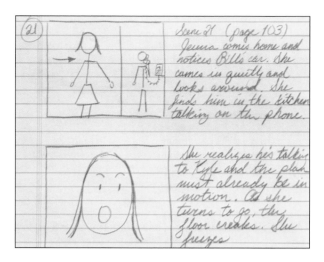

Though these storyboards vary in artistic merit, they differ little in the amount and quality of information offered. You can see the spatial relationship between your actors. You can imagine suitable locations and work out your screen directions and eye lines. Storyboards allow you to anticipate problems and correct them now with your eraser rather than later with your checkbook.

If You Want to Be Professional about All This

When I was eight and announced I was going to be an artist, my father wasted no time talking me out of it. He told me artists ended up poor, living in cold, drafty garrets...that don't allow pets. The pet thing clinched it. I steered my career course back toward ice cream man/astronaut. I think the truth is my father realized I was no Michelangelo and decided that bubble needed bursting. I know people who don't storyboard because they "can't draw." That's no excuse. It doesn't stop me and it shouldn't stop you. Storyboarding forces you to visualize every shot, and visualization is another critical key to proper planning. If you don't usually "think in pictures," exploiting the storyboard process is especially helpful. Having storyboards to show a client who has difficulty "picturing" is priceless. When it's time to draw storyboards, do like I do, crank some appropriate tunes, get the script in your head, grab a box of crayons, and start drawing.

Storyboarding: From Stan Lee to stick figures

Cross referencing the storyboard with the script, you should be able to guess whether the shot will hold long enough to get through the dialogue. Some storyboards are very precise, with dialogue noted under each drawing. For me, a cross-reference number on the drawing and script is good enough. Pads of storyboard forms are available through television and film industry supply houses, though it's easy to make your own. Even most word-processing programs have enough drawing power to construct passable storyboards.

If you have any kind of digital snapshot camera, you can consider an alternative to traditional hand drawn storyboards, especially if you're handy with computer paint programs. By shooting frames or shooting frames and drawing over them, you can create very nice, very visual storyboards. There are drawbacks to this method. First, it's another shoot. You'll need actors and a location. Unless you own a very nice still camera or your DV camera has a still mode, you'll be limited by the snapshot lens, which is often fixed or offers a limited zoom. Still, if you have to convey your idea to a skeptical client, this might be your best bet.

Some of the best storyboards in the world are available in bookstores and on newsstands everywhere. Comic books and illustrated novels are fabulous examples of high-end, full-blown storyboards. Look at the illustrations of Marvel comics founder Stan Lee. His dynamic rendering of Spiderman's dramatic adventures could be translated panel for panel, shot for shot to film or video. Many illustrated comics have actually made the jump to contemporary films. Sam Mendes turned one graphic novel into a hit movie, casting Tom Hanks in *Road to Perdition*. Page through the book and watch the DVD at the same time. You'll see they follow closely.

Today, technology has allowed movie directors to take storyboarding to a new level. It's become just one step in a process called previsualization or pre-viz. Filmmakers are using computer generation and shooting DV to create moving storyboards they'll match shot for shot, edit for edit in the final film.

Budgets

There are two good reasons to always do a budget. The first is to see what it might cost to do a project based on your vision of the finished product. The second is to track the actual costs of your production against your projection.

Sometimes, working with agencies or large production houses you'll see five-line budgets that list preproduction, production, postproduction, talent, and travel. That's not a budget and it serves no purpose when you're doing battle in the production arena. A true budget lays out every day rate, every rental, even every tape cassette.

In the past I've made the mistake of saying, "OK, they'll never go for the aerial if they think it's this expensive. On the other hand, they expected the animation to cost more than this. So I'll leave the aerial low and bump up the animation and at some point take the overage on animation and pay the shortfall on the aerial." You can bet that at some point in the process they'll drop the animation to save money, thus erasing your pad for the aerial. Bottom line, don't submit a line item budget unless you're darned sure every line is realistic and you can live with line item cuts.

A Budget-Building Checklist

There's a downloadable Excel-based budget form on my website (www.petemay.com), but for the time being, let's just look at the major budget areas you need to cover.

+ **Personnel:**
  The producer, director, writer, videographer, audio recordist, makeup artist, grips, gaffer, production assistant, etc. This item is sometimes divided up into the above the line or creative participants and the *below the line* or technical crew.

+ **Equipment:**
  The rental rates (or if you own it, the monthly payments) on all the production equipment you intend to use.

+ **Talent costs:**
  The narrator, the actors, dancers, clowns, and jugglers, as well as their wardrobe and per diems (per-day expense reimbursement).

+ **Travel expenses:**
  Hotels, rental cars, meals, tips, and all the incidental costs of travel.

+ **Craft services:**
  The catering, snacks, and drinks. If you have a crew, you must feed them.

+ **Record stock:**
  Your field tapes, the discs you'll archive to, the copies of the master tape or disc on completion.

+ **Postproduction:**
  The rental of the edit computer, decks for digitizing and dubbing, music cuts or composer, audio sweetening.

+ **Art:**
  All the graphics and animation, even the storyboards.

+ **Rights and clearances:**
  The cost of renting the location, paying the city for a permit, and getting the local bluegrass band to allow you to use a cut off their new CD.

+ **Expendables and miscellaneous:**
  The gaffer's tape, labels, lamps, stamps, and gels—things you use up in the course of a production.

+ **Insurance:**
  Not even rental houses will touch you if you don't have insurance. The good news is riders for individual productions aren't too expensive and you just add it to your cost.

+ **Contingency:**
  Whether you're budgeting a six-figure extravaganza or your own little documentary, a 10 percent contingency will help you over the bumps.

+ **Tax:**
  A video producer is a reseller and that means you can apply for a tax-free number and avoid paying sales tax. That also means you have to do regularly scheduled reports of income and sales tax. I prefer to pay the sales tax and pass the cost on to my clients.

If you can avoid it, don't finalize your budget until you've seen a script. Any budget projections done before the script can't take into account talent, location costs, travel requirements, and twenty other budget lines.

If the budget must precede the script, the budget must be given the power to edit the script. For example, it's very easy to write in a "beautiful" aerial of the company campus at sunrise, but it's harder to write the check for the helicopter and camera mount after two days of rain have washed the "beautiful" from the shot.

Duplication and distribution aren't normally added to a production budget but if the client wants you to handle it, add a line or two. In general, a markup of between 10 and 15 percent is considered a fair profit.

A budget serves the purpose of drawing boundaries. If the client asks for something that requires an extra day of shooting, you can point to the approved budget and say something one of my favorite editors used to say when clients asked for the seemingly impossible: "I can do anything you can afford."

I usually include a line in the budget adding the cost of a high-quality dub of the finished product for my personal archive. In addition, I usually budget in entry fees for a couple of awards competitions. I think it tells my clients just how seriously I'm going to take their project.

Rights, clearances, and losing the farm

The mere mention of her name makes me shudder. She caused me a lot of pain and worry. Sometimes I wish I'd never heard of Cindy Crawford. See, the script involved a self-important investigative reporter who, going undercover, had constructed an elaborate and entirely fictitious life story. In assembling his fake family, he had chosen a pretty bride from a magazine spread and Photoshopped his head into the wedding picture and framed it. Besides looking really fake, he was the only one who didn't realize the bride he chose was Cindy Crawford. We shot it and edited it and screened the scene for friends. The joke played very well but all the while, through all the laughter, I had this sick feeling in my stomach. Finally, shortly before the project was to be delivered, I couldn't take it any more and brought in an entertainment lawyer. Her opinion boiled down to, "What, are you nuts?" It didn't matter that we never showed Crawford full screen. It didn't matter that she's a public figure and it didn't matter that we never even mentioned her name. All that mattered was that we had lifted and reproduced a copyrighted photo and were about to benefit from her image without paying her for the privilege. We were forced to rethink the joke and reshoot the scene scant days before the project's premiere. The fact is, music, movie clips, historical photographs, and darn near anything else you might add to a production that you didn't create yourself is likely to have copyright protection. To use any of them, you'll need permission from the copyright holder and will likely owe licensing fees, some of which can be very pricey, though considerably less than the cost of a trial with you as the defendant.

How do you know if the song or clip or photo you want to use is copyrighted? My advice is, assume that it is. Under U.S. law, all creative and original material has automatic copyright protection from the moment it's created, whether it's registered with the federal government or not. It's certainly nice to know you enjoy this kind of protection, but it's daunting to realize that so does everyone else. Even more daunting is the fact that some have legions of lawyers who do nothing but hunt down copyright violations.

Keep in mind that getting the rights to use even a segment of a song can require permission not only from the artist but all the people involved in creating that recording: the musicians, the composer, the arranger, the agents, the studio, and the record company. If you're determined to use prerecorded commercial music, search "music, licensing, copyright" on the Web and you'll find a dozen agencies that'd be willing to walk you through the process for a fee.

Fair use is no use to most

The fair-use rule is an often-misunderstood aspect of U.S. copyright law. This rule was created in the belief that unauthorized use of copyrighted material can benefit society if it's used for education, scholarship, or to inform the public. If you're a classroom teacher, a research scholar, or a news reporter, you're probably already enjoying fair use. For the rest of us, it's complicated and difficult to justify (www.copyright.gov/help/faq/faq-fairuse.html). A small piece of copyrighted material used in a noncompetitive manner for the benefit of the public might pass muster, but before you make that leap, you'd better be confident about arguing the point in front of a judge, jury, and the copyright holder. My feeling is, play it safe. Get permission and pay the fee. Picture yourself on the other side of the argument. You'd want others to use your material fairly.

The only creative material we can all use free and clear is material in the public domain. But again, this is limited, and tricky. As of this printing, anything published in the U.S. before 1923 is considered in the public domain, but of course this doesn't cover a movie version of *Romeo and Juliet,* or a rock band's rendition of *Home on the Range.*

Tip: It's Worth Checking

+ For more information on copyright you can visit the website of the U.S. Copyright Office at www.lcweb.loc.gov/copyright. Copyright records from 1978 to the present are searchable online.

+ Another good resource regarding copyright issues is www.nolo.com, where you'll find translation of legalese into plain English.

+ Be sure to check the copyright laws in your country if you're not sure they're the same as I've outlined them here.

▶▶

▶▶

Other material that's considered public domain is material created by the federal government. But note that it's only material that's created *by* the federal government. If the material was produced *for* the federal government, it may be copyrighted.

Chapter 4:
On Location

Lighting Makes the Difference

Lighting isn't just illumination. It sculpts the subject, conveys emotion, directs attention, and pleases the eye. What makes a portrait shot by a professional better than your average snapshot? Well, it isn't the fake garden swing. It's lighting.

News photographers, often running and gunning, rarely have time to set up lights. So what do you get? Sun Guns. In the video world, a brand as well known as Kleenex, Sun Gun is the name given to any on-camera, battery-powered lights mounted directly above the lens, and they're dangerous...not physically, aesthetically. The problem is any light mounted on the camera, whether a news shooter's Sun Gun or your snapshot camera's flash, will throw substantially more light on objects close to the camera, often rendering them radically brighter than anything else in the frame. Sometimes these objects are hit with so much light they're rendered bright white. There's no detail, no depth, just a white, shot-spoiling blob. Well, blame it on physics.

Don't be frightened. Lighting is all very intuitive and I'm not going to ask you to do a single calculation, but you must grasp this stuff if you want to get good at lighting. And believe me, you want to get good at lighting. There's a law that governs light intensity called the inverse square law that states the intensity of radiation received from a point source (that point source would be our Sun Gun or flashbulb) is inversely proportional to the square of the distance from it. In plain talk, light falls off very quickly as the subject gets farther away from the light. For example, if we have a light source 3 feet (0.9 m) from a surface, then drag it back to a position 6 feet (1.8 m) from the surface, the light level doesn't drop to half ($\frac{1}{2}$), the light level drops to one-quarter ($\frac{1}{(2\times2)}$ or $\frac{1}{4}$). See how simple? Physics doesn't always hurt.

Applying today's lesson, the white blob in the foreground got pounded with photons and was overexposed. The person the proper distance from the camera got the proper amount of light and was properly exposed. Objects in the background don't show up at all because the light fell off to nearly nothing. Now let's take today's lesson into the lab. Ninety-nine percent of the art and science of lighting comes down to balancing various sources to yield a pleasing picture or draw the eye to an important detail.

Lighting equipment

Maybe someday you'll own lighting equipment, maybe you won't. There are lots of ways to make use of natural light and cheap reflectors—bounce cards of white foam core, mirror tiles, and the like. Still, if there's not *enough* available light, like in interior rooms or a studio, or the available light needs to be balanced or supplemented, you'll need to turn to lighting instruments.

The big stuff—studio-style lighting instruments—can be costly. Top-of-the-line portable lighting kits are pricey, too. Then there are the specialty instruments for specific lighting challenges, situations you might only encounter once a year. Not to mention the stands, arms, knuckles, cords, cases, and gels. Your credit card company would love you.

I'd like to tell you you'll never need all that stuff, but I can't. There are clever, on-the-cheap ways of accomplishing some lighting setups. I've seen articles suggesting you can make your own light stands by filling two liter buckets with cement and inserting two meter lengths of copper pipe before it sets and voila! They may be cheap but I can't see how, having such narrow bases so prone to tipping, they would be effective. The fact is, few of the makeshift methods offer the pure, refined efficiency and utility of professional equipment.

My feeling is that there are too many varied lighting situations and too much equipment out there to own it all, so I rent. It serves my clients and me well. Of course, I spend a lot of time shuttling equipment back and forth to the rental shop, and sometimes the kits aren't in the best repair and there are a few kits I've rented so many times I could have owned them but, we choose our paths. You'll find yours.

Orson Wells on the set of *Citizen Kane*. Tremendous intensity was required to throw light any distance in the amount needed to satisfy early film stocks and later, lazy video pick-up tubes. By the 1930s, lighting instruments had Fresnel lenses and dish reflectors for focusing and barn doors to help limit spill. In short, they worked and looked then like they work and look now and there is still little reason to change.

Serious instruments

Today's cameras, microphones, edit systems, and monitors have all benefited from miniaturization and the digital revolution. Not so for lighting instruments that have remained essentially the same since the Kliegl brothers introduced their first motion picture lights (called klieg lights) in 1911. Indeed, the history of motion-picture lighting is told through names like Century Lighting and Mole-Richardson Co., still leaders in the industry today.

My point here is if you think you might be interested in buying professional lighting instruments (and you've seen the prices new instruments command) you might look to the substantial used equipment market first. Fixer-upper lighting instruments may not look great, might have busted knobs and burn marks,

they'll require relamping, and maybe even rewiring, but the specs and parts are surely available. The same goes for the more portable lighting kits. Companies such as Lowell, Arri, and LTM offer light kits of varying capability and cost. The problems with used kits tend to be surmountable—missing barn doors, stuck stands, broken latches, and the like—requiring mostly parts and time.

If the convenience, confidence, and predictability of owning your own equipment are especially attractive to you, let me offer a short list of my favorite instruments; equipment that has, in my opinion, stepped into the future. This is an expensive proposition, but if you owned this kit, you'd be set for many production situations, most documentary situations, and every conceivable home shooting situation twice over.

Kino Flo

A significant advance in the science of lighting was the development of fluorescent fixtures for video and film lighting. Of course, fluorescent lamps have been around for half a century or more, and lighting directors have long been aware of their soft nature and substantial throw. However, there were problems as well, including noise, flickering, bulkiness, and, most significantly, color temperature of the light.

A company called Kino Flo was one of the first to overcome the big issues by engineering tubes that are color balanced for both daylight (5,600°K) and tungsten (3,200°K) and

mounted in lightweight, versatile instruments with remote ballasts. The result is a particularly user-friendly lighting tool that draws a fraction of the current that an incandescent lamp of similar throw would require. In addition, fluorescents stay cool, something actors and makeup artists appreciate. The unique design of the Kino enclosures provides integral barn doors that fold over and protect the tubes when the lights are stored. Fixtures come in 4-foot (1.2 m) and 2-foot (0.6 m) lengths, and four-lamp and two-lamp configurations. In addition, there are 9-inch (23 cm) lamps perfect for automobile interiors and even smaller, pencil-sized tubes great for tabletop work. There are other manufacturers of fluorescent fixtures but Kino Flo is the best known.

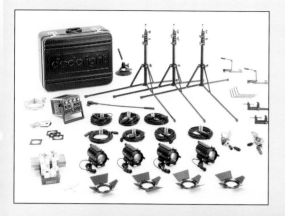

Dedo

My favorite lighting kit is made by Dedo, and it's a marvel of engineering created by German director of photography Dedo Weigert. An entire Dedo lighting system consisting of four light heads, four stands, a power unit, and all cables is designed to fit into a carrying case that's just 22.5 × 17 × 10.25" (57 × 43 × 26 cm) and weighs 45.4 lb (20.6 kg). Each universal light head has a lens system that delivers the illumination of a 300 W lamp from a 100 W lamp. The halogen lamps used are easy to change and last many times longer than tungsten lamps. The lamps actually run on low power distributed at three switchable levels through standard audio cables from the main transformer (able to accept all international voltages). As I said, they're a marvel of engineering.

Chimera

The bigger the source, the more flattering the light, and that's what Chimera delivers. Chimera makes a whole line of collapsible, lightweight fabric boxes that deliver a big, soft, pleasing light. The shape of the Chimera is maintained by spring steel rods that fit into a variety of "speed rings" designed to work with various manufacturers' lighting instruments (or even with bare bulbs). The inside of the Chimera is lined with reflective foil fabric and there are a number of accessories—grids, honeycombs, and louvers—to alter the characteristics of the throw. Other manufacturers make similar products, but Chimera is recognized as the lighting industry standard.

Dimmer

Cookie

China ball

Lighting on a budget

Saving money on lighting usually begins with the notion that commercially available sources are too expensive and, therefore, we must find ways to improvise cheaper lighting instruments. This is a dangerous concept. Though there are exceptions, LEDs and fluorescents being the most notable, generating heat is a consequence of generating light. The brighter the lights, the more heat. That's what makes improvising with light dangerous. For instance, one very effective lighting technique involves a china ball. These flimsy paper lanterns can provide an effective soft source if you use a higher wattage bulb than their rating would allow. There are aerosol flame-retardants available from stage supply shops but they do not guarantee the balls won't still burst into flames given the right conditions. So why take a chance? Well, the dime store paper lantern will cost a tiny fraction of what a professional china ball costs! Using vellum paper for diffusion or colored cellophane instead of professional gels falls into the same category—cheap, but at what price?

My own informal surveys have found that there are relatively inexpensive professional alternatives to much of the industry standard equipment, sometimes 60 percent cheaper! Let's say I'm looking for a back light on a stand. On the high end, I could choose a nice Mole-Richardson focusable Teenie-Weenie 600 watt open face with barn doors and a true 3,200°K tungsten lamp. I could then buy a Matthews Century Stand (C-stand) with a boom arm that would allow me to swing the light out behind my talent, nearly 10 feet in the air. All together, that professional rig would run $480. I found, giving up some of the height, the focus knob on the lamp, and going with lesser-known brands I could stay with professional equipment but spend only $200. On the low end, I could buy a halogen work lamp with no ability to boom or focus, no control of the light's throw and no guarantee of the light's color temperature for $75. I think the best buy, with its balance of price and functionality is the $200 package. In the upcoming section called "What's the point of lighting?," I'll show you how to cut that price in half by making that one $200 package do the work of two $200 packages.

Your grip kit

I sail. I sail on Lake Michigan. Lake Michigan can be very cold. In my sailing bag I always keep a pair of gloves, ear warmers, and an extra pair of socks. That's in addition to the suntan lotion, Swiss Army knife, CD wallet, tea bags, and all the other things I just might need on the boat. Be prepared, right? Well, a gaffer, someone who lights for a living, carries a bag, too. So should you.

I'm a realist, and I know some will go bargain basement no matter how strident my warnings, so maybe the compromise is compromise. Save where you can, but spend when safety is at stake. That said, here are a few places where you can save safely, trading functionality for affordability or time for money.

+ **Dimmers.**
A standard wall-mounted dimmer and a basic ground-fault protected wall outlet can be combined to make a portable rheostat for controlling incandescent light sources. Build your dimmers into heat resistant boxes, use a sufficiently robust AC cord, be careful of amperage ratings, and ground the box.

+ **Shot bags.**
Many lighting setups are based on the idea of booming instruments into place. This puts a rotational moment on the stand and boom and creates a tipping hazard. This is countered by using the weight of shot bags, so named because they were often filled with lead or iron shot. If you have strong canvas and a very stout sewing machine, feel free to make your own bags and fill them with sand. The cheap, cheap alternative to shot bags is to fill old, plastic milk jugs with water and tie short lengths of rope to the handle for hanging. The problem is that these jugs just aren't resilient enough for repeated use and will begin leaking. On top of that, you're looking at having puddles of water around a maze of electrical sources! Bad idea!

+ **Cable ties.**
Professional cable ties are expensive. Hardware store Velcro ties are not.

+ **Apple boxes.**
Though technically not lighting equipment, apple boxes are usually found on the grip truck so they fit in this list. Three-quarter to one-inch (2 to 3 cm) plywood is sufficient for building your own apple boxes.

+ **Aluminum foil.**
Spray glued to foam core or pressboard, aluminum foil makes a dandy reflective surface. Scrunch and form aluminum foil around a photo flood to direct its throw.

+ **Diffusion frames.**
PVC pipe and corners make perfectly serviceable frames for stretching diffusion material.

+ **Cutters and flags.**
Used to knock down light levels or shadow small areas, cutters and flags are easy to make at home. Make frames or buy cheap plastic poster frames, add black felt for flags, black fiberglass screening for cutters. Spray them with flame retardant and keep them a sufficient distance from your light sources!

+ **Photo floods.**
Found in hardware stores as clamp lights, they are supplied with a spun aluminum parabolic reflector. Choose ceramic sockets for heat resistance; add a color-balanced photo flood bulb.

+ **Cuculoris.**
The more common term is "cookie," a cutout used to break up light or even simulate a pattern like venetian blinds or window mullions. Feel free to make your own. Even professionally designed cookies appear to be cut out of thin pressboard and spray painted black.

+ **Clamps.**
Hardware stores are full of screw clamps and spring clamps. Just be sure not to use plastic clamps on hot surfaces.

+ **Fluorescent fixtures.**
I've mentioned the popularity and effectiveness of Kino Flo fixtures. Though you probably can't rival the engineering panache of the real fixtures, there's nothing keeping you from mounting a bank of four fluorescent tubes on a light, reflective surface and making your own. Be careful of color temperature. Though they're a little more expensive, it's worth buying tubes that are corrected to 3,400°K, 3,200°K if you can find them.

+ **China ball.**
Instead of a paper lantern, spend the extra for a Plexiglas globe. Try to find a ceramic base for your lamp. A great how-to can be found at videouniversity.com/china.htm.

+ **Bulk purchasing.**
Form a buying group for lighting supplies. Everything from blackwrap to gels is cheaper in large quantities.

+ **Gloves.** For the combination of protection, heat resistance, and durability, leather is best. When handling hot lights you sure don't want anything that might melt.

+ **All-in-one tool.** Leatherman and Gerber make nice ones. The idea is to always have a knife, screwdriver, and pliers handy.

+ **Clamps.** Pony (spring) clamps, Mafer (screw down) clamps, you'll need them constantly.

+ **C-47s.** Speaking of clamps, miniature spring-action organic cellulose clamps (wooden clothespins) are in constant demand as well.

+ **Tape.** It looks like silver-colored duct tape, but gaffer's tape is much better. It's cloth backed and strong, but it tears when you want it to, sticks when you want it to, and releases when you want it to (without taking the paint with it). Spend the extra—get the good stuff.

+ **Rope.** There is no substitute for good cotton rope.

+ **Black wrap.** Black wrap is thick anodized aluminum foil. It's fireproof, nonreflective, flexible, and reusable. Extend a barn door, form a snoot, or use a blade to cut a pattern for a quick gobo (in this case, an object that casts a shadow of a defined shape).

Lighting techniques

What's the point of lighting?

Shooting documentaries, I've had a chance to meet a lot of interesting people. One was Art Linkletter, a legendary performer and king of daytime TV in the United States throughout the 1950s and 1960s. An affable, buoyant man, he welcomed us into his corner office above Wilshire Boulevard in Los Angeles with warm smiles and robust handshakes all around. He watched as we rolled in our cart full of gear, pointed out the AC outlets, and announced he'd be down the hall until we'd finished setting up lights. I set camera while our cinematographer, Robb Fischer, went about lighting. He fiddled with the sheers, propped up a bounce card, and set one tiny eye light and was done. Linkletter was clearly surprised when we asked him back in less than five minutes. He sat in his desk chair as I held a monitor, showing him the results. Mr. Linkletter, a veteran of the days of searing studio lights and floodlit sets, was impressed. He watched, eyes fixed on the monitor as he turned slowly, testing the shot and finally announced, "I look pretty darned good." That's Robb Fischer's knack. He makes people, scenes, products, everything he shoots, look pretty darned good. What follows here are important lighting tips and techniques excerpted from a recent interview I did with Robb. The scene is an early spring afternoon in an open, airy, high-ceilinged coffee shop, lit by windows all along the storefront.

How do you approach lighting a scene?

"The main thing to me is using available light and then controlling it. Some people start out thinking, 'OK, where should I put the lights?' The first thing I ask myself is, 'Do I have to light?' I immediately look for the natural light, for contrast. I like putting someone in the brighter part of the room, letting the background be darker and that's easy to find naturally. In here, it would be up near the window. Generally, any situation where there are windows there's going to be light enough to shoot it with a DV camera. You have to find the right situation. Then you just need to control the light—direct it, block it, bounce it. The most important tools for me are control tools—flags, black cards, fabric, anything. I've used a black jacket hung over a stand to see if I could get rid of some of light (reflecting) back. It's called negative fill. A white card is positive fill."

"I'm a big fan of using natural light. Turn on a light and things look lit. Here, now your key light is that big sky out there. Bigger sources are better because they look more natural, and the larger you can make the source, the more flattering the light, the more real. When you make the light softer by, say, clip[ping a] diffusion [filter] onto a light, you're scattering the light but the source is the same size. That's one of the reasons the new fluorescent fixtures like Kino Flos look good—how big they are."

So you're not thinking in terms of textbook lighting schemes—the key light, the fill light, the back light? (For definitions of these terms, see Glossary, page 178.)

"Traditionally, backlight is for separation. [There are lots of ways to get your subject to stand out from the background.] You can use focus, letting the background go soft, and you get separation that way. Sometimes, there's different light on a face and white balancing on it might make the background cooler. Now you're getting color separation. If the person has dark hair and you put him against a light background, you get separation that way. I like using compositional separation unless the environment suggests backlight. If you have a [really bright] window [in a shot] and you give them [an equally bright] light from behind, that's motivated. Otherwise, it becomes a style. A hot light seems correct because it's pleasing, even though it doesn't seem right for the environment. It's fashion.

"I hate setting up lights and the minute you turn on the light, you change the scene's ratio [when one area of the scene is much brighter than another]. Then, to light somebody, you have to have enough light to light the background because you've got so much light on their face, the background is dark. That [means adding even] more lights.

"I mean I always prided myself on needing little. I always talk about how every light can do two things, so three lights become six lights. One of my favorite things—take a bed sheet on a frame or a rope. Put it 90° from the person, put a cheap, open-face light through it. The bedsheet knocks the level down a lot, spreads the light so you won't get a harsh shadow (remember, the larger you can make the source the more flattering the light, the more real). I aim the light so two-thirds of the light goes through the bedsheet and the other third misses the sheet and goes over top and hits a bounce card for fill. You don't need a separate fill light to get your balance right, just the fill card.

"I try to use the light and its spill. In a portrait, I'll boom a mirror behind the person, spot the light, aim it at the mirror for the backlight, and let the spill from that light light [the person] directly. It's a matter of shaping. I'll take a backlight and aim it so half goes onto the background, breaking it up with blackwrap and clothespins. I'll do a similar thing: put a light off at ¾ and behind, giving the person an edge light [while at the same time lighting a reflector that's placed opposite that light, in front of the person—that serves as a key light]. So you have the light do two things."

Besides getting double duty out of your lights, can you share any other cheap tricks?

"My favorite cheap trick is called Celotex. It's insulation—it's an inch thick, lightweight, and rigid. One side is matte silver and it's just the best reflector. It's shiny, but not enough to be specular.

It's got a nice quality to it. If you've got a situation like this with just ambient light through a window, you can grab that ambient light and throw it right back into [the subject's] eyes, put a piece right over the lens."

"Another one is a china ball, the cheapest, easiest source for light. The thing is, you always need a dimmer [with one], because you need control.... So many people just put a light up. You need to think how balanced it is with your background. You still need to control that light, and a dimmer is the easiest way. If you do use a dimmer, be aware that as the light dims, the color of that light will become warmer, but that can often be a good thing. The other way to control it is to back it away [from the subject], but the more you back it away, the harder it becomes, the more shadows you get. You're always better off using a bigger source of light closer to somebody. It's always more flattering to have that source as close to the person as possible. And the china ball mimics the shape of the face—it is round. If you see it in their eyes it looks good, pleasing."

And that's half the battle, isn't it—making the lighting pleasing?

"The thing that'll never change is the esthetic: for certain scenes, if you want to sculpt the look, you still need the light. Not every situation's going to look right without adding light. Especially situations where there's a lot of daylight. Again, it's controlling it or accepting it. If it works, let it become part of the look.

"Of course, then there's the question, 'What do you want to say?' That's part of it, too. How do you want the scene to feel? Should the person be sitting out of the light, isolated, or do you want them to feel like they're in this bright, open environment, part of the action?...What are you trying to say with that image, within the story? Do you like realism or impressionism? Do you like a shot that's degraded or [soft] focus, or is your intention clarity? Art? Emotion? If you're on a big shoot, you recreate all [that] you know, because then it's controlled. As time passes the light is constant, but if it's there already...You need less light if you develop a good eye."

Develop a good eye?

"The first thing you have to do is develop your eye, specifically for lighting. Everywhere you look. Everyone's got all these images [inside their heads, such as], 'sunlight pouring in the kitchen in the morning,' but what does it really look like? What does a vinyl floor look like, how does daylight look when it's hitting your cheek, how does light really work? You create this library in your head of images you want to light. Also, look at films that you like and see how they treat light; the details, shadows, don't just look at the overall image—take it apart."

Bedsheet set up.

Bedsheet shot.

Celotex setup.

Celotex shot.

Keep the china ball close to your subject. For best results, use a dimmer.

A China Ball is an easy way to deliver a refined and subtle lighting effect.

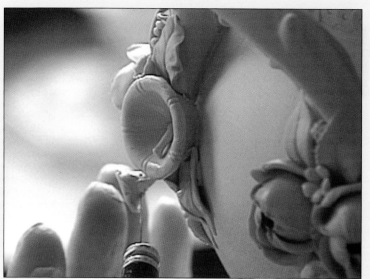

Sometimes natural light is the perfect light. Recognizing this takes a trained eye, which develops over time through trial and error. Testing lighting conditions will help speed up the process.

Three-point lighting

Though your first choice should be using available light and control tools to bounce, limit, and redirect light, there are the times when you can't talk Aunt Cynthia into the chair by the window. With that in mind, we're going to go over the textbook basics of lighting. Besides, you'll hear these terms tossed about all the time and you'll want to be able to get in on the conversation.

The principles of artificial lighting were developed with the first cameras in the nineteenth century but they still hold true today. Essentially, it's a magic act. You're creating the illusion of a third dimension, of depth on a flat screen, but you're using light and shadow instead of smoke and mirrors. OK, sometimes you use smoke and mirrors too, whatever works to deliver depth and texture to the audience.

The tried-and-true formula for basic lighting is known as three-point lighting.

Key light
The first light set up in the three-point system is the most important one: the **key light.** Think of this light as your indoor sunshine. It's the brightest light on the front your subject, traditionally set up about 45° from the line drawn between your subject and the camera. The light should strike the subject from above, again at a 45° angle, though you'll adjust the angle to flatter the face. Don't exaggerate a long nose, a jutting brow, or hair shadows. The key light can be set up on either the right or left side of the camera depending on the situation. If either side will work in the location, again choose the side most flattering to the subject or the side that yields fewer unpleasant shadows on the background.

Fill light
The second light in the setup is called the **fill light** and it does just what the name implies—it fills in or softens some of the harsher shadows created by that bright key light. Outdoors, where the sun is your key light you often use a reflector or bounce card to create a fill light. The fill light is placed 45° from the camera, opposite the key light and set at half the intensity. Some very subtle and pleasing lighting effects result from substituting reflected light for the direct beam of an instrument.

Back light
The third point in a three-point setup is the **back light.** This is a smaller, lower-wattage light placed directly behind the subject, in line with the camera, to create a visual separation between the subject and the background. The light should be aimed at the back of the person's neck and then adjusted to create a subtle rim of light around the subject. Blondes and people with thinning hair often need a bit less backlight. There's often a fourth light in the three-point formula, the **background light** pointed, as the name implies, at the background. Its purpose is to create further depth and separation.

Two-point and one-point lighting

This age-old formula of four basic lights, set at the proper angle and intensity, will give a scene the depth and texture it requires. But when age-old formula meets age-old problems like time, location, and situation, photographers often find themselves with fewer options. Enter two-point and one-point lighting.

Two-point lighting works. In a two-point situation, it's best to take Robb Fischer's suggestion to heart and try to get double-duty out of your instruments. The most obvious and effective choice is one we've already discussed, setting a bounce card on the opposite side of the subject, creating fill light from the key light. It's also possible to borrow some fill light by redirecting spill from your backlight, whatever provides depth and dimension. As always, keep the lights high in order to bury shadows below the camera's eye, but not so high as to create "raccoon eyes" on your subjects, that is, deep, dark brow shadows.

Above left: In a studio setup, if the background light is eliminated, the subject will be suspended in visual limbo. Limbo lighting relies on the background being dark enough to be invisible.

Below left: This age-old formula of three basic lights, set at the proper angle and intensity, will give a scene the depth and texture it requires.

An example of a two-point lighting setup with a key light and a bounce card fill. By making the bounce card the key light, and using the original key light as a back light, the effect will be more flattering.

The result of a two-point lighting setup with a bounce card fill and a back light.

Interview setup

In situations where there's more than one subject, take a basic face-to-face, tête-à-tête, in which two people sit opposite one another, one's key light is the other's back light and again, you'll need bounce cards to steal some fill light. Cutters, flags (objects that block light), and half scrims (half circles of metal screen mesh) are especially useful in situations where you're trying to squeeze out every last bit of illumination from a limited number of sources.

One-point lighting

At the very least, it's difficult to achieve *pleasing* results with one-point lighting. Set head-on (as in flash photography and the news camera's Sun Gun) the subject's features are flattened and lost. Moved off-axis, the subject regains some depth but severe shadows are introduced. Your best bet with one light is to set it at as you would a key light in a two-light situation, using spill on a bounce card to provide fill. If you can squeeze out a little extra reflection, you might be able to provide a bit of back light as well. Otherwise, you'll need to use color, contrast, or focus to pull your subject off the background.

Contrast

Sometimes the extreme contrast of a one-light setup is exactly what you want. The stark contrast of light and shadow is often used as a visual cue the character on screen is being pulled in two directions or hides a dark secret. The traditional interrogation scene is often a single-light affair. Used in other situations, like a children's story hour, the stark contrast of one-point lighting might seem out of place.

Always wear your headphones; it's the only way to troubleshoot sound issues before it's too late.

How to button down your location for clean recordings

+ Wherever possible, keep all doors and windows closed, preventing noise and conversation from entering the set.

+ Unplug the phone; be sure all cell phones and pagers are silenced.

+ Turn off or unplug any systems or appliances that cycle. That includes refrigerators, humidifiers, fans, water fountains, heaters, and air conditioners. I've heard sound people suggest that to be sure you plug it back in before the food spoils, put your car keys in the refrigerator.

+ Turn off computers and anything else with a cooling fan.

+ In commercial locations, have the paging system quieted.

+ Turn off radios and central music systems. Even at what you might consider an acceptable level, you'll hear the music skip with every edit.

+ When shooting at a dining table, try to keep dish and silverware noise down by putting a pad under the table-cloth. Avoid using ice cubes if possible or substitute prop cubes.

+ Moisten paper bags with a spray to lessen paper noise.

+ Stop recording when planes pass overhead.

+ If people are watching, be sure everyone understands there's no talking allowed—not even whispering—when the camera is rolling.

+ Keep plenty of those cheap, quilted packing blankets handy to muffle the noise of reflective floors and walls, creaky chairs, or the talent's shoes tapping away on the footrest.

Sound Thinking

Take a perfectly clear, crisp video image and whack away at it. Turn it black-and-white, make it look like old film, tint it, distort it, add stripes, dots, dirt, whatever, and it's a "look." It's "cutting edge!" It's evocative, daring, emotional, challenging! Funny though, we don't like our audio "challenging." We don't see it as at all artistic to have to lean over and whisper, "What did she say?"

I'll tell you right now, if you intend to cook up great sound tracks for your productions, you need to start with the best ingredients, like top-quality field recording.

The principles of audio recording

Your goal in recording audio should be to make it clean and crisp, free of coloration, noise, and interference. To achieve that level of audio excellence, you'll need to develop an ear for trouble. Try listening right now. Do you hear a computer whirring away or a fluorescent buzz? Maybe you hear kids playing outside, a truck going by, or a plane flying over. On your recording, those sounds are simply noise. While they can be appropriate atmospheric elements when *added* in just the right spot, you don't want to have to deal with the dilemma of misplaced sounds in your edit. The quality of your field recordings will depend on how well you manage your location, the choices you've made regarding microphones and their placement, and how conscientious you are about nipping audio problems in the bud.

If you have someone else riding audio for you, make sure they wear their headphones; it's the only way you'll ever know! You can't see audio problems on a VU meter, and there are many, many audio problems out there, all manner of distortion, noise, and interference just waiting to ruin your shoot. Even in situations where you're not setting your own microphones, where you're simply tapping into someone else's audio feed, maybe at a press conference, piano recital, or wedding, there are potential problems. The most common is the difference between line level and mic level feeds. Without getting into millivolts and decibels, line level feeds are usually 15 to 20 times "hotter" than mic level feeds. Line level is often preferred in distributed audio situations because most low-level interference is overwhelmed and rendered imperceptible. Some camcorders offer the choice of line or mic level inputs but many more do not. If you're not ready with a "pad" or resistor to knock the line level down to mic level, you're in trouble. A 50 dB line attenuator from your local audio supplier is usually effective. An adjustable pad is even better.

Achieving Balance

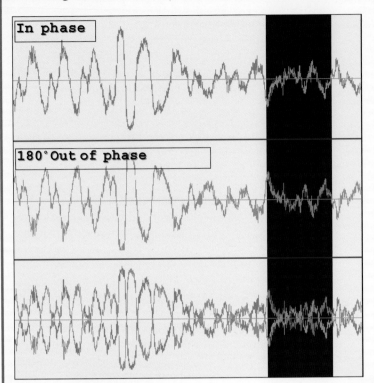

In phase

180° Out of phase

Balanced cables take advantage of an audio principle called phase to fight interference. Look at a graph of an audio signal and you'll see peaks and valleys. Take two identical signals and lay them over one another and if they're in phase, the peaks and valleys will add together; out of phase, the peak and valleys will cancel each other. On a balanced audio run, the signal is intentionally split with half moved 180° out of phase. At the other end of the run, the signal is recombined, put back into phase. Any audio interference picked up along the run would be introduced into both cables equally but when the proper phase is restored, the interference will cancel itself out. Remember, if there is a single unbalanced cable or connector in a run, the entire run is unbalanced.

Three-conductor (balanced) XLR or Canon connectors.

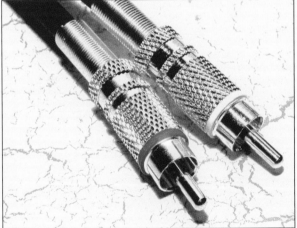

The ubiquitous two-conductor (unbalanced) RCA cables.

I keep a bag of adaptors in my grip kit. Not just a few RCA "Y"s, but a lot of adaptors. I mean, *a lot of adaptors.* I can connect stereo audio to LP gas, that's how many different adaptors I have. If you intend to shoot documentaries or events, you should do the same. The major audio connectors in use today are the RCA, XLR (or Canon), mini plug, and, to a lesser extent, micro mini and ¼" (0.5 cm) phone jack. Minis, micro minis, and phone jacks come in stereo and mono. If there's a male and female I have both.

Levels, latitude, and technical quality

To understand the technical aspects of digital audio, it's instructive to understand how digital audio differs from analog audio. Let's refer for a moment to a graph of an audio signal over time, those familiar peaks and valleys. Imagine for a moment, you are hiking up the side of one of those peaks. You might alert me to your position by describing the slope your hike has taken, citing altitude over time. I'd be able to figure out roughly where you are and trace the curve of your progress. That's the analog method. The next time, I'm going to give you a handheld GPS (Global Positioning System) and I'm going to ask that at timed intervals you call out your precise position. Rather than drawing the curve, we're going to plot points. The more often we record points, the more accurate my read of your progress. That's the digital method and is roughly analogous to digital sampling rates. If you called out your position 48,000 times a second, you'd be recording at a sampling rate of 48 kHz, the rate audio is sampled on DV camcorders in the two-channel mode. Music CDs have a standard sample rate of 44.1 kHz, slightly less accurate than DV audio.

To carry this analogy a little further, let's say that every time you reported to me you offered not only your position but the temperature, the wind, the composition of the ground beneath your feet, the color of the rock, etc. This deeper, more precise information equates to the increasingly accurate reports available as audio bit depth increases. Just as the more information you feed me in each report, the more accurate my picture of your experience becomes, the higher the bit depths sampled, the more accurate audio reproductions can be. DV capture and output is done in 16-bit audio. This 16-bit rate refers to the number of "conditions" you could report to me about your position on that theoretical mountain climb. In this case, the number 16 represents 65,536 numbers per sample, or 2^{16}.

Stick with me now as I beat this hilltop hiking analogy to death.

Imagine that there are issues with reporting information from above a certain altitude. In the analog system, having traced your curve, I've got a good idea of where you're heading and though I might be inaccurate, I could note your likely position. In the digital system, if I don't have your reported position, I would

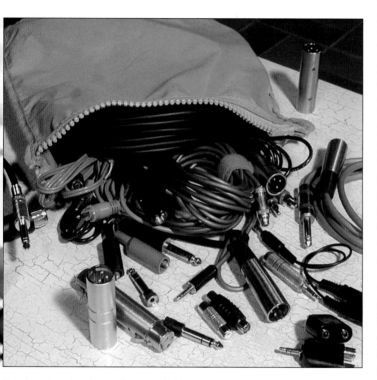

Keep lots of audio adaptors in your grip kit.

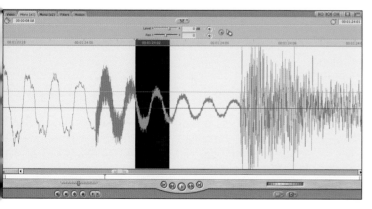

A graph of an audio signal over time.

Analog VU

Analog VU (volume unit) meters are graduated from –30 dB or –20 dB on the low side to +3 dB, maybe even +7 dB on the high side. The numbers change from negative to positive at the zero point, also the target point for your average loudness. It's acceptable for peaks, the hottest moments of audio, to shoot up above zero and into the red zone of the meter.

Digital VU

A digital VU meter's scale runs from –∞ dB on the low end, up to zero on the high end. In the digital world, zero is an absolute, never-to-be-crossed threshold. No information exists above zero. Therefore, it's critical to set your average loudness to a number that will allow sufficient headroom for your audio peaks. Most systems in the U.S. suggest setting to a 1,000 Hz tone at either –20 dB or –12 dB. You'll need to check. In Europe, –18 dB is often chosen. In any case, it's incumbent upon you to consider the dynamic range of your audio (taking it back to our peaks and valleys, the difference between the highest and lowest altitudes on your hike) and allow enough room for your audio to peak below zero.

simply not record any information at all. Translating this report to audio, we would hear nothing but a crackle or scratch whenever the information ran out. The curve would be flat on top.

This represents a substantial difference between analog and digital systems. Analog systems are somewhat forgiving of over-driven audio. Some of it may even be salvageable. It would probably be distorted, but it would also probably be salvageable. On the other hand, digital systems are absolutely intolerant of overdriven audio. The curve is clipped harshly at zero. There is no information to read, no sound to reproduce. That's why it's

important to understand how to set levels when recording audio in the field.

Most camcorders offer two mic inputs. If you need to use more than two mics, you'll have to use a mic mixer. Mixers often offer multiple inputs, sometimes mono, sometimes stereo. Two words of caution: First, be careful what you choose to mix because it can't be unmixed and the shy, quiet person may forever be overwhelmed by the loud, brash person. Second, monitor the audio going into your camera, not coming out of the mixer. A small point, but ultimately, one is important and the other isn't.

Automatic gain control

Most DV camcorders are equipped with a helpful little function called AGC (automatic gain control) or ALC (automatic level control). These automatic controls take the pressure off you, as both shooter and audio recordist, by constantly adjusting levels, compensating for moments when your audio peaks out of the acceptable range. That's the helpful part. The bad part is that when the audio is particularly low. Say you're in a hushed office setting or a quiet field, when there is no dominant audio, the AGC will search for something to amplify. It might latch onto the hum of a computer or the constant buzz of cicadas and begin boosting until the sound reaches average loudness. Then, depending on the reaction time of the system, if any closer sound presents itself, the AGC will overcompensate, dropping the gain way down in an effort to avoid overdriving. Now, I don't want to completely dismiss the AGC as worthless. It is set-and-forget and most of your audio will be usable. Indeed, on some camcorders there's no alternative. However, if you have the option of taking control of your audio levels manually, especially when recording voice or music, do it. When simply recording natural sound, if you have the option of taking control of one channel and leaving the other to the AGC, that's even better. You're covered.

Microphone types and when to use them

I recently supervised the taping of a large anniversary event staged by a local manufacturer. Each crew was outfitted with a very nice,

new DV rig. It was a four-day event and at the end of each day, I studied the footage each crew delivered, trying to keep track of our progress and plan the next day's needs. I was immediately struck by an interesting audio phenomenon. On the screen were three people tossing in lively, impromptu comments about the event, not a situation where I'd expect a lone photographer to try and mic the partiers. This is a job for the camera mic. The person on the left spoke and I could hear him fine. The person on the right spoke and again, passable audio. But when the person in the middle spoke, I could barely hear what he had to say! It was clear the manufacturer was more concerned with producing a "true stereo" effect than providing the kind of audio pickup pattern that most video makers would appreciate—a concentration on the audio source front and center in the camera lens.

Most every camcorder, whether high end, high def, or the least expensive DV pocket model, comes with a built-in microphone. When you're just looking for general ambient sound to accompany your images, this on-camera mic is often sufficient. If you harbor any thoughts of doing professional work or being recognized as an accomplished amateur filmmaker, that same camera mic is entirely inadequate. You must have other options.

Once you begin investigating your choices, you're going to find a dizzying array of mics available each with complex diagrams of pickup patterns and frequency response. I'm going to spare you all the minutia and get right down to what you need to be effective in the most common shooting situations you'll encounter.

Shotgun mics

Whether you're catching spontaneous comments or shooting cover video of some activity, it might be important to you to limit your recording to the sounds that are right in front of your eyes. This is best accomplished by using a shotgun. The shotgun mic is unidirectional, meaning it records in one direction—the direction it's pointed. The long-barreled design of the mic, though susceptible to reflected sounds, cancels and rejects most audio that approaches from the sides. Though shotgun barrels are quite thin and fragile, they're rarely seen without windscreens designed to lessen wind noise. Windscreens vary from a plastic blimp to the fake fur covering that has given rise to shotgun nicknames such as the "hairy Harry" or "mammal on a stick."

Shotgun mics are predominantly condenser-type mics and require power. That power is either, as in the case of some permanent mounts, stolen from the camera (phantom power) or supplied by a battery. It is a lifelong ambition of mine to reach the point where I can say, "I always remember to turn off my shotgun mic." Until that day, I will keep extra batteries on hand.

News shooters always have a shotgun mounted on their camera but shotguns are very popular production mics as well. Properly positioned short shotguns provide a pleasing and natural rendering of the voice.

Lavaliere mics

Lavaliere microphones, or lavs, are tiny, usually omnidirectional (or nondirectional) microphones designed to be used close to the sound source. Often called tie-pin or clip-on mics, they're ever present on news broadcasts and talk shows. Look carefully at the host's lapels and you'll find one, on live shows two, just in case one goes down. Lavalieres are condenser mics and require power. Some can phantom power off the camera but more often, batteries are needed so keep spares in your kit.

Stick mics

Another common and useful mic, handy to have in your kit, is a basic omnidirectional stick mic. These are usually dynamic mics, meaning their design is based on a moving coil in the field of a permanent magnet, and thus don't require batteries. These lollipop or ice cream cone mics are the darlings of the news business, often seen with station identification flags, and are chosen not for their sensitivity and fidelity but for their ruggedness. I recall seeing an ad campaign for one of the most long-lived and popular, the EV635, in which users were encouraged to send in stories of mics that had survived fires, falls, and being run over by trucks, yet continued to function. Because of their news pedigree, using a stick mic can add an air of immediacy and journalistic integrity to your production.

PZM mics

The last mic I'll suggest is not the most common or functional but can be indispensable if you find yourself taping meetings or depositions or indeed any situation where it might be impossible or inconvenient to individually mic a large group of people at a table. The Pz or PZM is a boundary effect mic, designed to use the entire surface upon which it's placed, a tabletop, the floor, or a wall, as a pickup. The mic is commonly suspended upside-down, just above the surface in its housing. It relies on reflected sound and offers a better response than you'd get from putting a couple of stick mics on stands around that same table.

Wind heard through most mics is not the pleasing, whispering wind of song and story. It's noise. It's scratchy, loud, unpleasant noise that blocks out what's being said. Be sure any mic you intend to use outdoors is equipped with a windscreen. I know the windscreens offered by microphone manufacturers seem expensive but they're designed for aural transparency and tend to fit better than the cheap ones that keep getting lost.

Here you see a lavaliere microphone clipped to the sweater in the same direction in which the woman is speaking.

Stick mic

Making sure a microphone is placed in the correct spot is vital to achieving quality sound. Lavalieres are designed to be placed roughly 6" to 8" (15 – 20 cm) from a person's mouth.

A final word of advice: don't buy these mics! At least not right away. Mics are expensive and can vary widely in quality, response, and reliability. Frankly, one of the most important factors in choosing a mic, fidelity, is mostly a subjective choice. You might not like the same mics I do. So let someone else take the hit for the product when it's brand new. You pay the fractional, and usually reasonable, cost of renting. Try a few mics. See which sound best to you, and then buy.

Booms, clips, hair, placements, and tricks

Choosing the proper place for a microphone is at least as important as choosing the right microphone. Some mics are designed to have an optimal distance from a source, but more often it comes down to a balance of aesthetic considerations, including presence, the desire for perspective, and the exclusion of extraneous sound. Begin by disregarding anyone who claims good, clean audio is available from any mic placed more than 2 meters from the on-camera speaker.

Lavalieres are designed to be placed roughly 6" to 8" (15 – 20 cm) from a person's mouth. Altering the placement can lead to "proximity effects," discernable differences in mic quality due to distance. Sound changes over distance; the lows and highs begin to roll off and room presence creeps in. Because minor changes in distance can alter the mic's sound, it's important to consider the speaker's potential movement when placing the mic. If the

Tips: Mic Placement

+ Consider the subject's movement. Will walking—or even turning—change his or her distance from the mic?

+ Silk is notoriously noisy. A mic will pick up a cotton blouse moving against a silk bra or a silk tie moving against a polyester jacket lining.

+ Secure potentially noisy clothing layers with pieces of tape turned back upon themselves to present two sticky surfaces. Small pieces of gray-colored, cloth-based gaffer's tape work best.

+ Be aware of noisy necklaces, bracelets, and pins.

+ In an effort to avoid accidental contact with the mic, remind inexperienced speakers of the mic placement before rolling tape.

+ Take into account nervous habits like drumming or fingering hair or clothing when you place the mic. Bracelets and watches clacking against a table can produce a frightful sound.

+ Don't allow mic connectors to hang loose. This puts unnecessary stress on connections and can cause noise if they bump against chairs, etc. Tape the danglers down. If the connection is on the talent, clip the connector to their belt or ask them to put the connector in their pocket. If the belt is out of reach or the talent might constantly toy with a connector in their pockets, use an Ace bandage or leg warmer to press the connection discreetly to their body.

+ Always make a short strain-relief loop in the mic cord. The loop will help counter accidental tugs as well as deaden noise transmitted along the mic wire. When using lavalieres, tape a strain-relief loop in place or use the teeth of the mic clip to hold it.

To get a mic into place, a boom (a large piece of studio equipment to which a mic is attached) may be used. Here, the operator is using a fishpole, which is a portable version of a boom. The fishpole has a shock mount on the end of a light-weight rod allowing him to position the mic without interfering with the shot.

mic is clipped to her left lapel and she turns from left to right, the distance of the mic from her mouth can be significantly altered. Every time she turns, the difference will be heard. Keep this proximity effect in mind, too, if, for example, she'll be talking to someone on her left throughout a segment—it would be best to clip the mic on her left side.

Shotgun mics are a bit more forgiving but still benefit from consistency in distance from the person speaking. Again, changes in distance introduce added reflections and noise, even in relatively quiet locations. If lighting or other considerations prevent the shotgun from being brought in above the speaker, try coming in below but be aware, this angle of attack could invite everything from ceiling fan to airplane noise. Remember, shotgun mics are directional. The speaker simply shifting from side to side in his or her chair could move in and out of the aim of a fixed shotgun mic.

When placing your mic, whether it's a shotgun, lavaliere, or a handheld stick mic, the best sound, with the fewest popping P's and hissing S's, is obtained when the subject speaks *across* the mic's pickup, rather than *directly into* the mic. With shotguns and handhelds, try to point the mic at a 45° angle to direction of the voice.

To get a mic into position it is often "boomed." A boom is a large piece of studio equipment to which the shotgun, or any other mic, is mounted on a rotating head at the end of a telescoping arm. The operator can then place a mic in position from a great distance off set. The portable version of a boom is the fishpole. A fishpole has a shock mount on the end of a lightweight rod and allows an audio operator to get in close without interfering with camera or lights.

The sound of silence

Let me offer a few final words about the absence of sound.

First, it is very frustrating to get into the edit and find that there is no natural sound, not because the mic wasn't turned on or plugged in but because the photographer and associates talked the whole time. Try to remember to keep the talking and extraneous noise to a bare minimum when recording sound.

Lastly, silence is not silent. Even when no one is speaking or moving a room has a sound, something we call "room tone," or "ambient noise." When recording on location, especially when doing production, record a minute of this ambient room tone. Have everyone in the room be deadly still, open up the same mic used for the interview or action and just roll. When you're in the edit, cutting between speakers or cutting the comments of one speaker, it's critically important to have some "buzz" to fill in the dead spots between words.

Hiding Lavalieres

In dramatic productions and even some industrials, you may decide it's better to have the lavaliere hidden. Here are some tips and tricks that might help you get away it.

+ When hiding a mic, try hard to find a placement where its sound pickup is open to the air. If tape is being used to secure the mic, be careful not to block the opening.

+ If the mic is to be attached directly to a person's skin, use clear surgical tape.

+ Depending on the camera angle and movement, a lavaliere can sometimes be taped to one of the temples of a person's glasses.

+ One of my favorite mic placements is the hair placement. Hair is quiet and offers complete concealment. With a hair placement, it's easy to get the mic an acceptable distance from the speaker's mouth while avoiding all clothing noise.

+ The first few inches of the mic cable can pass handling noise back. Build in a strain relief by taping a loop of cable where it won't be tugged or moved.

+ Clever sound recordists may have favorite trick placements like slitting the inside of a pocket and sticking the mic through, placing a mic in a hat brim, a fake pen, a wired earring, and others.

Wireless Mics

When the speakers are going to be moving around, whether it's Granddad showing us his gardens or actors moving about a set, a wireless mic can be the perfect answer. Though we often speak of wireless mics as if they are a single unit, a wireless rig actually consists of a microphone, maybe a lavaliere, or possibly a stick or shotgun, attached to a transmitter, feeding a wireless receiver. Now, there are dedicated wireless lavs, but my personal experience has been that the low cost, hard-wired units are ineffective and lack fidelity. Besides, it's infinitely more versatile to have the option of attaching your stick mic or shotgun to the same sender as the situation dictates.

Here are a few pointers that will help you get the best performance possible out of your wireless transmitter and receiver.

+ Keep your batteries fresh.

+ Try to maintain line-of-site between the sender and receiver. Don't let objects, especially metal objects, come between the sender and receiver.

+ There are often gain controls on the transmitter and receiver as well as on your camcorder. Remember that when amplifying a signal, you're amplifying the background noise as well. This is particularly noticeable on low-level signals. Work for balance. Don't make any one unit do all the amplification. Try to work in the middle range of all three units.

+ Be careful when mounting a receiver on your camcorder. One position may be quieter than another. Experiment.

+ Some transmitters and receivers use their cables as antennas. If your reception is troublesome, try adjusting the positions of various wires. Try to keep sending and receiving antennas parallel to each other.

Rolling Tape

The day you begin rolling tape you learn two things: First, how well you planned your shoot and second, how well you juggle. Whether you have a crew or you're a one-man band, whether you're using actors or just shooting what you see, you'll be buffeted by a constant stream of choices. What will we shoot first? Should the actor wear the red hat or the green hat? Should I get in front of the action or stay behind? When will we break for lunch? You're the one who has to keep all the balls in the air.

The challenge in shooting professionally (or at the advanced amateur level) is getting things right the first time, making every image committed to tape usable, at least in a technical sense. You can decide whether one angle is better than the other in the edit, but you don't want the decision made for you because the other angle is out of focus or overexposed. Clients won't stand for it. Friends will tire of it. You can't afford it. Remember, if you have a crew, you're burning through your budget by the second. If you're shooting documentary style, you need to be aware that most things happen only once, and it's considered bad journalistic form to fake it or ask for a do-over.

My goal is to help you gather the skill and confidence you'll need to work calmly and quickly. If your client (or your older brother) says, "Isn't that shot too dark?" I want you to be able to answer, "No, it's perfect," and believe it.

If your shoot was well planned, you've thought through most of the questions and answered them already, freeing your brain to concentrate on recognizing opportunities and avoiding costly meltdowns.

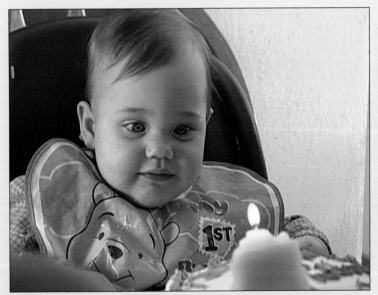

You might be able to relight the birthday candle for take two but it won't be as spontaneous or natural, and good luck trying to get the rafters over the rapids for a second shot, so make sure everything is ready to go the first time.

On some cameras the diopter is adjusted by rotating the view-finder eyepiece; on others there's a slider. Here, it's the lever on the underside of the eyepiece barrel. If it's not obvious, check the instruction book.

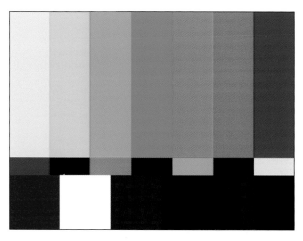

Split field color bars are a very useful feature when setting up your viewfinder. If your camera does not come with this feature, record some and play them back while you examine the viewfinder and the LCD panel.

"Roll tape! No, wait!"

I told Mr. Percival, my sixth grade teacher, I was worried that in front of the class, I would forget my presentation. He suggested I write my four main points on file cards, tape them to the four walls of my room, and refer to them as I practiced my speech. He told me if I ever lost my place in front of the class I could just envision the card on my wall and be reminded. It worked. So, when I got my first job as a news shooter, worried that in the ex-citement of arriving at a story I might lose my place, I made this list of things to do before I rolled tape and mentally hung each on a wall. OK, I used the floor and ceiling too.

1) **Set up the viewfinder**
2) **Check for unity (I'll explain what that means)**
3) **Check battery levels**
4) **Check audio meters and listen through headphones**
5) **Choose a filter and white balance**
6) **Expose and focus**

Other young shooters had to face the chief and explain why their video was blue or there was no sound, but not me. Thank you Mr. Percival, wherever you are.

Because one good turn deserves another and all that, I'm passing it on. Use my list and your own walls.

1) Set up the viewfinder

The purpose of setting up the viewfinder is to be sure you can trust that its image is a true representation of what's going to tape. Your viewfinder has a soft rubber cup around it called the eyepiece or eyecup. The diopter, a small lens just inside the eye-piece, allows you to focus the viewfinder screen for your eyesight. Be sure the camera's turned on and display information overlays the screen. I leave the lens cap on for this adjustment because I'm not concerned with the image, only that the display is in focus. Rotate the diopter through its range of focus, finding the sharpest setting.

On most DV cameras, brightness is the only viewfinder setup choice you're given, but it's an important one. What you want is a set of what's called split-field color bars. Some cameras generate these internally. If yours doesn't, record some and play them back while you examine the viewfinder and the LCD panel. Look at the three dark boxes in the lower right-hand corner of the screen. Darken the screen and then lighten it just enough to be able to see only the lightest of the three. Setting up to camera bars is way more complicated than just adjusting brightness and if you're lucky enough to own a camera and monitor capable of being set up to bars, learn how to do it right and do it every time.

A note to the aspiring professional: Pro video photographers, super-critical of focus, will usually prefer a black-and-white CRT viewfinder. Limitations created by LCD pixel size and/or dot masks make color screens harder to focus. Turning the color off doesn't change a thing. If you plan to go into business, consider stepping up to an analog viewfinder. The manual will detail a setup method. Learn it and follow it.

2) Check for unity

In a system at "unity," input equals output. As this term relates to cameras, "unity" means that anything that might modify the image is turned off. Scan your display and look for booby traps. Be sure the shutter is turned off, any video gain boost is turned off, any digital effects and digital features are turned off. If there's a 2× extender on the lens, disengage it. In cameras with a variety of shooting modes like manual, automatic, aperture priority, and shutter priority, it's worthwhile to declare one setting your unity setting. Automatic is a good choice.

3) Check battery levels

Have a fully charged battery on your camera and another one in your bag when you arrive for a shoot. If there's a question about having enough power (and you can't shoot with an AC adapter), bring your quick charger along and find a place to set it up as soon as you arrive.

4) Check audio meters and listen through headphones

Don't just listen through the headphones or just look at the meters, do both. Even if the lighting is great and the content is fantastic, if the audio is bad you've wasted everyone's time. Checking audio when you first grab the camera doesn't replace checking it while you're shooting, but knowing it was there when you first turned on the camera will make troubleshooting much easier later on.

5) Choose a filter and white balance

All light may look white but it's not. Light has color, measured in degrees on the Kelvin scale. Indoor, incandescent light is reddish (nominally 3,200°K), outdoor light (nominally 5,600°K) is bluer. Your camera needs to know what you consider white in order to render a true representation of all the other colors. That's why you "white balance."

As a news shooter, I'd grab my camera from its bag, set the filter wheel, and flip the white balance to "preset." So if someone shouted, "Quick! They're looting the Food King," I'd be ready to roll. That was then. Now, most DV cameras are equipped with auto white balance, circuitry dedicated to constantly assessing color temperature. Shooting all manual, moving from indoor to outdoor light required a slick bit of filter spinning and switch throwing. On most DV cameras, auto white balance takes care of it automatically and with surprising accuracy. The downside of constant white balancing is the system is ready and eager to make adjustments, regardless of how inappropriate. A camera

The idea is to start with a clean slate, then add whatever features and adjustments you think you'll need for the shoot. It's a good habit to zero everything at the end of every shoot. If more than one person uses the camera, it's just good manners.

struggling to define white might lose the splendid colors of a sunset. The same camera, given a mix of color temperatures from various lights indoors, might drift from one to another setting depending on framing.

If you feel you need to white balance, start by turning off the auto white balance and finding something white—a shirt, a sign, or that little white card you will, from now on, carry in your wallet or camera bag. Some folks will paste a circle of white paper inside their lens cap, which is only a good idea if your lens cap isn't attached to the camera by a short cord. With auto iris on, frame up on the white area you've chosen, nearly filling the screen. Hold down the white balance button on your camera and watch for a confirmation. If you're shooting in an area of mixed light, try to hold your white balance card so it catches the mix in the proper proportion *unless* you're looking for a color effect. It's possible to color your video by white balancing on something other than white. The trick is to white balance on a color opposite the color you desire. Look at a color wheel. If you want your picture redder, white balance on something green. This is a common trick when you're shooting under fluorescents, which have a greenish cast. The deeper the color you choose for your white balance, the more pronounced the effect. Most of the time, you're looking for a slight shift so if you want your video a little warmer (redder), choose a very, very pale green. The truth is, your camera may not accept a white balance on anything but a very, very pale color. Professional videographers will put a little

This shot drifted from blue to orange as the model moved away from the camera and more of the white background became readable. Feel free to use auto white balance when appropriate but be sure to lock in a balance if you're staying in one location.

Be aware—in the digital world, areas exposed above 110 percent are clipped and all detail is lost. In the edit, you can adjust the overexposed white shirt on your talent all the way down to a dingy 60 percent, but you'll still never see his buttons and collar. They're just plain gone.

square of pale, colored gel (often ⅛ Plus Green or ⅛ CTB) over a small white card. You can get these little squares from a company called Rosco. They'll send you a Cinegel swatchbook, more commonly known as a Jungle Book, free if you visit the company's website (www.rosco.com). (To say thank you, be sure to buy the many gels you'll need from Rosco as well.)

6) Expose and focus

Technically and aesthetically, exposure is critical to your image. "Properly exposed" doesn't mean fully exposed. It's not necessary or even desirable to have exposure levels reach 100 percent in every frame. Some shots want to top out at 40 percent, dark and moody. Other times, overexposure works. With filtration, a blown-out window or doorway can be soft and ethereal.

Unlike auto white balance, auto exposure (or auto iris) has been around for decades on both consumer and professional cameras. The thing to remember is…it stinks and it always will! The circuits are designed to detect overexposure and underexposure and react appropriately. Unfortunately, the camera reacts without thought. If the cook's knife glints or a flashbulb goes off, if the speaker's glasses catch a reflection or someone walks through the background wearing a white shirt, the camera irises down, then up again and that looks, well, unprofessional. The problem is, the camera can't know whether any variance is momentary or

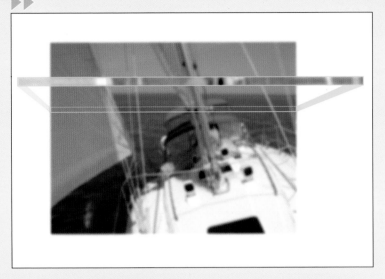
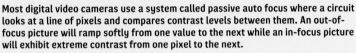

Most digital video cameras use a system called passive auto focus where a circuit looks at a line of pixels and compares contrast levels between them. An out-of-focus picture will ramp softly from one value to the next while an in-focus picture will exhibit extreme contrast from one pixel to the next.

a legitimate change in light levels without understanding the shot. To understand a shot, the camera would need a brain and the only brain nearby is yours. So, turn the auto iris off and learn to set proper exposures without it. Learn to work the zebra.

Many cameras offer a zebra pattern—superimposed diagonal stripes useful in judging exposure. The trigger point for the zebra is usually 80 percent (the traditional level of face tones), but some are set at 90 percent or 100 percent. Check your manual to be sure. If it's adjustable, choose 100 percent unless the camera also offers foldover. Foldover is a slick little function that turns areas exposed over 110 percent from white to black. With zebra and foldover you can note a range of exposure, say 80 percent and 110 percent, which further eliminates guesswork.

Momentary iris

Remember when I told you not to use auto iris? Here's when to ignore me. If your camera offers a "momentary iris," where it's engaged only while the button's pressed, that's fine, use it. It's helpful to see what exposure the camera suggests before you roll tape. If you're shooting scenery or wide shots where a brief lighting variation (like a white car zipping through the foreground) is unlikely, feel free to use auto exposure. If you're entering into a situation where you might need to keep one eye open for your own safety, by all means, use the auto exposure! Finally, if you're about to take a shot where you just don't have enough hands to do all the adjusting necessary, again, take advantage of the power of your camera's automated features.

The zebra pattern will alert you to overexposed areas and, with your viewfinder set up properly, you should be able to judge the rest.

Tip: Words of caution, when judging exposure, use the viewfinder with the rubber eyepiece rather than the foldout LCD screen. LCD screens are super sensitive to viewing angle and can often give you the wrong impression.

Auto focus

Unlike auto iris, I love auto focus! The system is clever and functional but still, there are times when it's best to turn it off. Auto focus tends to give more weight to objects in the center of the screen. If you intend to focus on an object frame left or frame right, auto focus may fight you. Low-light or low-contrast situations can confuse the auto focus circuit. A person cutting your frame doesn't hurt most shots, unless the camera decides to acquire focus on the intruder. Bottom line: Auto focus isn't always right. When it's not, focus manually. The proper way to focus manually is to zoom all the way into your subject (if it's a person, zoom into their eyes), turn the focus ring on the lens until you find your best focus, and pull back out. Unless there's a problem with your zoom lens, your subject will be in focus no matter what focal length you settle upon. If the subject moves closer to or farther from the camera, you may approach the limit of your depth of field, the area within which your focus appears acceptably sharp, and need to refocus. This is especially true if you're shooting telephoto, in low light or with a fast shutter.

Final points

- Don't assume because something looks like it's in focus in your flip-out LCD viewfinder, that it's in focus. Focus always looks better on smaller monitors. Your focus needs to be able to stand up to a big screen so zoom in, focus, and pull out.

- Shoot everything flat, that is, without sepia tones, mosaic patterns, stutters or any of the other cheesy in-camera effect options. Apply your effects in the edit, where you have better choices and more control.

- Be aware of your audio highs and lows. Consider the quality and listen for camera sounds. Compare your recollection of dominant sounds in the field to the realities of your audio on tape.

- Finally, with the viewfinder properly adjusted, the settings at unity, all the power you need, the sound coming in loud and clear, a good white balance, exposure and focus, you're ready to frame and roll. If you're new at this, roll often. Practice. Make your mistakes while it doesn't count.

The more you understand how and how well your equipment works, the better your decisions will be on location.

"OK, roll tape!"
Basic tips for shooting news style

- The world is your tripod. Lean, brace, prop an elbow, hang on the railing, do whatever is necessary to steady your shots.

- Use horizons and strong vertical elements near the center of the screen to be sure your shots are level.

- Tape is cheap. Allow shots to develop. Roll until the shot is done.

- Bracket your moves. Hold the shot for at least five seconds before the move starts and after the move finishes. You'll appreciate it in the edit.

- Bracket your exposures. If there's a question regarding what will look best in the edit, shoot it both ways.

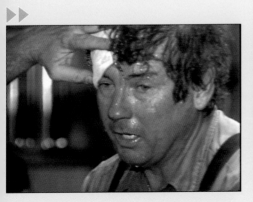

Shooting news style requires making quick decisions, recognizing shots, being open to possibilities, and getting the basics down before getting creative.

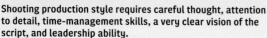

Shooting production style requires careful thought, attention to detail, time-management skills, a very clear vision of the script, and leadership ability.

- Shoot sequences: the man typing, the computer screen, his fingers on the keyboard, his hand picking up the phone, the man talking on the phone. Think in terms of shots that will edit together into smooth, sequential actions. We'll cover sequence shooting later when we examine the principles of editing.

- Shoot people as they transition from one place or activity to the next. You can't edit together the shot of the man typing and the shot of the man on the phone without the shot of the man picking up the phone. Sequences don't make sense without "connectors."

- Shoot *useful* cutaways. The essence of a cutaway is its value as a connector between shots in the edit. A useful cutaway doesn't contain anything in the frame that will raise continuity issues with the shot before or after. For example, in the list above, the tight shot of the screen would edit cleanly between the shots of the man typing and the man on the phone.

- Shoot for edit points. Don't simply follow the action; you'll have no place to edit. Let actions, people, and objects move into or out of the frame.

- Combine camera moves. If you're going to do a pan and a zoom, be sure both the pan and the zoom coincide, starting and ending together. It just looks better.

Basic tips for shooting production style

- Take stills of the location before you start moving things around. When it's time to put everything back the way you found it, no one will remember.

- "Spiking" means laying down a piece of tape to mark a spot. If there are positions to hit and objects moved during the shot, spike the start positions. In fact, spike everything!

- Walk your actors and crew through the shot, then walk them back to their start positions.

- When you're ready to roll be sure everyone knows. Yell "Quiet! Roll tape!" Be assertive.

- The photographer will respond "Speed," confirming tape is rolling. Get a nod from the audio operator then yell "Action!"

- If there's background action, yell "Background action" count seconds to yourself then yell "Action." Knowing the difference will help you with timing if things don't work out.

- If there's a camera move, call for it before "Action" as well (e.g. "Dolly" or "Boom").

Avoid the BIGGEST, MOST COSTLY MISTAKES OF YOUR SHOOTING CAREER!

+ When you finish recording a tape, don't rewind. Leave it at the end to help discourage accidental overrecords.

+ When you finish recording a tape, eject it immediately. If you don't think this is important, ask a rental company how many tapes it finds in cameras.

+ As soon as you eject your tape, look on the back of the tape and locate the record inhibit tab. Slide the tab left to expose the red color beneath. This will prevent the tape from being accidentally recorded over.

+ As soon as you finish popping the record tab, label your tape fully with the date, the project, and a number. Believe me, it doesn't take long to forget what's on the tape. It takes even less time for unlabeled tapes to disappear into the river of tape that surrounds the average videographer. Losing a tape is infinitely worse than not having shot the tape in the first place!

+ As soon as you've finished labeling the tape, put it with your other shot tapes, especially if you're shooting on location or traveling. Keep all your tapes together in the safest place you can think of. If you're in a hotel, consider putting the tapes in the hotel safe. When you're in transit, keep the tapes in sight and don't for a second lose your awareness of this video—it may be the entire reason you're traveling!

• If you have an extra person available on the set, log your takes with comments. Takes tend to look the same in the edit.

• Use a slate. They're cheap and you'll thank yourself in the edit.

• Roll camera long enough to record your comments on the take.

• When action is complete, yell "Cut!" Take control of the stopping and the starting of tape or something grand is going to happen two seconds after your photographer has already paused.

• Ask if anyone had a problem with the take. Decide whether fixing the problem is worth doing another take. If it is, make your adjustments quickly. Get everybody reset by yelling "Start positions."

Record inhibit tabs

• Once you've gotten a good take, get a safety—that is, a backup good take. One day you'll be a hero for doing this.

• Learn to recognize the point at which, no matter how many additional takes you roll, it's not going to get any better. Either figure out a way to break the shot into smaller pieces that are more manageable or give up and move on.

• Take production stills. It's amazing how quickly everyone will forget the lighting setup or whether the car was in the shot or not.

• Try not to roll back to look at shots unless you or someone who is very dependable is willing to take responsibility for recueing the tape. Nothing feels worse than rolling over a good take.

Tape labels

Secrets of Our Visual Language

One of the famous things Peter Mark Roget did was write a the-saurus. The other famous thing he did was in 1824 he described a phenomenon known as persistence of vision. Draw a big black dot on a piece of paper with a marker. Stare at the dot for ten seconds then shift your eyes to a clean part of the paper. The dot will linger. That persistence helps describe how your eyes see thirty individual pictures a second but your brain shows you a smooth, moving video image. Seventy-five years later, filmmaking began, and in the one hundred years since, filmmaking has developed a language of its own.

Filmmaking grammar makes it easier for the viewer to follow the story. A scene begins with a wide shot (WS) establishing location, and then cuts to a medium shot (MS) to introduce some action, finally cutting to a tight shot (TS) to introduce a character. That progression is an accepted convention, visual shorthand. If we see a TS before the WS, we're disoriented until we get our bearings. Of course, that might be the point of the shot. Since both film-maker and audience speak the same language, it's easy to make bold statements, toy with sly innuendo, or tell jokes. For in-stance, there's the one about Butch who swears there's no way that he'll dress up as Santa! Not under any circumstance, ever. Period! Cut to a shot of Butch dressed as Santa. Cue laughter.

Visual Grammar Primer

Our visual language helps both to direct the viewer's attention and supplement screen images with emotional undercurrent.

Color

Color is a powerful modifier in the book of visual grammar. We've come to see scenes tinted blue as being cold and scenes with a reddish, golden hue as warm. Blue is the color of winter; despair, depression, and all the things that go bump in the night. The golden color speaks to us of summer evenings, new days, family, home, and hearth. When this story changed and hope was introduced, the color scheme got warmer, reinforcing the message. We've all heard of the green room where television guests wait for their cue. Green is accepted as calming. Scenes that are predominantly green, especially green with foliage, are perceived as calming.

Face-ism ratio

When photographing people, we often speak of full shots, medium shots, head and shoulders shots, and close-ups. Studies have shown we like people more and care about them more when we see them shot in close-up. Turning that around, if I want the audience to like my character, I shoot more close-ups. That's the power of understanding visual grammar, the subliminal shorthand agreed upon by film-makers and audiences.

Settings

Surveys indicate we like and trust people shown in natural settings more than people in blank, corporate, or official looking settings. Understanding this, one might take advantage of this fact by placing a speaker in a natural setting.

Horizontal composition

Many people have spent years analyzing our visual language. For instance, take a screen and divide it in half horizontally. It's said a darker color above the line than below can invoke a depressed, closed in feeling, leaving the shot top-heavy and unstable. This is the language of the world around you. The dark below and light above is the natural state of the world, the division between earth and sky. The shot feels balanced, grounded, open, and happier.

Vertical Lines

You share many perceptions with your audience. Proportion, light, texture, and color prompt us to assign weight and mass to an object. Strong, parallel verticals can seem like bars on a jail cell or the strong soaring pillars shouting stability and respect. It's your job to assess your location and decide how they will be read, as stability or confinement. You do that by listening to your emotions and deciding how shots make you feel.

Often the best way to determine dominant lines and screen elements is to squint. Really. Look at a shot or graphic in your monitor through mostly closed eyes, denying the benefit of focus and brightness, and try to spot broad patterns of light and dark. Dominant diagonal lines from lower frame left to upper frame right are considered hopeful and triumphant, while the opposite diagonal is often assigned descriptors that imply retreat, failure, and sadness.

Strong vertical lines, especially convergent lines like you see looking up at a tall building, draw our eyes toward the top of the frame, toward the sky, toward the boundless heavens. If you invert the dominant lines, forming a V, the message turns around too. The resulting downward arrow can lead the eye and the mind into the abyss. So, should you commit all this visual language to memory? Don't bother. You already have.

The trick to using our visual language is to summon it to your consciousness and force yourself to think it through.

Composition
Framing

Years ago, I taught news shooting for a consulting firm that specialized in small broadcast markets. For financial reasons, their news photography ranks were filled with recent trade school grads and ambitious beginners promoted from other positions. Prior to my arrival, I'd ask that each photographer be ready with a half dozen minute-long packages we'd critique. My point is, I saw a lot of footage from inexperienced shooters and they nearly all made a mistake I call "centering." They'd find a subject (especially a human subject), zoom in and focus, zoom out and roll. There would be as much blank sky above as body below and equal space to the left and right regardless of what was included or excluded. The subject would simply be centered. These shooters completely skipped the critically important step of framing.

All three of these shots were taken from approximately the same position. The difference is framing. Framing is the conscious choice of shot boundaries for both aesthetic and narrative reasons. Before you roll tape, it's your job to inspect the image in your viewfinder and adjust the edges of the shot, sometimes by zooming, sometimes by panning or tilting, squatting down, or taking a step left or right. Your goal is to create the most powerful shot you can compose, while including important screen elements and excluding elements that detract from your picture and message.

Choosing a frame begins with choosing a lens length or focal length starting with the basic wide shot (or long shot), often noted in scripts and shot logs as WS (or LS). Though basic frame designations are often thought of in terms of how they relate to human subjects, a wide shot is a wide shot whether there's a person in the frame or not.

In the middle of the range of framings and focal length is the medium shot (or mid-shot) written as MS.

Finally there's the familiar tight shot or TS, also known as a head and shoulders shot. In Europe, the head and shoulders shot is synonymous with the medium close-up or MCU.

Clearly the three designations of WS, MS, and TS cannot cover the wide variation of possible lens length. For precision, we add to the list the extreme wide shot (XWS or XLS) (top) and the medium wide shot or MWS (bottom).

When framing, try not to cut shots at natural bodylines like the chin, bust, or knees. Shots that are more pleasing result from cropping these breaks in or out of the frame. On the other hand, shots cut at natural body lines can add an odd element of interest.

On the other side of the medium shot is the medium tight shot, or MTS (top), and the extreme tight shot or XTS, also known as the close-up or CU (center). Obviously there has to be an extreme close-up or ECU as well (bottom).

A shot should always include sufficient headroom so as not to feel clipped. A good rule of thumb is to allow 10 percent of the frame above the subject's head. This usually involves moving the person's hair very near the top of the frame. In close-ups, it is perfectly acceptable to crop out some hair or the hat.

Scenic shots can have too much headroom as well.

The first cousin of headroom is "nose room," also referred to as leading space or looking space. In a conversation, you'll leave nose room in the direction the subject is looking and talking. Resist the urge to frame up by centering the shoulders. Center the eyes and then leave a little more looking space. If the person turns from one direction to another, adjust the nose room with the turn.

When following a subject in motion—a car, a boat, a person, anything—it's important to lead the frame. Leaving an area for the object to "move into" enhances the feeling of forward motion.

Shooting buildings, objects, or a person head-on is boring and often unflattering. The alternative is a three-quarter shot. Three-quarter shots add depth, interest, and dynamism to shots.

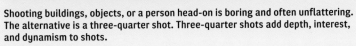

Inspect your frame and crop in the camera. Sometimes the smallest element of a scene can be the most interesting. Resist the urge to always include the entire object or even the whole face. It's a matter of emphasis.

Television is a horizontal medium. It's not possible to turn shots the long way. When faced with vertical objects, try to find ways to balance the frame. Of course, if interesting clouds or trees or architectural details surround the object, this may be unnecessary.

Tip: Underscan and Overscan

Understand the difference between Underscan, the full television image, and Overscan, the image as reduced by the frame around a typical TV screen. Generally, you should assume that 10 percent of the image will be lost. It's critical you experiment with your viewfinder, shooting and examining the results to determine whether you're seeing Underscan or Overscan. Ten percent one way or the other can be the difference between good and bad framing.

Look for foreground, midfield, and background, especially in scenics. A shot that fills all fields shows more depth, adding interest. Soft foreground elements such as flowers and trees can take the edge off angular structures or make a shot look cozy. Strong foreground elements can force the eye to centers of interest. Often foreground elements can be used to help hide or deemphasize unwanted elements from the frame.

Rule of thirds

We've discussed the error of centering, a mistake made by many beginning photographers who fail to frame their shots. There is a similar mistake made when, even after adjusting the frame for proper headroom and lens length, the subject of the shot remains dead center. This is a violation of the rule of thirds, a centuries-old principle that warns us that symmetry does not produce the most effective composition.

The rule of thirds is based on an ideal standard of proportion devised by the ancient Greeks. They called it the golden mean. This principle of composition, used in art and architecture for centuries, states that a picture should not be cut in half but in thirds, divided by two sets of horizontal and vertical lines. The four intersections created by the lines provide geometric balance and here is where a subject of interest should be placed. Keep this rule of thirds in mind as you shoot. It gives you a good base to work from and provides a variety of composition options.

Both of these images clearly illustrate the rule of thirds. By placing the focal point off center, a more aesthetically pleasing look is achieved.

When shooting a landscape, resist the urge to place the horizon at the center of the screen. Think about what you want to emphasize and place the horizon higher in the shot to show more land and ground the shot, or lower to show more sky and open it up.

Centers of interest

Try to pretend, wherever you are, through some metaphysical hic-cup, you've just been dropped into that scene. You wouldn't take in the scene as a whole. You'd glance around, assessing and in-specting. Your eyes might lock onto the teacup and creamer, dart to the window then jump to the computer screen aglow in the corner. Each of these scenes within your scene is a center of interest. If you were to show an audience a wide shot of your scene, they would go through the same process, looking around, drawn from one center of interest to the next. As a photographer, you must inspect a scene in your viewfinder and assess the centers of interest for dominance. In that way, you can determine where the viewer's attention will be drawn and decide whether that path, from one center of attention to another, suits your message.

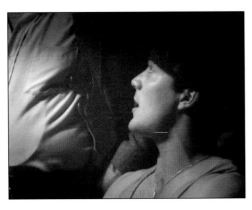

When this scene is flashed on the screen, the viewer's eye is drawn first to the brightest area, the actor in the chair, the primary center of attention. It takes a mo-ment for the audience to shift to the second center of attention and notice the gun in the detective's belt. If the gun was intended to be the primary center of at-tention, the shot might have to be framed differently or lit differently.

When framing two shots to be edited back to back, consider where you've left your viewer's eye in the first shot and take advantage of that position when framing the second shot. You don't want to jerk the viewer's eyes around the frame.

The path from one center of attention to another often follows the dominant line in the picture. Roads, rivers, and tracks are natural paths. You can use your under-standing of dominant lines and centers of interest to direct the viewer's eye.

Elements of the frame

Pictures tell so much of the story that writers often specify not only *who* will be seen but also *what* will be seen. The hidden report card, a wall of trophies, the dirty dishes in the sink, the uniform on the bed, the baby monitor, an opulent office, a crumpled wedding picture; all these screen elements "talk" to the viewer as much as the dialogue. Collectively, they're known by the French term *mise en scène*, the surroundings of an event. Often the *mise en scène* amounts to a sort of visual cliché, establishing the scene by offering image cues that speak without words.

This is a driveway turned into a park by the addition of a few benches and a trash can.

We know this couple has a young child because of the toys scattered around in shots.

This single shot—nothing but some bark, a couple of leaves, and some moss—can establish a location in a deep, primeval forest. Sound and a blur of green behind the character will fill in the rest of the picture.

We know this is a business meeting and not a dinner party because of the blueprints and mugs. We surmise it's a "creative space" because of the loftlike feel and less than businesslike furnishings...and the fact that just about everyone is sucking on a lollipop.

A living room becomes a designer's studio by the addition of a drawing table and tools.

The *mise en scène* is developed by getting to the essence of a location and its dressing. What makes an art gallery an art gallery? It doesn't take a lot of art, but it does take open space, plain, white walls, and some little printed legends. Four tables with matching tablecloths and centerpieces establish this location as a restaurant. Of course, the sounds of dishes and conversation round out the picture.

Camera Placement

Camera placement starts on a very practical level. You anticipate the action, the emotion, and dialogue, then decide where you're going to put your camera to record it most effectively. Do you want the viewers to feel as though they're in the thick of it? Handhold a camera close-in. Do you want the viewers to feel as though they're separated from the action, merely passive observers? Place the camera far away.

One shot, one placement, one decision, may be preordained by the space and situation. The challenges change when there's the opportunity for a second angle or a camera move. Now one position doesn't have to do all the work. Shooting news or documentary style, you're given the chance to show a detail, close up, or come around the table to see how the other person reacts.

In a dramatic scene, a second placement affords the opportunity for a telling glance, a funny aside, a secret revealed, or another interpretation of the situation. Now it's time to use your understanding of our visual language to convey the visual impression of respect, fear, fun, love, or lunacy.

Angles and eyelines

While some angles look better than others and some angles are more flattering than others, choosing a camera angle is mostly subjective. Eyelines are not. If you want the audience to understand that two people are looking at each other, their eyelines must match. If one is looking down, the other must be looking up at the same angle. If one is looking down and the other is looking straight, the implication is that one is reluctant to meet the other's gaze. That's a story point and shouldn't happen by mistake. When there is only a single subject in your frame, the eyelines must make contextual sense. Simply put, what are they looking at? Choosing the camera angle requires an answer to a similar question, "What are you looking at?"

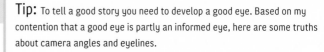

Tip: To tell a good story you need to develop a good eye. Based on my contention that a good eye is partly an informed eye, here are some truths about camera angles and eyelines.

+ When shooting a single shot or interview, looking up (slightly) at people imparts respect. Don't look up enough to see up their nose. This doesn't hold true when the person is looking down (e.g. writing, working on the computer, etc).

+ Kids like being "looked up to."

+ When shooting a single shot or interview, looking down (slightly) at people diminishes their stature and makes them seem smaller. Not so with true high angle shots where the single person is not the sole center of interest.

+ Still, it's best to look down (slightly) at people who are self-conscious about double or sloping chins.

+ When in doubt, look them right in the eye.

+ Try not to position people to appear having odd shapes and objects "growing out of their heads."

+ When shooting interviews, the most pleasing eyeline is close to, but not into, the camera. Try to have the person conducting the interview very close to an imaginary line drawn between the subject and the camera.

+ Avoid having a person on camera reading something that's just off camera. It is immediately obvious and mildly disconcerting to have someone who should be making eye contact with the viewer through the lens, looking slightly *off* camera. Force them to either memorize their lines or ad-lib.

+ If people are not supposed to be talking or relating directly to the camera, tell them, warn them! It is immediately obvious when someone looks into the camera, just as obvious as when you look up and see someone staring at you.

Shooting a documentary, the news, or a bar mitzvah, you may not have the advantage of seeing the location before the shoot. You have to think on your feet. If you have any say in the matter, try to steer things toward areas with light and shadow, color and opportunity. Outdoors, I may be describing the park bench in the shade. Indoors, the hallway stairs or landing might offer more intriguing angles than you'd find in a foursquare room. No matter what you're shooting, your goal is to make the shots look as good without stepping over the boundaries of appropriateness.

There are two ways that I can tell whether you're going to be an effective videographer or not. First, you'll give yourself away if I can tell how tall you are by your video. Some people don't realize they not only have knees, their knees are critical to competent shooting. Try alternate angles—high angles, low angles. Look for ways to stack people and objects. Find foreground and work it into the shot.

 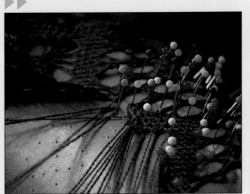 

The second way I can tell whether you're going to be an effective videographer is if you think your shoes are nailed to the floor. When I look for a wide, medium, and tight shot, I don't expect that all three will be shot from the same height and the same distance and the only difference will be a zoom. That's not three shots, that's just one shot framed differently.

When choosing camera angles, there are many conventions. In interview situations, it's the shot/reverse shot. Reverse shots are often done "over the shoulder," helping fill the frame and defining the physical relationship between the subjects.

I own action figures. You know, the articulated, hard plastic kind: Star Troopers, Young Elvis, that sort of thing. I own them because sometimes I shoot special effects and eyelines are important. In this case, one little figure stood in for Mel and gave Mary someone to look at. I was able to use an inclinometer, an inexpensive building tool, to measure the angle of her eyeline and duplicate it in the studio later. Though I don't shoot miniature people often, I do figure out shots for my storyboards and work out complicated 180° rule changes from time to time.

Kneel down or lie down, but get down to their eye level (or lower) when shooting children. Shooting the tops of children's heads, in addition to being less flattering, eliminates all the joy of seeing their expressions.

Respecting the 180° rule

Breaking the 180° rule

The 180° rule and screen direction

You're a shooter walking into a meeting. You assess the room. There's a group leader in the front, people on either side of the table, a screen in one corner, projector opposite, and coffee in the back. Seeing this wide shot orients you. To convey that orientation to your audience, you need to follow one particular convention now and for the rest of your shooting career. I've already mentioned it briefly in this book, and because it's so important, I want to go into a bit more detail about it. It's called the 180° rule and, though it's critical, even experienced videographers get it wrong. That won't happen to you because I'm going to make it very easy.

We'll start small, with two people talking. Imagine a line drawn from one person's face to the other's. If you stay on one side of the line, confining your shots to that 180° sweep, you will never break the rule. Why is it important? Because shoot these two from anywhere on the chosen side of the line and one will be facing screen left and the other facing screen right. They are "facing" each other.

If you cross the line for a shot, you'll end up with two people facing the same way. A viewer, denied other information, wouldn't know they're talking to each other.

Now let's apply the rule to a big stage show (right). Draw a line between the performer and audience and stay on one side of that line, the performer will always be looking at the audience and the audience will always be looking at the performer.

Edit together audience shots from both sides of the line and screen direction is lost. Going to a straight-on shot of the performers redraws the line, allowing you to shift then to the other side.

In the shots above, all the cyclists are headed in the same direction, but because some shots are taken from one side of the line of action and others from the opposite side, screen direction is reversed for one group of riders. That might not be a critical failure for a charity ride but it would be confusing if we were videotaping a parade. And what about two trains on the same track? The story relies on screen direction. The viewer must know whether one train is following the other or they're headed directly for each other.

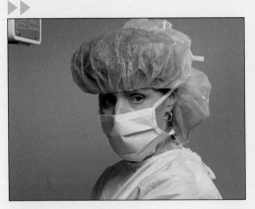

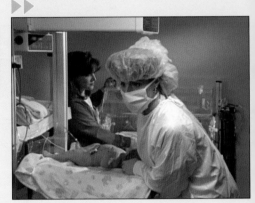

In a production situation, the assumption is that in a complicated conversation you'll have the edit figured out before you ever shoot. That's the right way. Still, if you're not sure whether it's going to be doctor-nurse-patient or doctor-patient-nurse, you'll need to shoot the reaction from both sides. Draw the line between the doctor and the nurse and see where the patient should look, then draw the line between the doctor and patient and see where the nurse should look. Again, the line is simply between the last two speakers.

In the two previous examples, the line has been simple and unchanging. Now let's go back to the boardroom. Here, it's clear that when the group leader is speaking we can draw a line between that leader and the person nearest the leader of the far side of the table. Stay on one side of the line and you're golden. However, as words and glances bounce around the room, how will relationships be maintained? What if a comment from the leader begins an exchange between two people halfway down on opposite sides of the table? The answer is very simple. The line is always drawn between the last two people who interact. Always! It's that simple. Don't let anyone confuse you by making it more complicated than it is. The line is dynamic. The line moves, but it moves in a simple way.

Now, here's how people get mixed up. If you're shooting this meeting documentary style, you don't know how the editor is going to assemble the conversation. Maybe the second and

fourth comments are good but the third is off topic. What are you to do? The answer is, be sure to shoot people *who aren't talking*. Shoot the leader while the others go at it. Shoot the quiet guy on the end of the table. What you want are shots of the people who aren't talking but are *turning their heads*. You want someone looking left to right and right to left. These are your cutaways and will "turn" the 180° line for you.

Let's look at another important application of the 180° rule before we move on. The 180° rule defines the 180° line, also called the line of action. The action might be conversation, as in the examples we're looked at so far, or the action might be dueling pistols or fisticuffs. In the case of physical conflict, the line of action is more critical to the telling of the story, though no more complicated than before. Whether it's a foot race or a car chase, screen direction is equally significant. The line of action is drawn between the racer's beginning position and destination.

The 30° rule

Amateur videographers often make the mistake of using too much camera movement; they use the zoom too much, they tilt too much, or pan incessantly. It's a little ironic that one of the most common jump cuts is created by not moving the camera or zooming enough! The rule that's violated is called the 30° rule, though many know it as the 30 percent rule. In any case, the problem arises when there is not enough variation from one framing to the next. The solution is, when you move the camera, move it by at least 30° and if you change the framing, change it by at least 30 percent. Having shots that vary in size and perspective will make the editing process easier and give the final product a more interesting and professional look.

Sequence shooting, talking, and turning

The time to begin planning for your edit is in the storyboard phase. The day the camera rolls you should already know how any character you've scripted is going to get from here to there, your camera positions and most of your edit points. If you're shooting news or documentary style, chances are you won't know what's going to happen until you see it happen. That's why it's important to plan when you can and know how to react appropriately when you can't.

Edit points

To shoot documentary style (or home video style), it's critical to learn the skill of dissection. You must become capable of rapidly analyzing people's actions and slicing them up into shots. Any activity, from sailing a boat to dialing a phone, can be disassembled into individual movements. In this example, the lift operator drives up, begins filling the tank, spills some fuel, and has to clean up after himself. In real time, the whole process took about five minutes. In a video presentation, there's no time for real time. The answer is to divide the larger action into steps and shots. It's called sequence shooting and when done well, it allows the editor to adjust the screen time devoted to the action. It's important to choose camera angles that allow subjects to enter and leave the frame or to choose angles where discontinuous actions won't be noticed. For example, in the shot of the man's face as he pumps the fuel, we have no idea what his hands are doing. This trick allows us to cut from a shot of the nozzle going into the tank, then to his face, then to pump with the nozzle being replaced. The editor can decide whether the edited action should take four seconds or forty seconds.

Cutaways

An essential derivative of the sequence shooting method involves shooting cutaways. A cutaway is literally a shot that cuts away from the main action. Cutaways are intended to allow the compression of time without creating jumps in the action. A cutaway shot of a reporter listening will mask the edit between two nonconsecutive sound bites. In the case of shooting interview cutaways, it's usually best to keep the cutaway shot similar in composition to the shots it's joining. There is no logical way to edit together a series of shots where a man is on one side of the creek and then the other without the shot of the water flowing between.

Transitions

One of the most critical errors inexperienced videographers make is to shoot actions without shooting the transitions from one action to the next. It is actually far better to shoot the transitions between actions than to shoot the actions!

Let's consider for a moment a woman baking cookies. We have a medium shot of her spooning mixed batter onto a baking sheet. We also have a medium shot of her putting the baking sheet into the oven. The problem is there's no logical way the editor will be able to join those shots without a transitional shot or a cutaway in between. What might work? A shot of batter-dabbed hands picking up a towel, using it, then dropping it again. A shot of the woman's face moving, clearly turning from one activity to another might work, too. A shot of the clock or a timer would do it. However, a videographer thinking ahead would have offered a better solution. The videographer should have seen he or she was backing the editor into a corner by delivering two back-to-back medium shots without a transition. If the videographer had ended the first shot by allowing the woman to pick up the baking sheet and exit the frame there would be no issue. If the shooter had begun the second shot on a closed oven door and allowed the woman to enter the frame, again, no cutaway necessary! A good videographer thinks about edit points when he or she shoots.

Talk and turn

A popular technique for breaking up long narratives is a variation on sequence shooting called the "talk and turn." This one-camera shoot involved several long stand-ups, difficult to cover. We would have our talent walk, addressing the camera, and on a certain word, turn to where the camera was going to be. We'd then move the camera and have the talent repeat the tail end of the previous standup, looking at where the camera was, turn on the same word, and continue talking to the camera now in the new position. The challenges are threefold, first to be sure you know where the new camera position will be and second, to be sure the talent always turns at the same point, on the same word. Finally, if you're shooting the second shot at a different time than the first shot, be sure the talent turns in the right direction! Done well, it's always a nice, clean, tight edit.

Coverage

Before we move on, I want to introduce a film term that relates to this concept of shooting sequences. It's called "coverage.' When the budget exists, rather than break a scene up into sequences of individual shots, directors sometimes shoot coverage. The idea is to shoot the scene or the action from a variety of camera angles and sort it all out in the edit. There are obvious advantages and disadvantages of this method. It's time consuming, costly, and it requires people to perform the action or run the lines the same way over and over again and that can wring the spontaneity out of any scene. On the plus side, there's always somewhere to go in the edit. If you didn't catch the essence of that look when the camera was there, you probably caught it when you moved the camera over here. It's not the best way out of sequencing a scene, but it is a way out.

Camera Movement

In 1896, Alexandre Promio fixed a Lumière camera to a gondola and amazed the world with a panoramic tour of Venice's Grand Canal. That day marked the transition of camera as passive observer to camera as active participant. Cameras haven't stood still since. Over the years, cinematographers and videographers have invited us on a wild ride, allowing audiences to run, drive, fly, swim, fall, and float in space. The remarkable evolution of camera movement has relied upon inventive technicians who've devised all manner of complex rigging, stabilization, and support. Today's shrinking DV cams are freeing themselves from all mechanical restraint. I believe portability, combined with a new generation's precocious understanding of digital video's possibilities, promises viewers many years of stunning, soaring, provocative movements yet unimagined.

Movement is classified by whether the camera itself actually moves or merely its field of view. Beyond that, moves are further sorted by direction; up, down, left, right, or a combination as we'll see in boom, jib arm, and crane shots.

Pan and tilt

A tripod consists of two parts, the head and the legs, often sold separately. The legs have everything to do with how high, how low, and how stable the camera can be but nothing to do with movement. The head allows rotation around two axes to produce the camera movements known as the tilt and the pan. I'm going to take you to a children's playground to help you get this straight.

The merry-go-round or roundabout spins on a vertical axis. That same movement of a tripod head would produce a pan. A pan is named by the direction the lens moves. If the lens moves left, it's a pan to the left. Now imagine a teeter-totter or seesaw. The seesaw rotates around a horizontal axis. That same movement of a tripod head would produce a tilt, again named for the movement of the lens, either tilting up or tilting down. Grasp the difference and you'll never make the mistake of using uninformed phrases like "tilt left" or "pan up."

One other important point about tilts and pans—they're unnatural. Don't believe me? Try panning with your eyes. Stare straight ahead and turn your head. It feels unnatural, right? The way we actually pan is, as our head turns, our eyes jump ahead, locking on a shot until the head catches up, then jumping again. We don't see every inch of a pan. We see a series of individual shots cut back to back. The same is true, though to a lesser extent, with tilts. Our eyes want to dart ahead, preceding the movement of our head.

Track, truck, and dolly

Where pans and tilts involve a movement from a fixed camera position, tracking shots and dolly shots involve moving the camera. Simple. Now let's mix it up a bit. Just as a cameras pan left and right but tilt up or down, there is a technical distinction between tracking and dollying. In the truest film sense, a camera "dollies" in or out, but "tracks" left or right. The verbs are simple. The confusion arises from the fact that a tracking shot, moving left or right, will likely be done from a dolly. In a TV studio, where cameras are semipermanently mounted on big, heavy pedestals, movement is called "trucking," whether in, out, left, or right. Of course, I can't resist mentioning that a dolly often runs on tracks (thus the name "tracking shot") and early film dollies were often called trucks!

Tips: Tilting and Panning

+ Shoot it wide and move slowly. If you move slowly enough, the viewer's eyes can follow naturally, darting ahead.

+ If you're not using a tripod, practice your pan before you record. Fix your feet and pan from the waist. Try not to make the end of your move a strain. Start wound up and unwind toward your final frame.

+ If you're not using a tripod, practice your tilt before you record. Fix your feet, shoulders' width apart, elbows close to your side, camera at neck level. The eyepiece viewfinder is easier to use than the foldout LCD. Try not to make the end of your move a strain. For a tilt up, start bent over and straighten up toward your final frame.

+ Find visual motivation for your pan. Let motion within your screen draw the camera along; a passing car, a pedestrian walking by, or a part on the assembly line. The pan looks more natural if there's a subject in the frame.

+ Let text motivate your movement. We're trained to pan naturally when reading.

+ Choose purposeful camera movements. A pan might be the best way to illustrate the spatial relationship between two characters or objects. A tilt might be the best way to emphasize the height of a structure or the distance from ground level to the bottom of a hole.

+ Pans are difficult to watch. You'll detract from your message and annoy your audience if you simply throw in pans for the sake of movement. If a shot is boring, it's going to be just as boring with an added pan. Limit your use of camera movement unless you're doing a music video or "art."

+ Give every shot that includes movement a beginning and an end.

+ Record enough of your camera moves. As you roll tape, hold your first framing for ten seconds, make your move, then hold your last framing for ten seconds. In the edit you'll have six choices: taking the starting shot, the starting shot with the move, the move alone, the ending shot, a move into the ending shot, or the whole move from start to stop.

Panning　　　　**Tilting**

This shot involved a move from a second story window, down to and then along the sidewalk, requiring a crane mounted on a dolly running on a stainless steel track.

Next time you see television coverage of a bike race, watch the wide shots for a cameraman sitting astride a motorcycle, facing backwards, poised for shots like this.

This Steadicam move involved snaking our way up and down aisles and around corners through a warehouse. The alternative, laying and leveling 50 meters of dolly track could have taken most of the day.

This truck was part of a TV show opener. It involved a dolly move along the desktop, and finished with a ped down and a zoom into the shot on the TV that's beginning to appear in the upper-right corner of the last frame. The zoom would continue as we'd dissolve through to a matching shot on set.

Let's review. A tracking shot involves a left or right movement and is usually shot from a dolly, unless we're talking about high-speed tracking shots that might be shot from a car (sometimes specially designed) or even, in the case of bicycle races, a motorcycle. Technically, a dolly shot is either a move toward or away from a subject, but the truth of the matter is, any shot from a dolly can be called a dolly shot and you're not going to confuse anyone.

A whole lot of high-end dollying and tracking isn't done from a dolly or a truck but with a Steadicam. These expensive, difficult-to-operate stabilization rigs bring to professional film and video cameras a similar kind of image stabilization that you already enjoy in your DV camera. Dolly and tracking shots, though diffi-

cult to accomplish with perfect precision, add an extra dimension to a shot, where the movement in space give viewers a feeling of "being there."

Most high-end dollies offer the ability to raise or lower the camera by approximately a meter (about three and a half feet). This up and down movement is called "pedding," as in, "Ped up a few inches." The term "ped" is derived from those big, heavy pedestals on which TV studio cameras are mounted.

You'll often hear people suggest a couple of no-budget dolly substitutes. One is a shopping cart. The camera operator climbs into the cart and the dolly grip pushes. The obvious problems with this approach are, first, the small wheels aren't going to roll smoothly on any but the smoothest of surfaces. Second, those darned wheels hardly ever roll quietly, even on the smoothest of surfaces. The other more-effective method involves renting a wheelchair. Medical supply houses offer them and since their rentals are usually long term, they might be nice and let you borrow a chair for a day free of charge. If the local supply house isn't forthcoming, try garage and rummage sales where older models are often had for a song. Wheel chairs are more manageable than grocery carts and the bigger wheels mean it will roll more smoothly.

Luckily, again owing to the fact that cameras have gotten very light and most have optical image stabilization, perfectly acceptable tracking shots can be done "handheld." There are two methods of doing handheld tracking shots. One is to walk forward with the camera pointing 90 degrees to your body. The problem with this method is being able to see the viewfinder, especially outdoors in bright light. The method I prefer is "crabbing." Crabbing involves walking sideways, one leg crossing in front of the other. That gives me the smoothest movement. One other tip: anytime you're moving with the camera, you get a smoother result if you keep your knees slightly bent.

Stop zooming!

There are few things that shout, "I'm new to this business!" more clearly than the herky-jerky use of the zoom without reason or motivation. Beginning videographers often fail to allow a shot to start, where every three seconds or so, they're tapping the zoom control and lurching in and out. To me, this behavior indicates either a lack of confidence in ones' ability to properly frame a shot, or a lack of understanding of the basic photographic aesthetic. Try to think of the zoom lens the way professionals do—as a variety of fixed focal length lenses. The zoom makes it easy to switch between primes, so to speak, but the switch—the actual zoom—is like a scenery change in a play, not something normally shown to the audience.

Of course, the greatest advantage and most common use of the zoom lens is to obtain critical focus in manual focus situations. Zoom in, focus, then pull back, and if your zoom lens is working properly, every focal length in between telephoto and wide angle should be in focus as well. When auto focus is turned off, it's important to use this method to focus your every shot. However, aesthetically speaking, I know of only four reasons why I should ever see a zoom.

A moving camera can add interest and excitement to a shot. The sense of motion can be exaggerated by designing the shot to include foreground elements that pass between the camera and subject. When designing a move, remember the motion of the camera doesn't need to parallel the motion of the subject of the shot: the camera can take an independent path, cross the path of the subject, or can circle or dolly towards a stationary subject.

+ The Art Zoom

The art zoom is motivated only by aesthetics. Snap zooms fall into this category. A snap zoom, difficult on cameras without professional-quality TV lenses, involves a zoom so fast it blurs. Another zoom used only for effect is the depth zoom, or foreshortening, where a camera is dollied toward the subject as the camera zooms out (or vice versa). The depth zoom is often used to indicate disorientation or to suggest a break with reality. Art zooms, like most special effects, should be used infrequently. Overuse diminishes their effectiveness.

+ The Pinpoint Zoom

A pinpoint zoom is motivated by the desire to accentuate a detail in your frame. A pinpoint zoom will pick someone out of a stadium crowd or accentuate the price card in a retail display.

+ The Revelatory Zoom

A revelatory zoom reveals a detail by including more information in a display. A revelatory zoom might begin with the shot of a driver at the wheel. Pull out and we see the driver is stuck in an awful traffic jam. Maybe we see a person reading a book. The zoom out reveals he's sitting on the roof of his house.

+ The Framing Zoom

Start on a head and shoulders shot of someone walking toward you and the closer the subject gets to the camera, the wider the lens needed to maintain that framing. Watch motor racing and you see this zoom at every turn. Shots often begin telephoto, zoomed way in as the car approaches. As the car nears, the camera operator zooms out; the lens is at its widest as the car passes the camera position. Once past, the camera operator zooms in, going telephoto again as the car recedes in the distance.

Tip: In the case of motivated zooms, just as in the case of pans, tilts, dollies, and trucks, a shot should have a smooth beginning and end. Ramp into the zoom and ramp out of it. Don't simply zoom until you hit the stops!

Dutch angles, booms, cranes, and the new world of camera movement

Here's the accused, hastening along, head slightly bowed, surrounded by his legion of lawyers. If you're seeing their faces, chances are there's a news photographer walking backwards in front of them. It's called "backpedaling." News photographers backpedal a lot, leading to a fair number of falls and collisions. Still, being a former news photographer and given a situation where I needed a face-on shot of a person walking, I began to backpedal. Then I noticed another fellow shooting the same thing, with a very similar DV camera. You're probably aware that on DV cams with a foldout LCD viewfinder screen, if you turn the camera on yourself, you can turn the screen so you can see yourself. This fellow working next to me had his camera turned that way, shooting backward over his own shoulder, watching the shot in his viewfinder while walking safely forward! Why didn't I think of that? The point is, light, flexible, DV cams have ushered in a new era of camera movement.

Lightweight cameras with image stabilization have made many shots formerly reserved for higher-end productions quite possible.

Dutch angles

Dutch angles are shots where the horizons are skewed for effect, sometimes to indicate things are out of kilter, or dreamlike. It's a common comic book convention for introducing dynamism to shots, though today it's become a popular style. Dutch angles used to be difficult to shoot, especially moving dutch angles. With a heavy camera on a tripod or dolly, you needed a compound head, essentially a tripod head on another tripod head, to get tilt in two planes. With less need for a tripod, it's easy to hold a shot at a dutch angle.

Dutch angles

Cranes you can ride, booms you can't, but either one allows the camera to reach new heights—high angles, low angles, sweeping arcs, overheads, and the like. A "boom down" or "boom in" is a traditional move used for establishing shots, welcoming a viewer into the action. Using a crane or a boom usually required a lot of setup time and considerable cost. Today, thanks again to the decreased weight and built-in stabilization, it's much easier to simulate boom and crane shots.

I've seen some credible boom work done with a DV camera mounted on the end of a lightweight aluminum monopod designed for still camera use. The videographer then operated the monopod boom like a mic operator handles a fishpole, both arms extended straight overhead.

It's a great time to be a videographer working in DV. Nearly any angle you can imagine, you can shoot; dollies, booms, point of view (POV), macro close-ups—you're free to design shots that were out of the reach of low-budget storytellers not long ago. Still, just because you can, doesn't mean you should. Once the wow factor wears off, you must ask yourself the same questions filmmakers have asked since camera movement became possible: "Does this shot advance my story?" Ask yourself, "Does this camera angle, this camera move 'say' what needs to be said?"

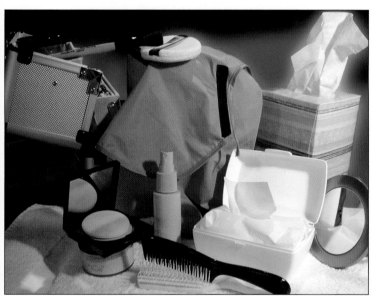

Makeup

So imagine yourself in the middle of a video project, say, a fund-raising video for the local school, and you're making a shot list of the interviews you've completed with various alumni and school officials. The location, the lighting, everything's looking good, but then you get to the principal's interview and, what's that? It's his shirt collar. It's flipped up in back. Maybe it's not worth redoing the interview but you know the principal will notice and in his or her eyes, this error will diminish the success of the interview. How could you have missed it?

On big-budget movie sets, the director relies on many eyes to keep track of the details. Makeup, lighting, sound, each person concentrates on one aspect of the shoot so the director can concentrate on the next shot. But as a videographer, you may often find yourself working as a one-man band. So along with the shooting, the lighting, and possibly conducting the interview, it'll be up to you to make sure your subject is looking good.

When shooting informal interviews, soundbites out on location, or a live event you're certainly not going to whip out the powder and hairspray to groom every subject, but for those more formal set-ups, preparing subjects to be interviewed involves more than clipping on a microphone. These people will be in front of the camera. They won't be able to see how they look. They'll be depending on you to make sure they look their best.

If the person is bald or has a shiny nose, tell them you're going to apply a bit of powder to take the shine off. Take the time to drape a towel or makeup cape over their suit or dress before applying the powder. Use a light touch and a disposable puff. Have a comb handy to straighten any flyaway hair. Check to see if their collar and tie are straight and smooth. If a man's suit jacket seems bunched up in back, have him sit on the edge of his jacket to help keep it down. This should all take just a few minutes. You don't want the subject to feel they look wrong. Be professional. Be self-assured. Your directness and poise will make the subject feel confident they look fine and these few adjustments are made for the camera's sake. Your attendance to these details should actually help set the person at ease, knowing you're concerned about helping them look their best.

Tip: Keep a small makeup kit handy for formal interviews.

+ Comb and small brush
+ Small hand mirror
+ Hairspray
+ Makeup cape or large towel
+ Translucent compact powders in several shades
+ Disposable powder puffs
+ Makeup remover pads
+ Tissues

The Tough Stuff

Shooting food

A while back, I started a little file in my computer where I collected phrases, little things said by family and friends that struck me as humorous. For example, I never thought my parents could visit France so much that one day I'd hear one say to the other, "I'm all Paris-ed out." One day my mother-in-law mentioned in passing (and in truth), "Stalin's daughter borrowed my rake." I also made an entry the day my wife declared, "We've got enough biscotti in this house to choke a horse!" The later, uttered on having completed a shoot for a bakery, speaks to one of the difficulties of shooting food. Food on camera doesn't often act right, and even less often does it look right. If you've ever grabbed a fast-food lunch, peeled back the wrapper and thought, "This can't be the same special I saw on TV," I'm not telling you anything you don't know. Be it the span of a huge buffet or the frosting of a single cupcake, shooting food so it looks natural, fresh, and appetizing has its unique challenges.

Any commercial or industrial video that has food in the starring role, say, for a restaurant or bakery, would ideally have the budget to hire a professional food stylist. A food stylist blends artistry and chemistry to make food look its best for the camera, sort of like a makeup artist for food. Their special bag of tricks is usually a large tackle box filled with an assortment of items and special effects, from butane torches and knives to fake ice cubes in various sizes, calcium chips to create steam in coffee, and tiny glass bubbles to float on beverages. Although some food stylist solutions have become almost legendary, like spraying stain guard on pancakes to help the syrup flow over them, or creating ice cream out of Crisco and corn syrup, the trend today is to use a more natural and realistic approach. If you're shooting food close-ups without a stylist, however, a few of their tricks could come in handy. For instance, glycerin spritzed on a glass of iced tea or a bottle of beer can help it look cold and fresh. Glycerin can also help meat look juicy. If you're shooting a close up of a piece of chicken or steak, undercook the meat to help it retain its texture, apply food coloring or Kitchen Bouquet to make it look cooked through, then spritz on a bit of glycerin to give it a juicy look. This type of thing is not an option of course for a scene where an actor is taking a bite of that same steak. For scenes where the food needs to stay absolutely fresh and edible, just make sure you have enough to cover several takes.

Shooting special effects: fights, blood, gunshots, ghosts, accidents, and superpowers

Special effects in movies today would seem to require a mind-blowing mix of pyrotechnics, animatronics, and fearless stunt performers. Actually, special effects have been evolving since the early days of film and include a variety of illusions and tricks. There are many easy and inexpensive, yet effective, special effects available to the amateur or low-budget videographer.

The most important thing about successful special effects is working within your limitations. Serious science fiction aliens are probably out of reach, but zombies are no more than a dozen egg whites and a bag of flour away. In fact, many amateur filmmakers are drawn to the horror genre because the effectiveness of a film lies in building tension and offering only glimpses of the movie's supernatural menace. In horror, as in most low-budget special effect work, less is more. It's often enough to simply suggest an event and allow your viewers' imaginations to do the rest. You don't have to show the fist connect with a chin or the bullet hitting a chest. Showing the after effects can be just as effective, maybe more so. Keep in mind that in scenes with special effects, the sound is often just as important as the visuals. Try watching a gun battle scene with the volume turned down and you'll see what I mean.

How to fake a fistfight

Well-designed fights can establish conflicts or provide dramatic, action-packed resolutions to clashes between characters. However, fight sequences that aren't carefully planned and properly executed can be laughably unconvincing.

+ First, choreograph the fight and plot it out with a storyboard. It's best to break the coverage of the fight up into many shots from various angles allowing you to craft a quick, action-packed sequence in the edit. Remember: the telephoto lens is your friend. The compression and foreshortening effect of the long lens will forgive the distance of the missed punch. Set up the shot correctly and be sure the reaction is properly timed, and you'll find a foot is as good as an inch.

+ If your actors will be breaking chairs and tables during the fight, use only breakaway furniture. Make the props out of balsa wood or Styrofoam, fitted together loosely with glue, not nails. Woodgrain painting kits are available at most hardware and home improvement centers. If your homemade props still don't appear real enough for your eye, consider orienting the shot in silhouette with backlight or shoot a real chair being swung around going to a close-up for the impact. The actors' reactions and added sound effects will complete the illusion

+ On the set, watch through the lens as the actors practice each swing, move, and fall. Make sure the camera positions allow the actors to miss each other by a reasonable distance to help prevent shoot-ending accidents in the heat of the action.

+ Shoot the scene without sound so you can direct the actors through each shot. Once the action is complete, record as many sound effects as you can in that same space.

How to fake a bullet hitting a bottle

In the movies, bullet hits are usually accomplished using explosive squibs embedded in objects. The squibs are dangerous and their use is regulated by government agencies most everywhere. So how can you fake a bullet impact without pyrotechnics? Have the slug "hit" a glass object.

+ Buy an old-fashioned, wooden-based mousetrap. Saw off the half of the base that begins under the trigger lever.

+ Tape a long nail onto the bar of a mousetrap (at a right angle to the bar), leaving about an inch extending from the bar. Paint the entire device black or, depending on your scene, an unobtrusive color.

+ Tie a wire onto the release catch. Use museum putty or gaffers tape to fix the mousetrap in place and set the trap.

+ Use a glass cutter to score an X near your estimated point of impact. Fill the bottle to be hit by the bullet with liquid and place it in front of the trap.

+ On cue, pull the wire. The nail will swing up and smash the base of the bottle.

+ Of course, the explosive sound of a "bang" added in the edit will be required to sell the effect.

How to fake blood, scabs, scars, and wounds

If you're thinking about shooting an action or horror script, one of the things you'll need is blood, and a lot of it. When movies were done in black-and-white, fake blood had to be made darker than the real stuff in order to look right. Alfred Hitchcock is said to have used chocolate syrup in *Psycho*. But in today's full-color productions, blood that looks realistic to the eye will look right in your production. There are many recipe variations for fake blood but here is a basic, universal concoction:

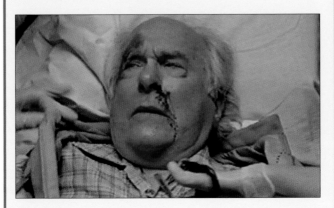

Fake blood

1 cup white corn syrup (golden syrup)
1 tablespoon red food coloring
1 teaspoon yellow food coloring
2 tablespoons water

Mix together to the right consistency. Certain red food coloring already contains some yellow. If your blood is coming out too orange, use less yellow. Add more water if too thick, more corn syrup if too thin. If you want it less transparent, add a dollop of milk. And just be aware that this stuff can stain clothes.

Fake scabs

Scab effects can be obtained by mixing unflavored gelatin with equal amounts of water. Apply it to the skin and work in appropriate food colorings before it sets. For added texture, paint corn flakes with food coloring, let them dry and attach to the skin with spirit gum. Darken areas with an eyebrow pencil and apply fake blood for the look of persistently runny sores.

Fake wounds

The most difficult part of constructing prosthetic makeup devices is making them light enough to stay in place without industrial strength adhesive. One method I've found effective is to create scars and wounds by laying a bead of hot glue on waxed paper or plastic wrap. Once the glue has nearly set you can use a Popsicle stick to sculpt it, possibly creating the "cut" running its length. Once it's cooled, cut around the prosthetic, leaving enough material for gluing. Again, affix with spirit gum, and then use foundation makeup to color the scar and blend it to the victim's skin. In the case of the wound, a bead of fake blood will make the wound appear fresh. Little knotted pieces of black canvas thread every half inch or so will give the appearance of stitches. Remember that spirit gum requires spirit gum remover.

How to fake a fender bender

Car chases and crashes in the movies require a lot of time, money, and coordination, not to mention the danger involved! But for the low-budget production, there's the classic camera shot known as the "crash zoom." To pull it off you'll need two vehicles, two drivers, and a street with a stop sign. This description involves vehicle #2 rear-ending vehicle #1 at a stop sign.

+ Sitting in the front passenger seat of vehicle #2, shoot a medium shot of vehicle #1 through the windshield as it moves ahead of you, including part of the front hood of your vehicle in the shot. A variation that works just fine is to shoot this shot POV (point of view) by sitting in the back seat of vehicle #2, behind the driver. Ask the driver to move away from the camera a little bit in order to clear your frame.

+ If your camera's zoom speed is adjustable, turn it to the fastest setting. As both vehicles come to a stop for the stop sign, zoom in quickly to the back end of the vehicle #1, shaking the camera a bit as you do. The vehicle doesn't have to stop abruptly because the camera does the crashing for you. It may not seem effective at the time, but when you add the screeching tires and crash sounds in the edit, you'll have your fender bender.

+ Additional shots to complete a sequence can be done while the vehicle is parked. Consider a close-up of a foot hitting the brakes, a shot of the driver through the windshield reacting to the impending impact, and possibly a shot of the driver of the second vehicle snapping forward at the waist, maybe even hitting the steering wheel (see "Fake blood" and "Fake wounds" on the opposite page).

+ For added realism, try this little trick. It'll enhance your sequence but cost you some money. Fill a medium clay flowerpot with sand. Cover the back of a mirror tile with duct tape then hot glue the taped side of the tile to a 1-meter (1 yard) wooden dowel. Plant the dowel in the sand. Set your camera, on its tripod off to the side of the path of vehicle #2. Remember not to violate the line of action! Zoom into the mirror (adjusting the angle of the mirror as necessary) so it appears the camera is directly in the path of the vehicle #2 then hit the mirror! Clean up any glass that breaks away.

+ Add the screeching tires and crash sounds in the edit to complete the effect.

How to fake a fire

+ Use a tripod. Disable auto focus and focus on the scene. Underexpose the scene slightly to make the flames appear brighter by contrast.

+ Set up a couple of lights with amber gels and have your assistants dance the light over the scene to simulate light from the flames. If the fire is outdoors, use gels over mirrors or gold tone reflectors to add light.

+ If the fire is outdoors, use smoke cookies (see recipe below) set in fireproof dishes to enhance the effect. Try the cookies first to gauge their smoke production. You may only need small pieces.

+ Set candles on a surface so the flames are visible in the foreground of your shot (not too close though!). If candles appear too controlled you might consider burning small pieces of cardboard (roughly the thickness of matchbook covers) fixed just below the lens level. Shoot the scene through the flames. When shooting keep in mind that the effect might be more realistic if shown in slow motion. If there are actors in the scene, consider having them move especially quickly through the burning area knowing you'll be slowing the action in post.

CAUTION: Any effect requiring smoke, flame, or kitchen appliances should be done with parental supervision.

This effect can also be used with miniature props like cars or buildings. Be careful not to give away the fact that you're toying with scale. A "giant" blade of grass in the foreground will give it all away.

How to make smoke cookies

Mix one part potassium nitrate (saltpeter) to two parts powdered coffee creamer. Use a tiny amount of water to bind the mixture, less than a teaspoonful for two dozen cookies! Form into small, cookie-sized disks. Dry the cookies for one hour in an oven set at 250°. When they're done, store the cookies in an airtight container or plastic bag since they'll quickly absorb moisture from the air and break down. To use, place the cookie in a fireproof dish, light an edge, and step away. Each cookie will burn for approximately three minutes, giving off a thick, white smoke.

Potassium nitrate is available in hardware stores as "powdered stump remover." That sounds toxic but it's not. Potassium nitrate is actually used as a meat preservative! Still, don't taste the cookies.

Also, though the smoke has the mostly pleasant smell of burnt milk, try not to breathe it in, and never use smoke cookies in confined spaces! Any effect requiring smoke, flame, or kitchen appliances should be done with parental supervision.

Disappearing act

The simplest special effect, used since the earliest days of film production, is the disappearing act. Be sure your camera is locked down and perfectly immobile. At the moment in your production when the person or object is to disappear, when the magician waves the wand, or the spell is cast, call, "Freeze!" While everyone else remains perfectly still, remove the object or have the person who's to vanish walk out of the frame. Call "Action!" again, having everyone turn, amazed, to the position of the missing person or thing. In the edit, cut out the time between "freeze" and "action" and you'll have harnessed the power of the jump cut and reproduced the original movie magic.

When shooting special effects that will require further finishing in the edit, it's always a good policy to work with lockdown shots, that is, shots where you have the camera secured to a tripod with the tilt and pan mechanisms locked. It's not that you can't work with moving shots and there are many edit systems that allow tracking and corner pinning but still, it's often not exceptionally accurate and motion discrepancies can be dead giveaways, obvious to even untrained eyes.

How to fake a ghost

To fake a ghost, lock down your shot, accurately mark the location, and use sandbags or heavy objects to keep the tripod immobile. If the camera moves at all, tilts, pans or bounces, the effect will be lost. If your camera came equipped, it is a good idea to start and stop it with the remote control rather than take a chance on moving the camera and losing registration. Decide who drives the action in your shot—the live actors or the ghost. Shoot the most important player(s) first. Block the shots so the ghost and real characters don't pass over one another. If the ghost is to pass through furnishings or doors, they'll need to be removed when you shoot that character's action. If there will be dialogue or interaction between the ghost and other characters, you'll need to do two other things before rolling tape. First, you'll want to split the audio going to your headphones and feed it to a tape recorder that you'll roll while shooting your first pass. The second thing is be sure you have a standard movie clapper to mark the beginning of the scene or begin your scene by having someone actually step up to the mic and clap their hands together once, sharply. Shoot your scene with your live actors or your ghost character alone. Once you have a good take, pause the tape recorder and rewind it to the beginning of the take you intend to use. This becomes your playback and all dialogue will be cued by this tape. Roll your camera and the audiotape playback and play the scene again with your other character(s). In the edit, you'll combine the two shots by doing a half-dissolve of the ghost character layer over the real characters, masking out areas where the real characters stand. The real characters will appear solid and will interact normally in the environment. The ghost character will appear semitransparent and will pass easily through objects on the set.

How to make someone fly

A very useful special effects technique available in all but the least expensive NLE packages is called the "key." We'll talk more about keying in the next chapter, but briefly, keying allows you to use an attribute of your video signal (usually brightness or color) to cut out portions of a shot and substitute portions of another shot. In this case, we'll shoot an actress with a solid green-colored background and tell the keyer that uses color as a reference, or "chromakeyer," to remove all green from that picture, replacing that color with a picture of the sky. Mixed together, it will appear that our actress is flying.

Start by looking for a way to suspend your actor off the ground. Here we've used a couple of sawhorses draped with chromakey green paper. Though commercial chromakey paints, papers, and cloths are available in green and blue, it isn't necessary to use them. In most edit systems, you can configure the chromakeyer to eliminate any color in the spectrum. The saturated green you see in the pictures here is often used because there is little chance there will be any other bright green objects in the frame that might be keyed out inadvertently. You can come close enough to chromakey green for this effect at most paint stores that will mix custom colors. Lighting is the next critical consideration. A good, clean key requires even lighting. There is a danger the edit system might fail to read the chromakey green if it falls in deep shadow. We set fans around the actress to blow her hair and cape around as if she's flying then simply told her to extend her arms and act like Superman. Remember that if she were indeed flying, the sunlight from above would light her so try to fix your key light directly above the talent. Shoot the shot of the sky from a compatible angle (don't shoot straight up into the sky if you're going to show a shot of the actor flying in a ¾ framing). We'll look at finishing and tweaking this effect in the next chapter.

Tip: If the special effects bug has bitten you, there are a variety of commercial effects supply retailers and special effects and makeup clubs. Most of the websites, including the commercial sites listed here, offer some tutorials and how-to articles.

Retail
www.fxsupply.com/
www.skylighter.com/
www.graftobian.com/

Hobbyists and Helpful Practitioners (with many more links)
www.detonationfilms.com/
www.geocities.com/Hollywood/Lot/9373/SCREAM/index.html
www.matthawkins.co.uk/

Chapter 5

Basic Principles of Editing

As a first-year engineering student, I took a course called Invention. The first day, our professor stated—only half kidding—that the purpose of this course was to allow the university to quickly appropriate the best ideas from the brightest students, who would undoubtedly drop out to become millionaires before graduating. Unabashed exploitation primes the economic pump in many college towns and, I've discovered, throughout the television industry. Take my first TV job. We all worked long hours at a miserable rate of pay in return for being allowed to, on our own time, and entirely without pay, produce programming of our own invention! The program we originated was called *The Television Live Radio Hour*, a studio music performance show simulcast in FM. For variety, we peppered the show with music by, and interviews with, headliners who often passed through town.

One night, we went to interview the members of a well-known national act playing the local coliseum. It took about a second to realize the band didn't take themselves, much less our college-age crew, seriously. The interview quickly collapsed into uncooperative babble punctuated by barking sounds coming from the band member who wore a rubber dog mask the whole time. It was actually a relief ten minutes in when the lead singer stood and announced they had to go and get ready for the show. One small consolation was at least we would be allowed to tape the performance. We set up and settled in but before the first song had ended, an apologetic roadie shooed us off stage and ushered us out. Angry and disappointed, we returned to the station where we handed the tape to the show's director, John Miller, and declared, "There's absolutely nothing here." Two nights later, John took me to school. Sitting slack-jawed and wide-eyed, I watched a clever, funny, and thoroughly entertaining segment and for the first time became acutely aware of the incredible power wielded by a video editor.

I was recently reminded of that night 25 years ago. While editing one of the first scenes of a feature film, I felt all that power again. In the film, the not-so-popular sister asks the popular sister if she really wants her to tag along to the party. The popular sister simply answers "Yes," but oh, how deeply textured that one word can be. Said quickly and clearly it can be an emphatic yes. Hesitate a moment and it becomes a qualified yes. A moment longer and it's a reluctant yes. With just a little pique, "yes" can even mean "no." That answer, that one word, would establish the tone of their relationship and affect the entire film. Editing's a big responsibility.

I would encourage you, as an editor, to experiment with the nuances of tone and timing. Try alternate reads and varied placements. Seven frames one way or another can make a world of difference. It often takes years of time at the edit bench before one can correctly and without hesitation place a line of dialogue or even a sound effect precisely, unerringly where it belongs. I'm looking forward to that day.

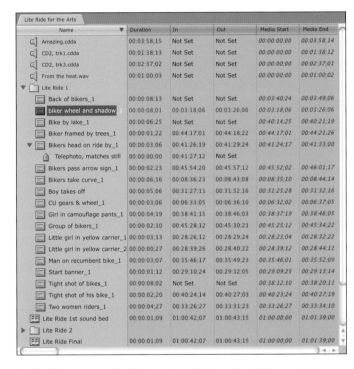

Logging bins can contain a little or a lot of information. This example shows a descriptive name followed by time code numbers. Other available columns include digitization information, shot descriptions, compression information, tape numbers, and much more.

 Tip: Basic Edit Protocol

To help prevent things going from bad to worse to downright terrible, here's my list of basic edit protocol:

+ Be sure the record tabs are popped on every tape.
+ Be sure every tape is labeled with a unique number.
+ Be sure every tape is accounted for.
+ Log every tape.

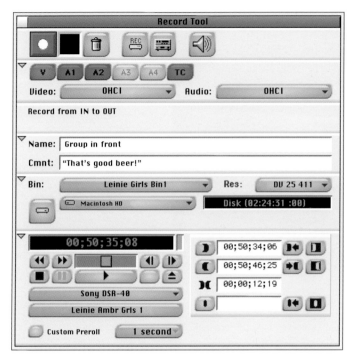

This is Avid's capture box, the model for most others in the industry. It allows the operator to choose tracks to be digitized, shot names and descriptions, media destinations, and whether the shot will be digitized immediately or just logged for capture later. This interface also includes all the necessary deck transport controls.

Timecode numbers

Tip: Pay Attention, Number Your Tapes!

Your camera assigns a timecode number (in hours, minutes, seconds, and frames) to each frame of video recorded. When logging tape, the edit computer notes the timecode number whenever you mark an in- or outcue. When digitizing footage, the edit computer finds that exact frame again by its timecode address. On some cameras, you're able to specify at what hour you'd like your timecode to begin. Often, videographers will match the start hour to the tape number so tape 14 might begin with hour 14 (14:00:00:00). However, on many cameras, the timecode simply begins at zero on every tape. Therefore, when the edit computer goes to an address, say 00:13:05:28, that address will exist on any tape inserted, even if it's the wrong tape! That's why it's absolutely critical you number your tapes and pay attention to those numbers when logging and digitizing. If you don't, as the playbill often says, mayhem will ensue!

The Mechanics of Editing

Assume you're shooting a documentary about Swedish arts and crafts. You have nearly an hour of footage of the carving of Dala horses. No one but another carver is going to be interested in watching that much unedited footage. The idea is for you to choose the best of your shots and string them together in an interesting and informative way, maybe add music and a bit of narration, and move on to glassmaking in Smaland. This, in a nutshell, is the edit process. Here's the step-by-step.

Step 1: Logging tape
The first thing you'll do is assess your footage in a process called "logging tape." Logging can be done on paper or directly into the computer. This often depends on how much tape there is, whether it's all going into the computer or just "selects," and whether you're sharing the edit computer. Note every shot, the timecode number where it should begin and end, as well as enough information to be able to recognize the shot by its log notes. Don't call shots #1, #2, #3, and so on. The bigger the project, the faster you'll get lost if you've done a sloppy job logging.

Step 2: Digitization and batch capture
Unless you record your footage directly into a computer or a digital file-storage medium, editing will require digitization—that is, transferring visual data from the camera tapes to the edit computer. If the logging was done on the edit computer, this may simply be a matter of telling the computer to record the shots in a process often called "batch capture." The computer will talk to the playback deck, usually your camera, through the FireWire cable (IEEE 1394). The computer will say, "Insert tape NYC uptown #1" and you'll do just that. The computer will search the tape for the correct time code address and will digitize the shot's audio and/or video as logged.

Step 3: Creating a timeline
Once the data is in the computer, you will need to create a timeline, a "blank document" where you will lay down your intended program. Your timeline is like an infinitely long piece of videotape with many open tracks for video and audio.

Step 4: Arranging your shots
Once you've created a timeline, you'll begin to arrange your media along that timeline by inserting or overlaying those images and sounds on the timeline. You'll choose where pieces of media begin and end, whether they overlap, and how they'll interact.

Step 5: Trimming, slippin', and a slidin'
As you begin laying media on your timeline, you will see the need to rearrange and adjust the positioning of your media. Adjusting the boundary between two shots is called "trimming." You might trim an edit a couple of frames one way or the other,

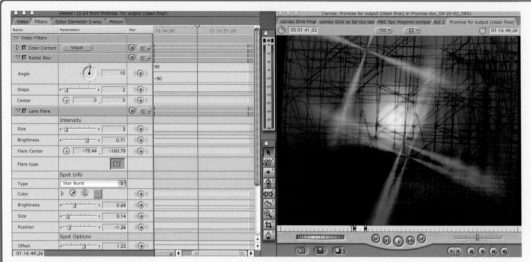

Different NLEs have different methods of adding special effects. Final Cut Pro uses a system of filters. The filter shown here creates a lens flare effect. All the parameters of the effect are adjusted in a pane under a filters tab in this viewer.

Special Effects Require Processing Power

You might want to add effects to your edited program, possibly changing the color of a shot or layering shots together (compositing). You might mix tracks of audio elements like music, dialogue, and sound effects. You may add words or titles to your program. Be aware that anything you do, other than simply playing one piece of media after another, requires additional processing power on the part of your computer. At times, you may ask more of your computer than it can handle in "real time." When this overload occurs, the computer will need to render the effects in order to play them properly. As processing power continues to shoot up, computers are able to handle many more streams of media and, thus, need to spend less time rendering, cutting down on the frequency of unpleasant little render breaks.

forcing one shot or audio clip to end sooner and the other to begin sooner. You are always free to trim audio and video together or separately. Uneven trimming of audio and video will result in what's known as a "split edit." You might also recognize the opportunity to improve your edit by moving clips, even groups of clips, along the timeline. This is called "slipping" or "sliding."

Step 6: Output

Once all your media is in place and you're happy with the look and sound of your project, you will "output" your project either by "printing to tape," burning it to a DVD, or possibly uploading it to a server for streaming over the Web.

Every nonlinear editing (NLE) system's graphical user interface or GUI (pronounced "gooey") is a little different. Every NLE's approach to the processes involved in editing will differ, too. There are many diverse and powerful NLEs on the market. I don't know which system you'll choose, and I don't know if you'll use that system the same way I would, so I'm not going to try and tell you "how" to trim or "where" you'll find the titling tools. I will assure you that every system will have a method of trimming and titling. Many will be similar in approach and function, but you're going to have to read the manual to learn your system. Every nonlinear edit system I've ever used has come with a practical and helpful tutorial program. I recommend you take advantage of this.

The Universal Principles of Editing

While editing mostly involves art and storytelling, it also revolves around organization and information management. After all, you can't produce the best possible edit if you don't know what shots exist, or worse, you know what shots exist but don't know where they are, or worst of all, you saw the shot once but think you accidentally erased it!

All NLE programs have some provisions for information management and allow limited searches. More advanced programs offer more advanced possibilities. Still, I was recently involved in a monstrously large shoot with dozens and dozens of raw tapes and found it faster and more efficient to do rough logs and pick usable shots, called "selects," before sitting down to begin digitizing shots. You can find my paper log sheets and a legend to help understand my principles by logging on to my website (www.petemay.com).

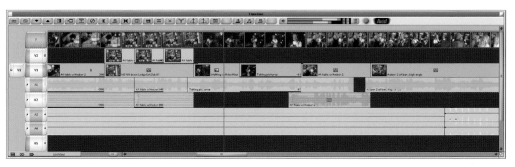

Arrange your media along a timeline.

Some NLEs allow editors to trim right in the timeline. Even many of those have stand-alone trim windows as well. The trim windows typically allow single frame or multiple frame trimming, some method of keeping track of the number of frames trimmed, and a preview button allowing the editor to examine the change before committing it to the timeline.

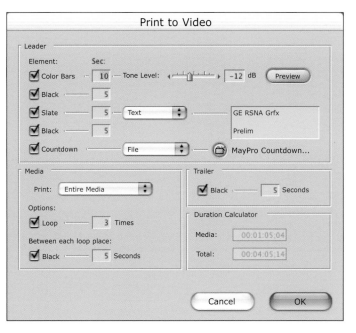

It may be called "print to video," "print to tape," "output," or simply "play," but the idea is to present your project in a linear format for you to watch and record.

We're Not Really Editing Video!

It is important to understand that in computer-based, nonlinear video editing, you don't actually lay shots on the timeline, you lay markers—representative links to the actual shots. When you play an edited piece on your timeline, the computer simply reacts to a series of commands that say, "Play clip #1 for 2.5 seconds, now play clip #2 for 4 seconds." The timeline contains nothing but "pointers." For this reason, although your media files are large and require huge amounts of storage space, the document that is your timeline remains relatively small, like a word-processing document.

It is also important to understand that computer-based, nonlinear video editing is a nondestructive process. If you move, remove, trim, or even add special effects to clips in your timeline, the original media you digitized is unaffected. So, go nuts! Try anything!

The Rules

Properly applied, "the rules" of editing allow an audience to follow the story being told. It's a convention of storytelling as old as motion pictures and is based on replicating reality. Many of the rules are designed to prevent you from making editing errors that fall broadly into the category of jump cuts. Jump cuts are edits that, visually speaking, defy the logic and physics of a situation. If in the first shot someone is standing at the sink and after one edit they're sitting at the table, they've jumped to the other side of the room, that's literally a jump cut.

One way to completely avoid a jump cut is allow the subject to exit the frame. Once out of sight, we're willing to loosen the rules of physics. If we see someone enter a front door and disappear inside, our visual language allows us to accept a jump to any room in the house by the time the door swings shut. We, as an audience, are so forgiving of these jumps, we will accept an edit between a shot of someone walking through the front door of the terminal at LAX followed by a shot of the same person hailing a taxi at Heathrow. This fact is easily exploited in your everyday shooting. As a news photographer, I did many last-minute features as a series of five or six on-camera stand-ups in which the talent entered frame left, spoke her piece, and exited frame right. Getting back to the station with only five or six edits to make was always appreciated as deadlines loomed.

The term "jump cut" has also come to include a number of edit errors that are simply aesthetic violations. A good example would be the 30° rule. As you can see, the angle difference between these two shots didn't meet the 30° test. It looks bad. It appears unintentional.

I've reversed the order of these two shots so you can see my point. In the shot on the right Brent walks toward the camera talking, then exits frame left. When he enters the next shot frame right he's carrying props. Once he's exited the first shot, we don't know where he's gone or what he might have picked up so we don't question the continuity.

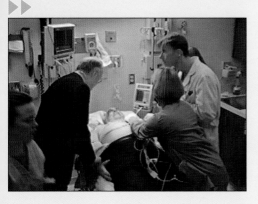 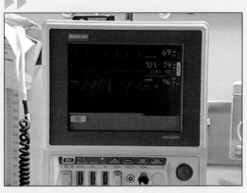 

  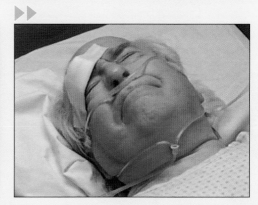

Good editing brings order and structure to a scene. For example, here, doctor #1 is tending to an accident victim; he looks up at the monitors wired to the patient. He notices an irregularity and indicates his concern to doctor #2. Doctor #2 glances at the monitors and then tells the patient surgery is needed. The patient grimaces when he hears this news.

When professional editors finish projects, they always have favorite edits. It won't be the edit that grabs attention, but the edit that defies detection. When the rules are followed, edits become transparent and allow the dialogue and action to shine through. It's unfair to say the editing will go unnoticed. People notice emotionally, in their guts—not in their heads. That's the power of a great edit.

Though the editor in this example was offered shots of the doctors from both sides of the 180° line, shots of the heart monitors from both sides of the 180° line, and shots of the patient looking at either doctor, the editor picked the shots that told the story clearly and concisely, positively placing each character in relation to the other. In the end, a viewer should be able to sketch out the relative positions of the players and know exactly who or what each one sees. If an actor is talking to someone screen left, the matching shot should have the other actor looking screen right. Success in orienting the viewer depends on having the right shots to work with in the first place, but still, when the photographer delivers a wealth of good shots, the final responsibility falls on the editor's shoulders.

Tips: Edit Rules

+ Obey the 180˚ rule.
+ Obey the 30° rule.
+ Establish a scene first with a wide shot. Then move into medium shots and close-ups. Work out of scenes by reversing this order.
+ Use close-ups to gain intimacy.
+ Don't edit in the middle of a camera move. Wait for the move to end or use a dissolve or wipe to cover the transition.
+ Be aware of continuity. If she's looking to her left in the first shot, she should still be looking to her left in the next. If his cigarette is freshly lit in the first shot, it shouldn't be down to the butt in the next.
+ Beware of technical errors such as flash frames—extraneous single frame edits usually left over from other versions of the cut.
+ Hold screen text long enough to read it aloud twice. That's usually more than enough time for viewers to read it to themselves.

+ Try to avoid cutting together very bright and very dark shots. The effect can be to leave the impression of a flash frame even if there was no flash.
+ Use your knowledge of centers of interest and principles of frame construction to lead the viewer's eyes to important elements of the frame.
+ Hold shots of easily grasped objects or symbols only long enough to grasp them. For example, there may be pacing reasons to hold a shot of a stop sign longer but a viewer will get it in a half second or less.
+ Let shots develop. As long as the subject or the situation is interesting, let the shot run. Unless you're editing to the beat of the music or the lines of dialogue, don't tie yourself down to fixed shot lengths.
+ Keep your edits tight. We don't need to see the entire gesture to know he's going to hail a cab or her entire brushstroke to know she's laying paint to canvas.
+ Break these rules as often as necessary.

Of course, edits aren't always intended to be transparent or even logical. Sometimes, viewers will tolerate being disoriented and tricked. Some commercial spots and many music videos break all the rules, often just for the impact. Still, it's important to understand the rules of editing in order to first, keep the viewer on board in traditional scenes and second, to obtain maximum visual effect when you do color outside the lines.

Got a match?

I'm originally from New York, and no matter that the odds are fifteen million to one, people who learn I'm from New York will ask if I know their school chum. We love connections. We want to know how *this* is like *that*. Her eyes are as blue as the sky and his belly shook like a bowlful of jelly. It is no wonder to me that people who study the art of editing have found that audiences enjoy connections created by the juxtaposition of images. They're called "matches" and they've been widely studied and categorized. There's the *match-on-shape, match-on-color, match-on-action, match-on-object,* and match on any other category one can devise. I would offer that any match could be further defined by purpose. Matches can support continuity, please the eye, and/or direct the eye. Let's start with the most common match, the match-on-action, widely used to support continuity and often used to simply please the eye.

Tip: It's obvious when an action isn't completed on the edit from one shot to the next. See someone take a swing at someone else in the first shot and cut to a third person standing still, unconcerned in the next shot, the effect can be jarring. Of course, that may be exactly the effect you seek. In a narrative story, that very edit could be a metaphor for the third character's lack of connection with the real world. It could also be a foreshadowing of a punch that third character may soon receive.

Match-on-Action

Considered most simply, a match-on-action is a continuation of a motion from one shot to the next in an effort to be true to real life, to support continuity. If someone begins to swing a sword in one scene, we expect the physics of that motion to carry it into the next shot. If the match-on-action isn't made, you're looking at a jump cut, that is, a cut that defies the logic and physics of a situation.

Talk and turn

If someone is seen pouring molten metal in the first shot, you should see the metal continued to flow in the second shot. If someone is turning in the first shot, you should see the completion of the turn in the second shot. Match-on-action is often used when narrators speak. You'll see the narrator finish a sentence, turn to his left, and continue with a new thought. This is the talk-and-turn trick we've discussed, a technique so common it's often mocked. Still, it's very effective.

Tight edits

One of the things I've learned while editing over the years is that it's not necessary to do a *perfect* match-on-action. I've often found I can remove two, three, even seven frames from a match-on-action cut and it actually looks better than the true match-on-action. For instance, I may have someone standing in one shot and then sit into a second shot. I found that if the simple action of beginning to sit, bending one's knees, shifting one's weight, is shown in the first shot, you can edit to the person nearly seated in the second shot. The same is true for turns, throws, and all sorts of other actions. Try it. I'm convinced the tighter edits actually look more natural.

Continuing movement

Match-on-action can also work as a match that pleases the eye." A match-on-action is a valid connector between shots of two different people, tying otherwise unconnected shots together by continuing a similar action from one shot to the next. In this situation, the action is begun by a worker throwing a case of beer and finished by a basketball going through the net. These are, of course, two entirely different actions but by matching the same relative motion in approximately the same position of the frame, the result is a smooth transition between shots.

Match-on-shape

We love shapes. We lie in summer meadows staring at the clouds saying, "That one looks like a bunny." We measure cars by similarities to other cars; we assign similarities to people who look like other people. We love our round pegs in our round holes. It's no wonder then that one of the most common associations in editing is the match-on-shape. Watch for it in commercials. You'll find the sports car's spinning hubcap edited to the spinning CD. You'll find the shapely woman's knee matched to the K in Special K cereal.

Shape repetition

An obvious and effective use of the match-on-shape was seen recently in a series of Volkswagen ads. The average everyday world is expressed in edits of square after square after square—a piece of toast to a boring office building to a floppy disk and so on. Finally, rebelling against the tyranny of shape is the new, rounded Volkswagen beetle, shown with its reflection, completing a perfect circle.

Circles

Circles are pleasing to the eye. They have no sharp corners, they represent a continuum, and they are common in nature. That's why matching on a circle shape is one of the easiest and most popular connections.

Dominant line matches

A match-on-shape can be loosely interpreted to be a match on dominant lines. The church spire in one shot can be matched to the woman at the bus stop in the next. The woman and the church steeple are certainly not the same shape, but they both create a dominant vertical line in the first third of the screen.

Objects

The ultimate match-on-shape is a match-on-object. Saxophone-to-saxophone works here.

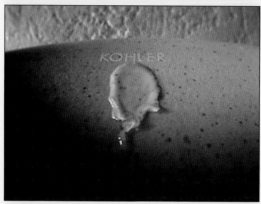

Match-on-whatever

Knowing people crave connections should open your mind to the possibilities of other effective matches.

These clocks vary in size, shape, and layout but are clearly matched as common objects.

A match-on-color can be effective. The golden tones of all three shots stitch the sequence together.

Matches can be metaphors, similes, references, or transitional devices.

The match here implies this hot car is like this everyday car you can own.

Here, the match is on the logo. We follow it from shot to shot in this animation.

Matches on dominant action also work well. Swish pan to swish pan edits, matched in direction and speed, are seamless. Flashes from cameras can connect a picture taker with a subject separated by miles or even years. It's always a happy occurrence when an editor finds the perfect match, but that discovery is made more likely when the shots are planned in the field. Be nice to the editor. Look around when you shoot. Any match will do if it pleases the eye.

Many magic tricks rely on the magician's ability to control the audience's attention. He wants you to look at the card in his left hand while he rearranges the deck with his right. An editor's job involves similar legerdemain. To accomplish the stunt of directing the viewer's attention, you pull tools from your bag of tricks. Analyze the centers of interest. Where is your eye drawn first? Second? Did you allow enough time for the viewer to make that little journey? Can you use one of the matches we've explored to direct the eye more quickly or precisely? In documentary or home video production, your efforts may simply result in making your audience's viewing experience more pleasant. However, there are times when it is more critical. If it's important for the audience to recognize something in the frame, be it the knife in the killer's hand or the valve being adjusted for the proper mix, it's your job to draw the viewer's eye to the action. There's no real science to it. There are no hard and fast rules. It's up to you to figure it out.

Breaking the Rules

"Rules are made to be broken."

"You must know the rules to break the rules."

There's truth in every cliché, but then that's a cliché, too.

The rules of editing are full of clichés, code, and universal visual shorthand. When we see a close-up of the matchbook sliding into her purse, we know we'll see the same matchbook again as the mystery deepens.

Understanding what the audience expects gives you the power to be different, to surprise, to confuse, to toss out the red herring, or rush them toward understanding.

Potemkin and *MTV*

Sergei Eisenstein, master of Russian cinema in the 1920s, would have loved MTV. Though MTV launched 50 years after the end of the Soviet Montage movement, many of the defining techniques of montage—quick cuts, rapid-fire imagery, visual metaphor, temporal tampering, and the collision of images—have become known as "MTV Style." Whoever gets the credit, montage breaks the traditional rules of continuity editing so effectively, it exists as a convention unto itself.

Collage art, where potent words and provocative images are juxtaposed in powerful ways, has the ability to act as a catalyst in the synthesis of both an emotional and intellectual understanding of a work. This same power to combine often disparate images in the fusion of new ideas exists in motion media as the art of montage.

Montage was, if not invented, then defined and refined by Soviet filmmakers of the 1920s, the most esteemed being Eisenstein. In his 1924 film *Strike,* Eisenstein intercuts shots of police firing on strikers with graphic images of a butcher at work, making what may now appear to be a facile analogy but was hailed as audacious and shocking in its time. Over the years, Soviet Montage Theory has become an accepted idiom of visual communicators. It's a common technique in commercials and music videos and can be a potentially sharp arrow in your quiver. Through montage, you might express the everyday pandemonium at Uncle Harry's house by intercutting shots of family hubbub and chaotic images of monkeys at the zoo. You could suggest the rebelliousness of customers who choose a new SUV by intercutting off-road shots with close shots of a child "coloring outside the lines."

Montage isn't just about visual metaphor, but toying with time as well. Shots are often cut together consciously employing rhythm or syncopation to intensify the edit's effect.

Again, we look to Eisenstein and his most venerated film, 1925's *The Battleship Potemkin.* The movie's Odessa steps scene, with its baby carriage sequence, is recognized as the defining moment of intellectual montage theory. Eisenstein uses a technique known as overlapping, where frames of action are repeated in subsequent shots to stretch time. In this case, troops firing on unarmed citizens kill a mother pushing a pram. As she falls, the carriage is sent careening down the steps. Other citizens try to rescue the baby but are each cut down by soldier's bullets, the horror of the scene amplified by each overlapping edit. The massacre on the Odessa steps seems interminable though the average length of each shot is less than two seconds. This is the power of montage and the reason Eisenstein considered it the essence of film art.

Tip: Rules for Breaking the Rules

+ Don't break the rules all the time or you lose the element of surprise.
+ Don't break the rules just to break the rules or you will lose potential impact.
+ Don't break the rules halfway. It could look like incompetence rather than audacity.
+ Don't break the rules without rewarding the audience for allowing you to break the rules. There needs to be a punch line or payoff, even if it's just a pleasant ending or resolution.

Creating a "look"

There's no telling what "look" is going to grab the public eye. Sometimes, the look is a result of a new TV technology. Remember "morphing," the transformation of one image to another by computer interpolation? Then there's speed ramping, where shots transition from fast motion to slow motion and back again so seamlessly. For some time, bad framing and drifting cameras were all the rage. There was even a time when the "look" was ordinary people shot in the most unflattering ways, as popularized by American commercial director Joe Sedelmaier and his "Where's the beef?" ad campaign for a fast-food franchise. No one can tell you what the next look will be but as a producer/director/videographer constantly buffeted by trends and sky-high expectations, I can certainly share how I see "looks."

First, don't fight it. If everyone is talking about a new style, you can be sure you'll hear (just after you hear your budget is cut in half), "Can we do something like [insert current multimillion dollar fad]?" I'll go back to something I mentioned earlier in this book: don't promise a big laser show if you can't produce. Obviously, a shaky camera look is deliverable at no extra cost but morphing might still be out of reach. This is when your creativity is tested. Rather than morphing, can you carefully match people's eyes and do dissolves? It might not be the *exact* look but copying a current trend is more homage than an attempt to fool people into believing you hired [insert current multimillion dollar director here] to shoot your daughter's wedding video or your boss's training tape.

If it seems impossible to even approximate the latest look, remind your client (or yourself) that looks are appealing because they're new. If the program you're creating is going to have any shelf life, it may be best to stay away from current looks. Maybe you should stick with a classic navy-blazer-khaki-pants kind of look, something that's not going out of style. Or, you could consider creating your own look.

Steadicam was invented and soon after that, sweeping POV camera moves swept the planet—another example of technology giving birth to style. Take that as a lesson. What do you have that can be exploited to create your own look? Optical image stabilization? Can you do an entire production based on a moving camera, interviews, cover, everything? Do you have a wide-angle lens? Can that form the basis of your look? Filters are another way to go. They're cheap and if you understand the situations in which their effects are most noticeable, and design your shoot to make the most of those exact situations, you've just created your own look.

But the best place to find for your look may be on your desktop. NLEs today offer many advanced special effects capabilities including digital effects (sometimes morphing), masks, selective focus, motion tracking, film look, and probably the most effective, color correction.

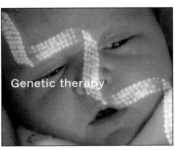

Genetic therapy

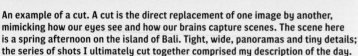
An example of a cut. A cut is the direct replacement of one image by another, mimicking how our eyes see and how our brains capture scenes. The scene here is a spring afternoon on the island of Bali. Tight, wide, panoramas and tiny details; the series of shots I ultimately cut together comprised my description of the day.

Transitions
What they mean and when to use them

As I've talked about the rules of editing, I've been talking about cuts, the simplest transition where the shot on screen is instantaneously replaced by another shot. This fundamental transition usually implies continuity and chronology, suggesting no time has passed; this is simply one angle, one view, followed by another.

The cut naturally mimics the way we see, locking in on an image, then darting to the next. That's partly why we perceive that no time has passed when one shot cuts to the next. Editors and directors make use of this fact. A cut between a shot of someone looking at the sky and a shot of the sky implies the person is seeing that sky. Intercutting—cutting back and forth between shots—implies two simultaneous but separate lines of action. A shot of a train moving screen-right cut with a train moving screen-left implies an imminent collision. Shots of someone in a waiting room intercut with shots of surgery imply that the person in the waiting room is holding vigil for the person on the operating table. Editors and directors will also take advantage of expectations created with crosscutting by changing the expected outcome of a sequence. See if this sounds familiar: We see images of the spy secretly searching an office intercut with images of the traitor arriving at the office, parking the car, and approaching the office door. When the traitor throws open the door, we expect to see the spy surprised. Instead, the traitor enters the office unaware. We cut to an exterior shot of the same office building and see the spy walking away undetected.

Simple cuts don't stand out when they join expected images or follow a simple narrative. Cuts used to join odd or discontinuous images can have a jarring or surreal effect. As in Eisenstein's *Potemkin*, quick cuts can be used to relate images in a montage. Very quick cuts, a frame or two in length, of slightly varied images is animation.

Dissolve

A dissolve is a transition where one video image blends with, and then becomes, a second video image. In a standard narrative sense, a dissolve usually indicates a passage of time, a change in location, or both. A dissolve is also called a mix, a mix dissolve, a cross fade or, by the cinema literati, a lap dissolve.

Half-dissolve

Dissolves are sometimes used to relate one shot to another. Half dissolves, where both (or many) images are mixed together and visible in some measure, can be used to show or imply a relationship between shots. Other times, dissolves are simply used to create a lyrical flow between images, especially when they're set to music. The tempo of the music will dictate the length of the dissolves.

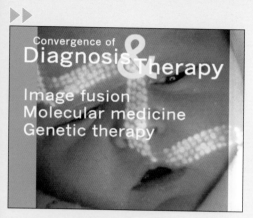

Wipes

Beyond the cut and the dissolve, most other transitions are lumped into the category of wipes. Wipes are similar to dissolves in that one image progressively replaces another. The difference is while dissolves deal with full screen images, wipes involve the incremental replacement of one shot by another. The oldest and most common wipe is the edge wipe, characterized by a traveling line of demarcation. In front of the edge is the first shot; behind the edge is the second shot.

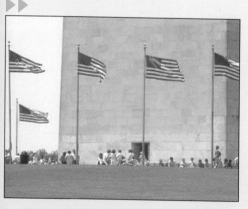

Soft wipe

The edge of a wipe can often be feathered and soft, almost as if a traveling dissolve moves along with the edge of the wipe. Some wipes have a meaning assigned to them. A clock wipe has come to mean a passing of time. A circle wipe harkens back to old-style film wipes.

Wipes are sometimes chosen because they relate to the movement or dominant lines in the shots on either side of the transition. You might choose a right-to-left vertical edge wipe because it would follow the motion of a person cutting the frame right-to-left.

Wipes

Generally, wipes mean whatever you think they mean, although they do suggest a major, but rarely somber change in scene or storyline.

This method of replacement is called the wipe pattern. Wipes can have colored borders of various widths, soft edges, rotation, and modulation in all sorts of combinations. Some NLE systems also allow wipes to be positioned, that is, to begin at a specific location on the screen. Wipes (and dissolves) are usually spoken of as having a "duration," expressed in frames.

Transitions can sometimes solve problems for you. If you cut between two shots that are too similar, it can appear to be a jump cut. Sometimes the shots are only similar in dominant line or brightness and even then, the edit could appear to be a jump cut. A dissolve or wipe could solve your problem by softening or eliminating the appearance of the jump cut. That's not to say you shouldn't be very careful while you're shooting; it's just that if you do get backed into a corner, a transition might be your escape route. An old friend of mine used to say, "If you can't solve it, dissolve it, if you can't dissolve it, justify it. If you can't justify it, well then…it's art."

What they can't do

Transitions get us from one shot to the next. Some transitions have meaning by tradition or association. We've covered how the passage of time, change in location, simultaneous action, and other information transitions can add to a story. Unfortunately, people try to force transitions to do things they can't or shouldn't be asked to do, such as make a program more exciting or interesting. Transitions can't replace content. Connect two boring interviews with an amazing 3-D particle storm and you're still left with two boring interviews.

With all this awesome transitional power comes an awesome responsibility. You must join with me and *all editors of good taste* and take this oath: "I, [state your name], promise not to produce videos, or stand by quietly and watch others produce videos, that seem to have no other purpose than to use every transition ever invented." OK, you've been deputized. Just so we understand each other, I have no problem with using a page curl as a transi-

where they've been and leave them with a nice feeling about the experience? Maybe that's your missing third act.

Don't Be Afraid to Kill

I've also heard it expressed as, "Kill your puppies." My puppy was an adorable 540° camera move in a busy clinic scene. It was a pain in the butt to light and took a half-dozen takes to get right. The day we shot it, already behind schedule and scrutinizing this ambitious undertaking, I should have killed it right there and then. Nevertheless, it was shot and survived all the way into the edit where I didn't want to kill it because it had been so difficult and costly to shoot in the first place. It took a comment from someone who didn't know the level of difficulty before I realized it had to go. So, in my case, that puppy was a shot. In your case, it might be the disarmingly clever retort or a great stunt; it might be as big as a concept or a small as a musical sting.

At every stage of the production process, you must be prepared to kill. Your eye must always be on the bigger picture. In editing, much like in poetry, there is virtue in efficiency. It's important to be able to forget who you are and what you have invested long enough to cast an unbiased eye on your work. Sometimes, I show a rough cut to someone in order to get his or her opinion and find myself watching a scene, hoping it will end before this viewer shows signs of boredom. That's a warning. If I've been successful at detaching my ego from the project, I should recognize a cut is needed.

Don't be afraid to kill puppies and don't be afraid to chase them into the next room. Sometimes, it isn't until the final hours of the edit that you see opportunities to make gross changes in structure. In the eleventh hour, I've seen the end become the beginning and the story benefit greatly.

Using Music and Sound

Violins. That's what does it for me. It starts with the distant sound of children's laughter and the whistle of a chestnut warbler in the garden. Inside, the summer breeze billows behind white gauze curtains. Grandma stands in the mostly empty room, moving boxes stacked about, pausing to look at that picture of her and grandpa outside this house back when it was new. The chorus sings, "Remember, remember," and the violins kick in. That does it. My eyes get salty and wet and Kodak can chalk up another direct hit.

We, most of us, anyhow, have buttons. There's the fright button, the righteous anger button, the funny button, and the nostalgia button, the one the Kodak folks have mapped so successfully. A good editor understands buttons and where to find them. I know where many are found and I've pushed my share. It's kind of fun, watching the other guy tear up for a change. Gratifying too, finding them. I could show you if you were here, but for the time

When it all comes together—the pictures and sound—there's some powerful manipulation possible.

being, let me share the fact that they're located mostly on your audio tracks. Sure, there are some sad ones right around the soft focus, and some happy ones close to the dog in a fish-eye lens, but they're tons of them beneath carefully crafted layers of natural sound, compelling music, and strong voices.

I'm not advocating that you find these buttons and start mashing away at will, but probably not for the reason you might think. I'm all in favor of bringing the occasional tear to the eye or smile to the lips. I think we can all use a little emotional goose now and then. What I object to is the lazy overuse and ultimate reliance on the formula. I'm not impressed by a piece that finds that old Kodak button, but find the pathos in pop or the comedy in classical and you'll be showing me that you understand the power—and you're able to use it for the general good!

Editing the Sound Tracks

You'll need one or two video tracks to edit a character-driven feature film, your aunt's life story, or a classic two-narrator training project, with no special effects, no titles, or just the normal back-and-forth of dialogue. You might separate characters onto their own tracks or put your B-roll on one and A-roll on another just for the visual pleasure of it, but it wouldn't be *necessary*. However, for a decent audio mix it'll be necessary to have six, maybe eight tracks. They fill up fast! Consider that you'll give up two right away to stereo music and two more to each layer of sound effects if they're in stereo as well. You'll want to keep each of your characters on a separate track and you might want a separate track for room tone. Did I say eight tracks? Maybe you'll need a dozen!

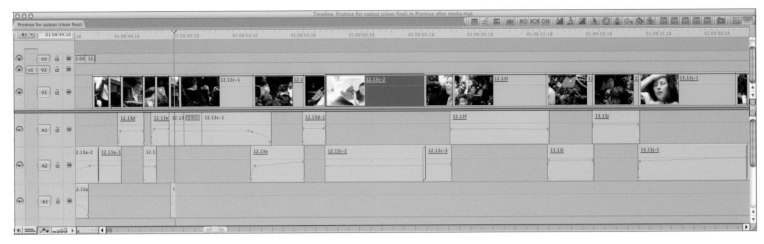

Checkerboarding

When recording actors in a natural conversational interplay they hardly ever sound natural to me. You'll see this exchange in your script:

CAROL
There is no way I'm going to sit around here while you and your gang of hooligans visit every pub between ...

BOB
(overlapping)
They're not hooligans and we're not a gang. We're a book club!

The script clearly indicates Bob is going to jump in and cut Carol off! But he never does. Carol always ends her line, trailing off unnaturally as Bob finally begins his. I say, good! As long as they're on single shots, perfect! If they spoke over each other on the set, you'd have no choice as to *how much they'd overlap* and, closely mic'd, you'd never be able to get either line clean. So it's better for you, as the editor, that they didn't perform the scene the way it was written.

Checkerboarding
I've cautioned you to keep various sound elements on their own separate tracks. But what about the situation in which Bob and Carol are mic'd by a shotgun and all their audio begins on a single track? Well, you'll want to do something called "checkerboarding." What you'll do is, once the dialogue is laid down, cut it up between lines, and move all of Bob's to the track below Carol's, so they look like the alternating squares on a checkerboard. You'll then go back and trim each line nice and tight. If the dialogue was recorded in a noisy location, you should also do a little ramp up and down on each cut, even if it's only a few

frames. I do that *on every cut of audio*, regardless. Your audience might never notice, until the mix is played on a high-end speaker system. Then you'll all hear the sharp edges.

Filling in the sound blanks
Remember that as you slide clips of dialogue around, you're changing the relationship of one line to another, tightening it up—maybe overlapping audio—and there's a chance we're going to hear extraneous words from this or another take sneaking through. OK, now remember when I insisted that at the end of a scene you record room buzz (ambient sound)? Here's where you use it. Under the checkerboarded cuts from the talent you're going to lay down an uninterrupted track of room tone to fill in the blanks.

Tip: Consistency Pays in the Mix

When you begin to edit your project, begin dedicating audio tracks to a single purpose. Put all the narration on audio track 1 and all of Mom's comments on audio track 2. Put sound effects on audio tracks 3 and 4, and the music on audio tracks 5 and 6. Then, be consistent throughout your production. You'll see why when you get to your mix. Let's say you learn that the narrator's voice competes with the music you've chosen. You might want to be able to add equalization or change the overall level of all the narration in the whole project at once. Imagine how difficult that might be on an hour-long documentary of the narration bounces from track to track all the way through!

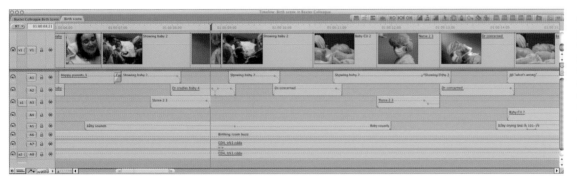

Tip: Mixdowns

NLEs will often be limited as to how many audio tracks can be played back simultaneously. Though audio, considered alone, is not nearly as taxing on the processor, dropped frames of audio will stop playback just as quickly as dropped frames of video. Luckily, most programs offer the option of an audio "mixdown." An audio mixdown takes the tracks you designate and combines them in either an invisible render file or sometimes mixes them to a new track entirely. Clearly, it's best to mix down the audio tracks that are most stable at any point in your edit. Changing any aspect of the audio inside the mixdown will negate its accuracy and require a new mixdown.

Tip: On professional audio mixing boards, you'll find a couple of buttons many timelines share—solo and mute. These two choices allow you to turn specific audio tracks on and off. Mute quiets one track at a time. Solo mutes every other track than the one you've soloed. Using solo and mute will help you find that annoying pop or tick you can't isolate any other way.

Split your edits

A split edit is an edit where the incue and/or outcue of your video differs from the incue and outcue of your audio. The result is the stairstep look. Split edits are often necessary if you want to hear the whole piece of sound (a sentence or sound effect) but you want to see some other image over the top. Split edits will also help fill in areas where the audio might be unusable on a neighboring shot. To me, split edits are most helpful in deemphasizing your edits. Try this sometime. Edit two shots back-to-back with clearly discernable and differing background audio. Review the edit. Now extend the audio from one shot under the other shot and listen again. If the audio and video edits aren't coincident, the edit is deemphasized. Add an audio dissolve and you'll hardly notice the transition at all.

Editing the music

Most edit projects involve music. Sometimes, it's a direct involvement as we see musicians on the screen or hear Uncle Jim talk about his favorite song. More often, it's less literal, used to suggest attitude and support the emotion of a scene. Music cues the viewer, building tension or lightening a moment. Since you'll use music in most of your productions, it's important to know how to use it effectively.

It's obvious that choosing suitable music for a scene is important. The favorites on your shelf might not always be the most

When editing cutaways, otherwise known as "b-roll," into a program, I always look for long cuts of background sound that can be played through several video edits. This will significantly soften those edits. Of course, turning it around, you can call attention to an edit by making the video and audio cut at the same time.

I added the yellow line to help point out the stair step look of a split edit. Split edits are especially useful when trimming up news stories. I like to backtime soundbites, starting the sound of the interviewee under the b-roll turning up to full sound as the b-roll finishes. The result is a very smooth and natural transition.

Louisiana Art Museum in Denmark

Vietnam Veterans Memorial in Washington, D.C.

appropriate; having a music resource to dip into is critical. It is illegal to use copyrighted music for any purpose without the copyright owner's permission. Even if you're simply putting your niece's favorite song under the dancing at her bat mitzvah, you're in violation. The law in every country in the world is very clear on this account. Further statutes are broken when you duplicate the tape for all your aunts and uncles, or worse, post it on the Web. Now, you might never get caught if it's all kept within the family. It's your decision, but I recommend you look for music that's created for the purpose of building soundtracks. Search the Web for "copyright-free music" and you'll find hundreds of sources offering thousand of cuts at a variety of prices, from one-time uses to total buyouts.

Music cuts

Music is often surprisingly forgiving of edits. I had a line in a script talking about the Louisiana Art Museum in Denmark. Talking about the wealthy farmer who founded the museum, the script line read, "He called it Louisiana, in honor of his first wife...and his second wife...and his third wife...all named Louise." I was able to take the music running under the segment, full of long, sustained notes, and simply repeat the note three times under his first wife, second wife, and third wife. The music edit added another layer of humor to the sentence and always got a chuckle. In another case, I was unable to find music with sufficient impact for a piece about the Vietnam Veterans Memorial in Washington. I did find a musical selection with a series of haunting flute passages. I was able to take just those parts, add long rests in between, and create a cut of music.

Locating edit points with music

Music cuts created for use by video producers are often recorded in convenient clip lengths of 10, 15, 30, and 60 seconds. That's great if you're cutting commercial spots, but isn't particularly useful if you're creating a family history or documentary. There's usually a full-length version of each song, too—two, three, or sometimes four minutes in length—but how often will you need a piece exactly four minutes in length? I find myself editing almost every cut of music I use. I like to maintain the original beginning and ending of most pieces because it sounds more natural than simply fading the music up and down. The trick then is locating edit points within compositions. My method involves markers. I'll cue up the music and listen to it all the way through a couple of times, tapping out the rhythm with my fingers. Most contemporary music has a regular rhythm established by percussion. Sometimes the beat is computer generated and you'll find it perfectly precise. When I'm comfortable with the tempo I'll run through the song tapping markers into the timeline. Go back and use the mark-in and mark-out buttons to time the measures. It'll help you map the song's construction. After that, it's a matter of locating edit points in the composition— places where the phrasing and instrumentation seem close. If you're careful about marking measures and picking edit points, cuts will often be perfect on the first try. If not, go into the asymmetrical trim mode (trim one side at a time) and begin tweaking. If I find the edit just doesn't work and a trim one frame this way or that doesn't help, I'll rethink my edit point. I'll ask myself if I should try slipping the clip a whole measure. Sometimes, even if you've chosen the right place to edit, the system isn't precise enough to handle trims less than one-thirtieth of a second (one frame in NTSC).

Tip: What You Hear May Not Be What You Get

It's important to understand the difference between audio monitoring and audio output. Audio monitoring is the configuration of audio channels you hear while you're editing. Audio output is the configuration of channels that will go to tape or disc. They are usually set independently in different control panels. It's entirely possible to hear channel one and two centered while you're editing and find the channels panned left and right when you output to tape! Don't make the mistake of assuming your output will automatically match your monitor.

I prefer to have most of my tracks centered, in the zero pan position (pan is like the balance on your stereo). One exception is stereo music. It's mixed to have channel 1 panned all the way left, channel 2 all the way right.

It's sometimes tempting to think it'll be cool to confine the person standing on the right side of the picture to the right speaker and the other person to the other side. Wrong. It sounds unnatural. That's not how you hear. Occasionally, it works to *exaggerate* the stereo effect with a sound such as a passing ambulance but even with a passing, pinpoint sound source, you hear it in both ears all the time. The only time I like complete separation of the tracks is when I'm trying to synch two music or voice cuts. It helps me to have total separation, left and right, in order to discern which source is ahead of the other. After I've got the synch, then I zero the tracks again.

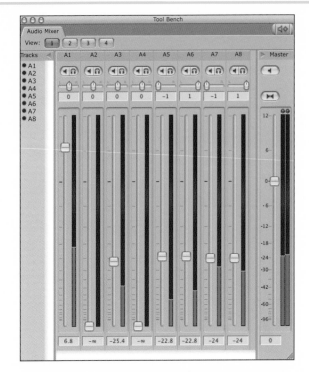

In this example, tracks 1 through 4 are being fed equally to the left and right monitors. Tracks 5 through 8 are two stereo pairs with channels 5 and 7 feeding the left speakers and channels 6 and 8 feeding the right.

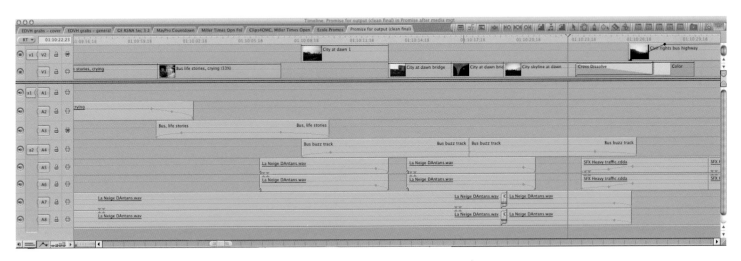

Once you've figured out the frequency of beats identified by the structure of a piece of music, it's not too difficult to edit it, shortening or lengthening the piece, repeating bridges, or even constructing an alternate ending.

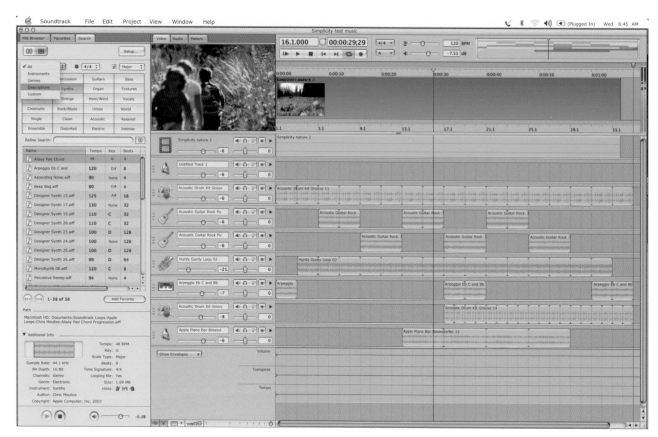

There are professional programs on the market today such as Sony's Acid and Apple's Soundtrack and a whole raft of simpler, free programs that actually allow you to compose and create your own copyright-free music by arranging prerecorded loops. Some are easier to use than others but the only thing I can play is the radio and I was able to record a usable tune my second time out of the box.

Tip: Beat It

There's an almost overpowering tendency to want to edit on beats. Try to resist. Edits on the beat emphasize the beat, drawing undue attention to the rhythm track. Edits on the beat can also seem unimaginative and pre-dictable. Try to draw out other aspects of the music. Maybe you can edit on phrases or solos. Of course, editing on the beat can be a wonderful way to surprise viewers by establishing a pattern and then breaking it.

Looking at a song's energy plot, it's easy to identify the sharp attack of each beat and even locate points where other instruments join in. Still, sometimes it's best to ignore the music completely, letting it work alone, establishing a mood or even a counterpoint to the edited images.

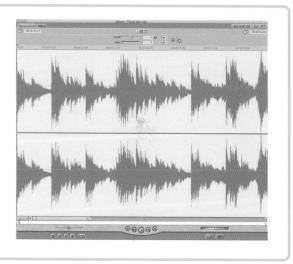

Soundscapes

Sound can turn an image completely. This shot of a teenage boy sitting in the backseat of a car could easily establish wildly different settings. What does it say if we see his dour look and hear the voices of other teens in the car laughing and joking? Maybe he's just broken up with his girlfriend or maybe he's just depressed. Now imagine the sound of a family singing. This poor guy might be a reluctant passenger on a family trip. Now substitute the sound of a police radio squawking in the background. Chances are he's an even more reluctant passenger on a more portentous trip. It's all in the power of sound, sound added and controlled in the process called "audio sweetening."

Consider how you can use the power of sound and sound effects. If you walk around your neighborhood on a sunny summer afternoon, you might hear children playing, a lawnmower, the ice cream man, maybe the occasional slap of screen door. A sound designer shooting a motion picture would think of all these elements, bringing them together to create the soundscape of the perfect, idealized summer afternoon. Maybe your family video could benefit from the same depth and sweetness.

Sweetening

Sometimes sweetening involves replacing real audio with sound effects. Without dedicated microphones close to the situation, the sound of this tiger behind a glass panel won't meet expectations. A professionally recorded roar might be exactly what's needed. In all my years of shooting, I've never heard wind noise from a camera mic sound like anything but distortion. If you want that lonely, howling cliché wind sound to help set the scene, you'll need to find a sound effect.

The mix

The final step in the sweetening process is the "mix." In the mix, you are literally mixing or combining all those dozen or more audio tracks into the stereo pair you'll output with your project. Your job in the mix is to listen critically to your levels, and adjust areas where the relative intensity of your sound tracks is out of whack. You might need to reduce music levels when the narrator is speaking. Other times you might want to boost sound effects masked by the music. You may detect conflicts in audio presence. Sometimes the deep, rich tones of the music and full, sculptured soundscape point up the tinny quality of the narration track. At that point, you'll need to go back into your timeline and adjust the equalization of the narration.

Sound effects can also help texture a documentary story. You hear the lionlike roar of howler monkeys in the distance, not once but a couple of times in this location. The purpose was to foreshadow and add weight to the subsequent soundbite of a tourist scared by the howlers.

The gentleman looking at the picture of the smoker actually coughed! It was a funny moment. Being way across the gallery, the sound wasn't very good. I didn't consider it too much of a journalistic misstep to share the humor of the situation with the viewers by taking a cough from later in the footage and dubbing it in here.

In addition to equalization, many NLEs offer a variety of audio filters and effects to correct or enhance your production. There are "notch filters" that allow you to eliminate annoying hums and whistles, sounds that fall in a relatively narrow frequency range. You're often offered echo and reverb to control the "size" of the sound. Some systems have noise gates, capable of pulling out unwanted background sound between voice cuts. In addition to the tools built into your NLE, there are often interesting and useful plug-ins that allow anything from pitch shifting to pop removal.

As I noted earlier, nonlinear audio editing is also nondestructive. The relatively easy-to-use and versatile audio tools found on most of today's nonlinear edit systems invite experimentation and offer even the amateur hobbyist a chance to achieve professional-sounding results.

Even after spending many hours tinkering with the mix, I'll watch the edit from beginning to end several more times before I'm convinced the sound track is complete. I usually "watch" once without taking my eyes off the VU meters. It's surprisingly easy to lose context during a production. Taken scene by scene, the mix is fine, but by comparing the beginning of the program to the end, you might be surprised to learn that occasional peaks are topping out near −6 dB early on but dangerously close to 0 dB by the end.

Special Effects

In the classic 1960s TV show *Bewitched*, Samantha, secretly a witch, made things appear and disappear with a wiggle of her nose or a nod of her head. The special effect used was the simplest special effect, the jump cut—simply an edit that defies physics. A prop is there, and then it isn't. All the producers had to do to make things appear and disappear was to lock the camera in position on the scene and roll a bit, take out the object and roll again. Edit the two shots back to back and the object inexplicably disappears. That's where special effects started way back at the beginning of the last century.

Now the opportunities for us to toy with reality have increased manifold. There are methods available to add people to shots they were never any part of. We can compress and expand screen time at will. Even one of the most remarkable effects of the 1970s, the *Star Wars* light saber, is available to the ambitious hobbyist as an NLE plug-in today. We would be shortsighted not to assume that the most remarkable effects we see today are but a few years beyond our present reach.

Still, there are a few, as universal as Samantha's disappearing act, that are here today and certain to be here tomorrow. That's where we're going.

Remember that without the time and money to create cinema-quality special effects, you're going to be faced with compromises and concessions. Whether it's a rocket launch, a light saber, or Mom walking through walls, all play better in short shots. Ask any magician—it's best not to give your audience too much time to pick apart your efforts.

Combining Shots Using Keys

Keying is the process of using attributes of the image, either color or brightness, to turn areas transparent, revealing another image underneath. Together, these layered images are called a "composite" and often the process of combining shots is called "compositing." The composite with which we're all most familiar is the weathercaster standing in front of a map. It looks like there's a map behind him, but in the studio all you see is the weathercaster standing in front of a green wall. Special equipment identifies everything in the scene that's green and substitutes video or maybe an animated weather map. This process of substituting another image in the place of a color is called "Chromakeying."

The most common color for chromakeying is green. Most any color can be used but there are several reasons why green is chosen more often than the second most common, chromakey blue. First, the chances of your talent wearing (or being put in a costume) this shade of green are limited. Second, the green component of a video signal preserves information better and that means better keys.

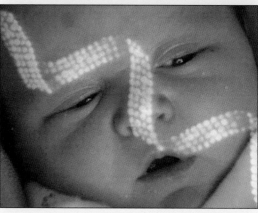

Keys allow many improbable composites, from Neo in *The Matrix* to a woman flying. It's always important to remember that effective effects begin on location. It's the old computer programming paradigm: Garbage in, garbage out. A chromakey needs to be properly lit to give the editor a fighting chance at getting a clean key, but to *sell the effect* it's important to think it through even further. The composite will ultimately have a flying woman streaking across the afternoon sky. The Sun would light her from above, and reflectance would fill in. The sky is blue and would add a bluish tint to her costume and skin. If you're careful, chromakeys can be very convincing effects, not limited to flying.

Luminance Keys

Keys based on brightness attributes are called "luminance keys." A luminance key inspects an image for the darkest areas and builds the key based on making those areas transparent. Here the Moon, bright against a night sky, was keyed out and inserted into this shot in a position the Moon couldn't possibly occupy.

Unlike chromakeys that are usually either on or off, a luminance key can be graduated, showing more of other layers through depending on how bright a specific pixel on the screen may be. This allows the key to "feather off."

Matte

The information developed by the computer's inspection of an image for luminance or chroma information comprises what's known as the "matte." Think of a matte as a sophisticated hole-cutter for video. If it's moving it's called a "traveling matte." Whether it's a luminance key or a chromakey, it's possible to specify whether the dark or light area should be cut and what source should be used to fill each.

Anything bright enough in comparison to its background will key. Backlit snow in the night sky will key. A burning match will key, perfect for fire effects. Here, we keyed a light-bulb originally shot against a black background. A flash paper fireball will key, perfect for making the Moon over Milwaukee explode.

Alpha channel

In many NLEs designed with compositing in mind, every shot has an automatically generated matte based on lightness and darkness within the image. This is know as the "alpha channel" and can be used for luminance keying.

Unfortunately, the method of setting up keys differs on nearly every NLE so you're going to have to get the manual and figure it out.

Color matching and color effects

Color correction. That's the problem. We call this powerful production tool "color correction," as if there has to be something wrong, something to fix. Some people call it "color grading," or "color timing." Either way, there are times when all we need to do is get the green out of the sky or match face tones from shot to shot. However, the advanced color correction capabilities of today's NLE systems offer editors the opportunity to take advantage of color as a property of the image, available to help tell the story, convey shades of meaning, or create a look.

Color is an integral part of our visual language, often affecting message. Here, as the message moves from, "I could have a brain tumor," to "It'll be cured by a new therapy," the footage transitions from the stark, wintry blue to the warm, hopeful, golden color of abundance and reward. This sort of story support through color isn't uncommon. Steven Soderbergh's Academy Award–winning film *Traffic* expressed a similar dichotomy between the emotional grittiness south of the border and the sanitized coolness up north.

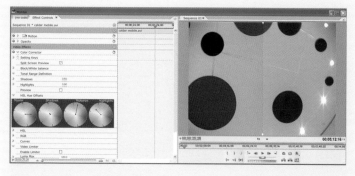

Three-wheel color correction allows the operator to deal independently with highlights, shadows, and the middle range. Moving the cursor toward the outer edges of the circle shifts the color balance toward the color noted.

Contrast range

Always begin your color work by setting your contrast range. If you hope the work you're doing will make it to broadcast, there are very specific limits to your whites and blacks (and chroma levels). You'll need to use your NLE's built-in scopes and whatever range-checking abilities your system offers. A waveform monitor, akin to a VU meter for video, is your primary tool for measuring brightness (luminance) levels. Scopes are generally laid out on a 1 to 100 scale. Your black levels shouldn't dip below 7.5 and your whites should top out at 100. Using scopes with your color correction tools, you'll begin to see the advantage of systems that allow you to boost, for example, only your midranges, so you can make your subject brighter without sending the sky over 100 percent. The 7.5 percent and 100 percent limitations aren't hard and fast. Like audio, there's usually no harm done if you occasionally peak a little above or below. Most consumer and prosumer cameras actually work on a 110 percent white clip, again, which is only an issue if you intend to go to broadcast. Not going to broadcast is not a license to disregard video levels. Whites, when overdriven, can bleed into your audio causing loud, grating distortion, or humming.

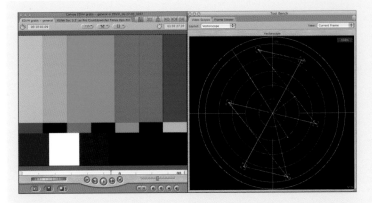

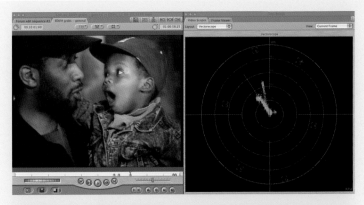

Vectorscope

Once you've adjusted your contrast range, taken your sky down to 100 percent, and pulled all the detail you want out of your shadows without turning your blacks gray, move on to your color. The tool used for checking color is the vectorscope and, like a waveform, is laid out on a 0 to 100 percent scale, which constitutes the boundaries of the amount of video bandwidth TV stations are allowed to broadcast, otherwise known as "legal limits." Again, if you're planning on broadcasting, be sure you're within these legal limits. Then adjust color balance. Look for an area of your image that *should be white* and adjust. With most current NLEs, it's simply a matter of clicking the eyedropper on a "white" area.

Be aware that if your system only allows hue-saturation-brightness (H-S-B) color adjustment, you really can't bring poorly white balanced footage back to white. In an H-S-B system, if you crank one color closer to where it should be, the others are shifted an equal distance away from where they should be.

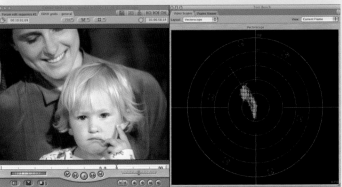

Here's a little support for the brotherhood of man: Regardless of race, human flesh tone values fall within a very narrow range of hues, so narrow, that vectorscopes are marked with a universal "flesh tone" vector.

The most common use of color correction is color matching. You might have shots of your daughter from a day last spring, her autumn birthday, and New Year's Eve. All three were shot with the same camera, but when edited one after another you'll see a tremendous variation in color. Color correction will allow you to bring the color values closer together.

When correcting between shots with the same location or same subject, try to find a coincident area, the same person, or the same wallpaper in two shots and start adjusting their colors until they match. Here, the subject was shot twice, the second time through a windscreen that added a blue cast. The bright highlight on her face offered a coincident area of color that *should* match. In this NLE, all that was needed was to point out the coincident area and the system took care of matching the other colors.

If you hope your work will end up on broadcast TV, and you're using a very inexpensive edit system without scopes and color checking tools, it's best to stay away from crazy color effects. Otherwise, experiment! Have fun toying with color as a method of communication. In their film *O Brother, Where Art Thou?*, the Coen brothers helped reinforce the desolation of the depression era setting by turning every lush, green field into a burnt brown color. Just be careful if you're working for a client. Unless you're doing family videos, music videos, or video art, it's important to remind yourself that the look can't take over. The message is still the primary driving force and must be respected.

Film look

It is a testament to our love and respect for film that even as high-definition technology continues to perfect the sharpness of the video picture, the question persists, "But, does it look like film?" Video is sharp and clear and less "moody" and is, therefore, seen as more pedestrian. Viewers may not understand the technical differences but still perceive the softer look of film to be more aesthetically pleasing. In the business, there's a certain "snob appeal" to working in film. There's always been a connection in the minds of film producers, even industrial film producers, with the glamour of Hollywood. Film production requires an arcane skill set, is far more susceptible to error, and far more expensive than video production, so I see it as ironic that the way to create a film look is to *degrade* your video. Now, before the film workers out there begin slamming this book shut in disgust, let me say this: Film is different from video and there is no way to gain the true advantages of film on video. Film has a far greater exposure range, maybe four to six stops! On film, you'll see detail in the clouds as well as in the shadows below, while on video you'll be forced to choose one or the other. Projected film (as opposed to film seen on TV) has far greater resolution than DV. Rather than offering the hundreds of thousands of pixels that make up a video picture, the small grain in film offers millions and millions of equivalent picture elements. However, what I've been talking about so far is film that's shot with all the exposure latitude offered by a refined daylight stock, and then projected on a big screen. Most of the film you see used on TV shows and movies is not shot simply to take full advantage of film's range. Cinematographers, in search of a "look," will use filters to add grittiness, romance, or mystery. So, when we talk about film look, we're talking about giving video some of the characteristics of altered film. Here's how.

Limited depth of field

Film look begins on location. Early on, I suggested you buy a set of neutral density filters when you bought your camera. The reason being you need neutral density filters to achieve one important aspect of film look: limited depth of field.Here's a simple, but important, proportion—the bigger the image collection plane, the less depth of field. Consider the difference in size between a frame of 35 mm film and the common ¼" (6.5 mm) CCD found in DV cameras. The CCD on a DV camera means nearly everything is in focus, especially when using the widest zoom setting—a distinct advantage to the average amateur shooter whose main concern is being in focus. However, it's a disadvantage to videographers like you and me. We might want to use focus to define centers of interest or to lift a character off the background. That's part of a film look. One way to decrease depth of field is to shoot "wide open" and that means limiting the amount of light available to the camera, exactly what neutral density filters do! If you'd like to take neutral density a step further, look into graduated neutral densities (ND) or grads. A grad is a filter that ranges from clear to an ND value. A grad might allow you to cut out the light in the sky and expose for the foreground, again, in an attempt to shoot with your iris wide open, which limits depth of field.

Persistence of vision

Film relies more heavily on persistence of vision and it shows. Standard NTSC video is recorded at 30 frames per second (PAL at 25), with each frame subdivided into two fields. So in NTSC, the video image is refreshed 60 times per second (50 times in PAL). Compare that to film "refreshed" at the universal 24 frames per second. Many DV cameras allow you to shoot in a frame mode, essentially a 30 frames per second rate with no update between fields. The result is a more blurred image, reminiscent of film.

Standard NTSC and PAL frames have a screen ratio of 4:3. For a movie, usually shot in a 16:9 or greater screen ratio, to be shown full frame on a 4:3 screen it is often "letterboxed,"—a horizontal band of black is added both at the top and bottom of the screen to effectively widen the aspect ratio.

Letterboxing is done so often that we've all come to associate a letterboxed image with film. Many DV cameras offer a 16:9 mode that can lend a film look. However, be careful. Sometimes, that ratio is achieved by simply masking a 4:3 frame, throwing away some of your picture information. Even if your camera shoots true 16:9, be sure your NLE can handle it before you find you've started a project you can't finish.

Diffusion filters

Diffusion filters are another way of adding that certain filmic something. Commercially available filters can add a glowing radiance to the bright areas of the screen and soften severe shadows.

Tip: Homemade Diffusion

+ An old trick to create diffusion is to take a piece of neutral-colored nylon stocking, remove your lens shade, and stretch the material over the lens. Hold it in place with a rubber band. Be sure you're not shooting too wide or you might actually see the stocking. Try other colors for other effects.

+ Another impromptu trick is to run your fingertip over an oily spot on your face (your hairline or next to your nose) and rub that oil on the lens. The same effect can be obtained without the possible appearance of nose picking by having a little bit of petroleum jelly handy. You can also try dappling clear nail polish, but in all cases *do not work directly on your lens element!* If you're going to mess something up, mess up that cheap UV filter, even with the face oil trick. I've been told there are elements in human oils that are corrosive to some lens coatings.

There are methods for achieving a film look in the edit but they require, as I stated earlier, degrading your video image. The quickest and most reliable is to buy a film-look plug-in for your NLE. These filters are amazingly effective, adding film grain in the shadows, scratches, gate jump, and even errant hairs! Some offer choices of aged film, old film, even specific film stocks.

Tip: Creating a Film Look *without* Buying a Film-Look Effect

+ Try to approach film's 24 frames per second rate through frame blending or deinterlacing. Frame blending involves combining video's two fields into a single frame. Deinterlacing does the same thing, but by throwing away one field and doubling the other. Blending is the preferred method but if your system only offers deinterlacing, copy your video clip onto two tracks and deinterlace one clip by choosing "upper" and the other by choosing "lower," then mix the two in a 50/50 half dissolve.

+ Crush your blacks by increasing contrast, thus darkening your shadows. For old film, try decreasing contrast, washing out your blacks. For really old film, try tinting your footage to a sepia tone.

+ Old film often jumped in the gate as it was projected. If you have access to effects in your NLE, try taking the occasional frame out of registration, allowing it to jump.

+ Old film prints were often poorly made. Try cycling your brightness up and down slightly over the duration of your clips. Add an occasional "flash frame," a very bright, almost white single frame.

+ Find some video of an old piece of black film leader. Play with half dissolves, non-additive mixes, and luminance keys, encouraging the grain and defects to show through. You'll find a full resolution DV clip to download on my website (www.petemay.com).

Animation

Do you want total control of your actors' every word and gesture? Are you willing to spend hours fussing over the tiniest details? Can you spare as many nights and weekends as it might take to build a matchstick model of the Tower of London? If you answered yes to all these questions, you may have the heart and soul of an animator.

All animation takes advantage of Roget's theory of persistence of vision to create the appearance of motion. There are three primary methods of animation: 2-D, 3-D, and 3-D computer animation.

2-D animation

Two-dimensional animation involves drawing picture after picture, each progressively different from the last. When the pictures are presented rapidly, in succession, the changes from one frame to the next smooth out and we see motion. Two-dimensional animation grew out of the early days of film when the public, hungry for the magic of moving pictures, took easily to seeing their comic strip favorites come to life. The first animated films were done on paper, with each picture redrawn completely from one frame to the next. The innovation of clear cellulose acetate film sheets (cels) simplified the production of animation, allowing backgrounds to be looped and various characters to be drawn independently or not redrawn if they don't move. From *Felix the Cat* to *The Little Mermaid*, a majority of the animation we've known over the years has been cel-type animation. Though most cel animation is done on computers nowadays, I don't include it as a separate category of computer animation because whether inked on cellulose, moved as paper cutouts, or sketched on a screen, the animation still involves two-dimensional images.

3-D animation

Three-dimensional animation involves the incremental movement and photographing of actual three-dimensional objects to impart motion. Characters are usually molded of a plasticine substance laid over wire skeletons. The characters then "interact" on tiny, 3-D sets lit just like any full-scale production. Nick Park's *Wallace and Gromit* series and other clay animation films fall into this category. Though clay animation dominates this style, I've seen incredible work done by moving furniture, dishes, and even people.

3-D computer animation

Three-dimensional computer animation involves the creation of objects that appear to reside in three-dimensional space. Their movements obey laws established by the animator with objects and body parts attached computationally rather than by wire and clay. Three-dimensional computer animation differs from all other animation because movement isn't made incrementally but by assigning beginning points and end points of actions and allowing the computer to "film the action," interpolating and rendering the "in-betweens."

It's possible to do reasonably smooth 2-D cel animation by holding images for two frames rather than one. Disney would never do it that way, but if you're going to give animation a try, that'll cut your work in half. This project, for a children's video, was drawn in a child's computer paint program, printed on paper, and shot, then edited together at 15 frames per second.

Registration
For animation to be perfectly smooth, the cels must be lined up perfectly from one frame to the next. This is called "registration." Historically, the most common registration method has been "pin" registration. A common hole puncher made for three ring binders will allow you to prepare your paper or acetate sheet for pin registration. You'll need to build an animation stand with pins sufficiently large to keep the paper from moving around on the pins. Though this will produce passable registration, it still won't be Disney-perfect. Luckily, as a matter of style, we've become accustomed to "jiggle" animation that's not perfectly registered.

Rotoscoping
Animation doesn't have to be done with drawings. This project was shot frame-by-frame with a digital snapshot camera. The frames were then painted in Photoshop and assembled. A whole genre of animation called "rotoscoping" involves shooting live action with actors, then painting the frames to look like cel animation.

Export and import of image sequences
Many NLEs support the export and import of image sequences, where moving video can be turned into a series of sequentially numbered stills. Once transferred to a paint program, the individual stills can be painted or composited with other image sequences and then reassembled into clips back in the NLE program.

Titling
Typography was at one time an excruciating, letter-by-letter art-card process. Today's computer programs make adding names, titles, and credits to a video easy, often allowing you to import text from word processing documents (such as your script) and even performing spell checks. What hasn't changed over the years is the importance of type and the powerful effect it can have on your finished product.

Lower thirds
When text is added to video, it's said to be "supered," meaning it's superimposed. Most videos will at least have a title at or near the beginning of the piece, but if your video includes interview soundbites, you'll want to add identifying information. These names and title captions added to soundbites are often referred to as "lower thirds," referring to their position on the screen. Whether or not you add names depends on the project and your audience. Wedding videos don't usually call for lower thirds, for example, but they might be useful to identify the speaker at a graduation. Lower thirds might seem inappropriate on home video projects but how many times have you turned over an old family photo to see who was in the picture and when it was shot? A lower third might serve the same purpose as those handwritten notes. Documentaries and business videos almost always require them.

Simplify for readability

When creating titles, don't overdo the font styles and colors. Develop a style and use it throughout. Some people don't like to mix styles, but I've seen it work nicely when compositional rules are followed. Readability is always your main concern.

Timing

Most times, it works well to dissolve text in and out. How long to hold a graphic depends on how much information is being conveyed. For lower thirds, super the text a few seconds after a person begins talking. If there's time I'll wait for a natural break in the soundbite before supering. Sometimes a soundbite is too short to have the lower third up as long as you'd like, but my rule is, dissolve the text in, read it out loud twice, then fade it out. If the video includes more than one soundbite from the same person, it's not necessary or even desirable to put their lower third in every time they speak. You'll need to judge this based on how many times they speak and how long it is between their bites.

> ## Tip: Get Your Lower Thirds Right!
>
> Although adding lower thirds comes toward the end of the editing process, it's a good idea to gather the information as you're shooting. You can keep a running list of people you've interviewed, writing down how they spell their names and, if needed, give their title. Better yet, don't depend on their handwriting, or yours! Get in the habit of asking them to give their name and spell it on tape. You can check their microphone level at the same time.

Placement

When adding any kind of text or graphics to video, it's important to stay within the title-safe area of the screen. Type that extends to the edges of your computer screen may be lost on some television screens. Your editing program should display a title-safe area that can serve as the margins for your text.

You'll choose the size of your font in terms of "points." This is the traditional way of measuring the size of a character. In print, 72 points equals an inch, but on a TV screen that means nothing. Consider that people might be watching on anything from a 5" (13 cm) screen to a 60" (153 cm) screen. Still, there is a limit to resolution. If a font is so small it's jagged and unreadable, you can blow it up four times the size and it'll be big and jagged and unreadable. Always go for readability, and that would usually mean stay above 18 points.

You'll often need to choose a background for your font page. Remember readability! Choose appropriate graphic and video backgrounds, but be sure they don't compete with your text.

 ### You can talk type

+ The word "font" refers to an entire set of letters within one style of type such as Helvetica, Courier, and Geneva.

+ Kerning is the adding or removing of space between letters to improve appearance.

+ Leading (pronounced "ledding") is the amount of space between lines.

+ Serif fonts have small lines extending from the main strokes of the letter that makes them easier to read. Sans serif fonts don't. For example, this type is printed in a sans serif font.

+ Cursive fonts look like handwritten script.

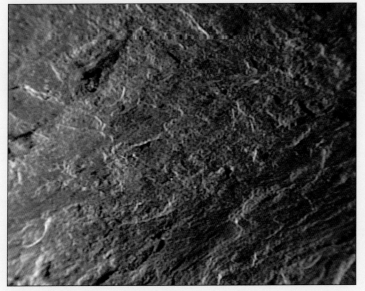

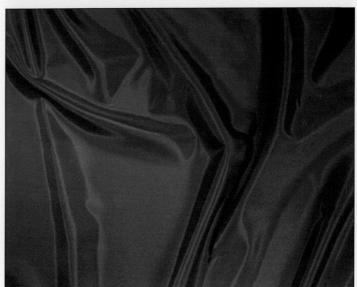

When choosing backgrounds, look around you. Maybe you can alter a shot on one of your reels. If you're shooting a special family event, maybe you can make a collage of memorabilia. This background for a Valentine's Day party is made up of lace and Victorian stickers. You might also try fabrics or textures from nature. Again, be sure the background doesn't compete.

Although the font choices may be mind-boggling, choose one that's both easy to read and fits with the style of your video. In general, you'll want to stick with one font style and color throughout the video. For titles, you can get creative but, as always, make sure it's readable.

Chapter 6:
The Finished Product

Abandoning the Edit

There's an old saying that an edit is never finished, just abandoned. The trick is knowing *when* to abandon the edit. I'll admit it's one of my weak points. I have difficulty stepping away if I'm not convinced the project is the best it can possibly be. You must do as I advise, not as I do. Consider the concept of *realistic perfection*. No client is going to pay you to tweak forever, so imagine the most money you'll probably bill and picture the graph. Look at the ascending line of increased quality and find the point where it crosses the descending line of pay per hour. Of course, you don't want to release a project that could *easily* look better. You'll have to consider word-of-mouth and return customers. Part of this goes way back to the budget process. If you've budgeted three days for an edit and you spend six, you cut your paycheck in half. If your client understands what can be accomplished in three days, agrees to pay you for three days, and then expects six days of work, your client is cutting your paycheck in half. It's a tough line to draw. If you figure it out, let me know.

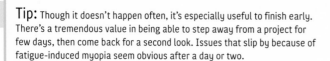

Tip: Though it doesn't happen often, it's especially useful to finish early. There's a tremendous value in being able to step away from a project for few days, then come back for a second look. Issues that slip by because of fatigue-induced myopia seem obvious after a day or two.

Deciding You're Done

+ I'm not an advocate of editing by committee, but sometimes extra pairs of eyes will see things your closeness prevents you from seeing. It's often helpful to arrange a screening where you sit in the front, watching the audience. Note deep breaths and fidgeting. Listen for snoring.

+ Did you make your point? Does your test audience agree? Ask questions. Find out if you've succeeded.

+ Are there errors? Watch the project from beginning to end at least three times. Watch once with your eyes on the VU meters. Be sure your mix is consistent. Be aware that some voices, sounds, and music can deceive you, appearing louder on your meters than they sound in the mix or vice versa.

+ Watch again with the sound turned off. Watch for flash frames. Think about where you're eyes are drawn on the screen. Be sure you haven't drawn the viewer's eyes away from something important.

+ Be critical of the especially dark shots edited back-to-back with especially bright shots. Sometimes wild luminance differences can give the impression of flash frames.

+ Watch one last time, staring right at the screen, this time with the sound turned up good and loud. Pretend you're someone who's never seen the video before and try as hard as you can to misunderstand.

+ Are there spelling errors? Nothing looks more amateurish than spelling errors. Don't expect repeat business from a client after you've misspelled that person's name or the name of the company! Check for spelling errors yourself, then invite someone else to double check your check.

If everything is in order, maybe it's time to release. Oh, yeah, that's the second old edit saying, projects aren't released, they escape.

Do yourself a favor and leave the cage door open.

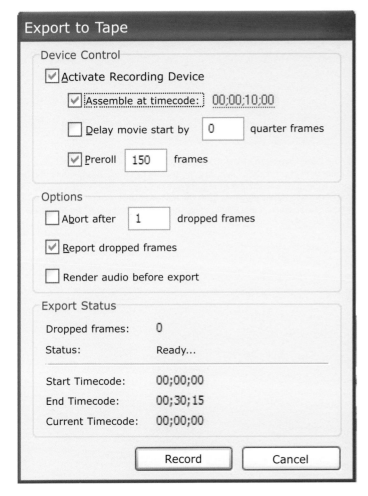

Export to Tape

Device Control

☑ Activate Recording Device

　☑ Assemble at timecode: 00;00;10;00

　☐ Delay movie start by [0] quarter frames

　☑ Preroll [150] frames

Options

☐ Abort after [1] dropped frames

☑ Report dropped frames

☐ Render audio before export

Export Status

Dropped frames:　0

Status:　Ready...

Start Timecode:　00;00;00

End Timecode:　00;30;15

Current Timecode:　00;00;00

[Record]　[Cancel]

Output
Print to tape

Now that you have all your shots edited just the way you want them, your audio sounds close to perfect, all your effects are mixed, your ducks are in a row and in full quack, it's time to get your video out there, where it can be seen by someone other than you. Here's where that FireWire link between your camera and computer will make things much easier than they've ever been for editors. The way IEEE 1394 is implemented these days, most DV camcorders are recognized by your computer, Mac or PC, as if they're long-lost friends.

You have a few ways to go here. You can print to analog media like a VHS tape, or you can move your footage digitally to DV tape from whence it came. If you want to record your video onto a VHS tape, just hook up your VHS tape machine to the same audio and video sources you're using for monitoring your edit, hit the record/play buttons on the VHS machine and play back your timeline. Keep in mind that before you start your playback, you may need to render any effects you've created. You'll probably find a Render All button in your software. If you have a slower system, this might be a good time to go get a cup of coffee, or if you have a really slow system, a long lunch. If it's a long program, you might just let it render overnight, a favorite technique of effects artists. After that, you're ready to print to either analog or DV tape.

To print to DV tape, use a tape onto which you have recorded uninterrupted video. This offers a continuous track of data that often makes everything go smoother. Put the lens cap on your camera, hit record and walk away for a while, at least as long as your edited project. Some people swear by recording black onto the tape, calling it "crystal black," but actually, any continuous video will do the same thing. Select "Print to Tape" or "Export to Tape" in your software, and you'll be presented with a number of options. The export choices you make will depend on the destination of your tape.

Export to tape

In most Export to Tape dialogue boxes, even on the most basic systems, you'll be asked to specify when you want your export to start, that is, how much black you want to see before first video. You might also be asked to set a preroll time. Preroll—time before the recording starts—allows your record deck or camera to stabilize its speed and confirm recording before your content begins.

If you're making a tape for personal use, be sure to roll your tape forward about 10 seconds so the tape will have a few seconds to pre-roll, thus stabilizing it for the impending recording.

Distributing on DVD

DVD is a wonderful distribution format! It offers tremendous video resolution—nearly twice that of the old VHS format—combined with CD quality audio. Not only are DVDs much higher quality than previous home video formats, they're cheaper to master and duplicate. Add to those advantages the fact that the saturation of DVD players, that is, the percentage of homes compared to the percentage of homes with DVD players, is on a powerful upward run. You're looking at an instant audience of people who can pick up your DVD, pop it into a nearby player, and enjoy. Whether you're producing videos with dreams of wide distribution or simply looking for a convenient way to share Megan's graduation footage with everyone in the family, DVD authoring is increasingly your best answer.

What about all that messy compression? You're in luck there, too, with most of the compression chores taken care of for you. In the early days of DVD authoring, you had to export all your files to a third-party application that would compress the video (MPEG-2) and create the proper audio files (PCM or AC-3). After that, you had to use yet another application to prepare your program for DVD burning. Now, on both Macs and PCs, this entire process can be taken care of by simply dropping your finished file onto an icon representing your DVD authoring package.

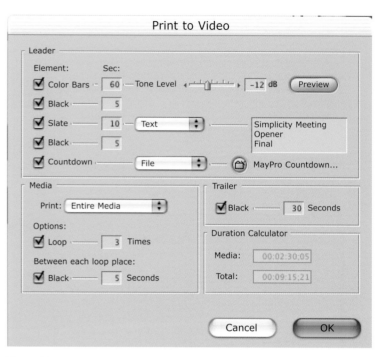

If your video is going to a TV station, it's always a good idea to first include a segment of color bars at least 30 seconds long, preferably a minute. This gives TV station engineers enough time to calibrate the video you're sending, so its colors will match all the rest of the videotapes they use. After the thirty seconds of bars, it helps to give them around five seconds of black just to give them a "launching pad" for the video.

Here's some more good news for you as a videomaker. Creating your own DVD is getting easier with every passing revision of nonlinear editing software packages. Some programs offer DVD Authoring from the Timeline, meaning you're able to place chapter markers, indeed, compose the entire DVD right from the edit timeline. Here, the NLE opens a track labeled DVD. With some software packages, a menu tool assists you in creating the interface of your DVD.

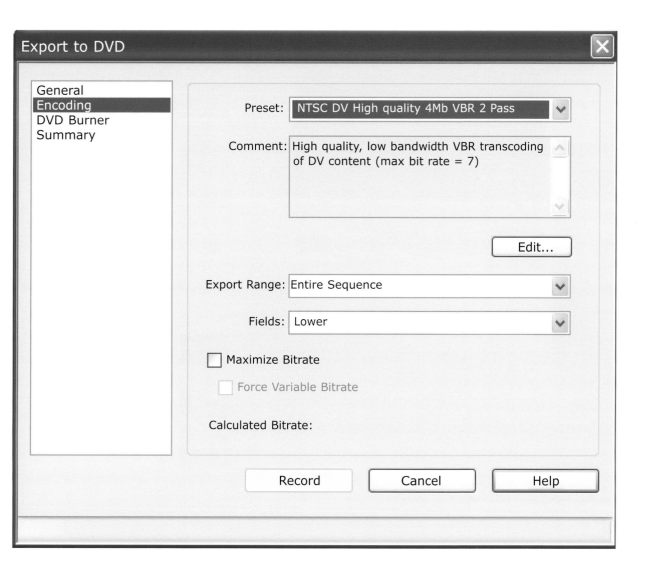

Export to DVD

In some cases, if you're not looking for fancy menus and all you want to do is lay your timeline's contents to a DVD, you can just select Export and you're given the option to export the contents of your timeline straight to DVD; no menus, no nothing—it just starts playing when inserted. No frills, but it's quick and easy. You can either go with the defaults or select compression rates, aspect ratio, and lots of other parameters. When you're ready, click record and you're off and running. Make sure there's a blank DVD in the drive, and before you know it, you'll have a disk to deliver to your client or post to Grandma.

Tip: Get a DVD burner that can handle all the popular DVD formats, like DVD+R, DVD-R, DVD-RW, DVD+RW, and even the CD-R formats. That way, you can be sure that your finished DVDs will play on just about any player. Many DVD writers feature software that's capable of DLA (drive-letter access). DLA will allow you to do double duty with your DVD burner, using it as a backup device that works just like any hard disk.

Pro-level DVD

If you're looking to create a pro-level DVD, that's a lot easier now, too. With most of the new, easy-to-use DVD authoring packages, gorgeous-looking templates are included, and some even include background music. These canned interfaces can give you an excellent jumping-off point for your creations. Where you go from there is limited only by your creativity. You can use moving backgrounds or animated picons (picture icons) where you can even put moving video inside the buttons. You have the ability to choose any typeface on your computer and animated transitions, letting you create clever ways to move from one screen to the next. Best of all, because of the increased resolution of DVD, your DV footage will look as good as it possibly can.

If you're going to create your own disk menus and buttons, pay close attention to the DVD authoring program's requirements. You'll usually have to supply a menu background and buttons to represent three states, the normal state (how the buttons look when the menu is untouched), selected state (how the buttons look when the cursor rolls over the button), and activated state (how the buttons look when the viewer hits OK or Enter).

Once your buttons are in place, you'll need to program their actions. You'll choose one button to be the default button (usually the primary Play button). You'll probably be required to designate the navigation path, choosing what should happen from one button to the next as the viewer presses the down or up arrows and the left or right arrows. This "programming" is programming in name only. It will probably involve graphic- or menu-driven if-then choices. Maybe you'll want to build in a default action as well, indicating that if the user doesn't choose a button at all in, say, thirty seconds, the disk will begin playing automatically.

The final step before burning your DVD will be testing a "disc image." Your hard drive will act as the DVD; you'll try all the buttons and watch the video segments. Watch them with a critical eye. Make sure your chapter markers are in the right place, listen to your audio, and generally become convinced you're ready to commit the project to disc.

Then hit the button and burn away. Within a short time, you'll be a DVD author, ready to wow the consumer market, dazzle the critics, or face the ultimate "tough crowd," your in-laws!

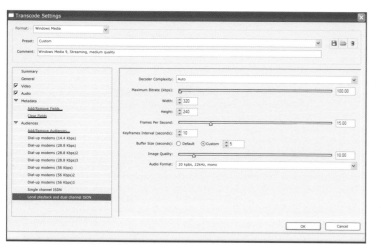

Web streaming

If you're looking to show your video to the entire world, then Web streaming is for you. Compression is the name of the game here, but you must squeeze your video down to a fraction of its original size for streaming—it'll be much smaller than that MPEG 2 file you'd make for a DVD.

Streaming formats

There are three popular format choices for Web streaming: Windows Media, Real, and QuickTime. All offer variations that can stream, that is, play while downloading, and all let you choose to create files that can instead be downloaded and watched later. Windows Media is the most common format, especially since more than 90 percent of all computers used on the Internet possess it as standard equipment. RealOne player is easy to download, though, and comes in second in popularity, with QuickTime trailing the two. All three can be played back and recorded on both Macs and PCs.

You might think that sending these huge video files over the Internet is like stuffing a basketball through a garden hose, and you'd be right. That's where codecs come in handy. The word "codec" is a shortened form of the two words "compression" and "decompression." Codecs are small software programs that make the sending of large files easier. The way they work is like this: You compress the video using a codec that makes it smaller and more easily transmitted, while your viewers decompress the file, using that same codec, so they can watch it. QuickTime, Windows Media, and Real are all simply wrappers for these codecs.

Many popular nonlinear editing packages allow you to easily export your projects to all three streaming formats, and also let you customize the bit rate and file size of your videos. The compromise you must make with streaming video is to make the frame big enough to see, while keeping the file size small enough so your viewers can watch the video without interruption. A common frame size for streaming video is 320×240, running at 15 frames per second (fps), half the frame size and rate of standard NTSC video. This would be considered medium quality and could be watched without dropping frames by viewers with an Internet connection that's at least 100kb per second. You can see that the size of the video files are immediately cut in half when you halve the number of frames in each second of video. Add to that the considerable savings achieved by halving the frame size and that big, wild video file becomes a little tamer.

If you'd like your viewers to see every frame of your video at a larger size and frame rate, you might want to prepare the file for downloading rather than streaming. A downloaded video file can't be watched until the entire file is present on a computer but, because the file is being read from your relatively speedy internal hard drive, you can be assured that most computers will be able to play back that file without interruption.

Compressing your final product for streaming is a lot easier than it used to be, with many nonlinear editing packages letting you simply export your files directly from that application into the streaming format of your choice. There are also more sophisticated third-party compression applications that offer more choices and control of bit rates, codecs, and frame sizes.

Streaming video is the great democratizer, giving anyone with a DV camera, an edit program, compression abilities, and an Internet connection the chance to speak to the world. I'd like to think, the more you've embraced the contents of this book, the better you'll become at video production, and the better you become at video production, the more people will seek you out, understand what you're saying, and embrace your message. So plan, shoot, edit, stream; let's hear what you have to say!

Tip: When compressing video for streaming, keep in mind that some users have a fast connection to the Internet, while others are still using dial-up for all their Web surfing. It's common to create two, or even three, different-sized files to accommodate various download speed capabilities of your potential audience.

Glossary

180° rule The 180° rule protects continuity and screen direction by establishing a "horizontal line of action" between two subjects. If all shots of the subjects are taken from one side of the line of action, when edited together, the shots will convey the correct spatial relationship between objects.

30° rule, or **30% rule** The 30% rule states that less than a 30% change in picture framing or camera angle will result in an undesirable jump cut when the shots are edited back to back.

AGC AGC, or Automatic Gain Control, constantly monitors and compensates for variations in audio levels. AGC is to audio what auto iris is to video.

Aliasing Look very closely at a sharp, diagonal line on a video screen. If it appears to stair-step, that's aliasing, sometimes called the "jaggies."

Ambient sound Tell everyone in the room to be dead quiet. What's left—the street noise, the air conditioning, the radio downstairs—that's all ambient sound. It's also referred to as buzz. The buzz is what makes a location sound like a location. While everyone is dead quiet, record a minute or so. You'll thank yourself in the edit.

Analog Using ones and zeros, a digital system re-creates frequency curves by saying very clearly if a point is on the curve or not. In analog signals, the circuits attempt to re-create frequency curves by describing the shape of the curve. It is imprecise and much is lost after a series of descriptions or "dubs." This loss is called generation loss. Because there can't be much confusion between one or zero, off or on, digital systems suffer negligible generation loss.

ANNCR In the audio section of a script, indicates announcer.

Antialiasing Antialiasing is the electronic smoothing applied to the undesirable artifacts described in "aliasing."

Aperture Aperture means, literally, "opening," the opening that lets light into a camera. The size of the aperture is determined by adjusting the iris. There's a direct relationship between aperture and f-stop. The higher the f-stop, the less light is admitted. Most cameras return the best image (technically speaking) in the middle of the range, about f-5.6.

Apple boxes Standard-sized closed plywood boxes used to do anything from getting a tripod up 6 inches (15 cm) to evening out the height of two actors standing side by side.

Apple boxes in the U.S. come in full (12" × 12" × 24" [30 cm × 30 cm × 60 cm]), half (6" × 12" × 24" [15 cm × 30 cm × 60 cm]), and quarter sizes (3" × 12" × 24" [7.5 cm × 30 cm × 60 cm]).

Artifact Artifacts are undesirable errors and distortions introduced into a picture by manipulations such as image adjustments, digital effects, compression and decompression, speed changes, and scale changes.

Aspect Ratio The aspect ratio refers to the proportions of the television screen and image. The ratio of normal NTSC width-to-height is 4:3. Widescreen is predominantly 16:9.

Available light Before any light is added, the ambient, natural light on a scene is the available light.

Backlight A light set behind the subject to enhance the edges of a subject and separate it from the background. The degree of backlight determines to what extent your subject is silhouetted. Backlight can also refer to a camera setting that opens the iris a touch, compensating for excessive backlighting on a subject.

Backpedaling Shooting while walking backwards is called backpedaling.

Back-story Everything that went on before we joined the story is called the back-story. The back-story often explains why characters act and react as they do.

Bandwidth Just as the diameter of a garden hose determines how many gallons per hour it can carry, bandwidth determines how big a signal can be pumped along the signal path. Lack of bandwidth explains why video can't be fed down a phone line without considerable compression.

Barn doors Four movable metal flaps attached to the front edge of a lighting instrument used to restrict the spread of illumination.

Bars and Tone Bars and tone are television industry standard signals used to insure record and playback consistency. "Bars" is short for color bars. With the proper monitoring equipment, specifically a waveform monitor and a vectorscope, playback can be calibrated to match exactly the levels of information as they were originally recorded. Tone is also a reference signal and, with a VU meter, can be adjusted for a consistency in audio levels.

Batch capture An automatic function of nonlinear edit systems allowing unattended digitization of previously logged clips.

BG BG is short for background. BG can be used to refer to background sounds or background as an audio level. Visually, background can refer to screen elements in the background as opposed to the foreground or it can refer to action taking place in the background of a shot.

Black balance An adjustment done to insure the integrity of camera black regarding luminance and color levels.

Black wrap Thick, black metal foil often used on the front of a lighting instrument to direct light in irregular ways.

Black Although one might call any blank screen black, "true black" is a video source, not the absence of video. Black must meet precise engineering standards and contains as much video information as any other frame of video.

Blown out Overexposed, sometimes intentionally.

BNC connector BNC stands for bayonet nut connector and refers to an industry standard twist-lock connector for coaxial cable.

Boom microphone Any mic (usually a unidirectional mic) mounted on a fishpole or boom.

Booming Using a mic on a fishpole or boom.

Bounce card Cardboard or foam core material, usually bright white, used to reflect soft fill light into dark areas.

Bracketing Varying exposure on successive takes to be sure you have one that's perfect.

Break Break is what you yell to end a take if it's not going well and isn't likely to get better.

Breakup Surfaces tend to look more natural when the light seen on their surface is more random. To accomplish this randomness, the lighting director will often call for a little "breakup" on a surface. See *Gobo, Cookie*.

Brightness A reference to the overall, average light level seen on a monitor screen. Also referred to as luminance.

Broadcast quality If a signal meets FCC technical broadcast specifications, it's broadcast quality, though the term has been hijacked to imply a level of aesthetic quality as well.

B-roll There was a time in broadcast history when, in order to dissolve between two shots on the air, each needed to be on a separate source, usually a film roll, an A-roll, and a B-roll. In today's nonlinear terms the A-roll and B-roll can be thought of as two video tracks in a timeline. The term has stuck and generally refers to any secondary footage used to cover interview or track. See *Cover*.

Buzz Ambient sound, often recorded to add under clean studio-recorded dialogue as a "buzz track" in order make it sound more natural.

C-47s Wood clothespins, commonly used for holding gels to frames and barn doors, so called because on traditional Hollywood budget forms they fall on line C-47.

Canon connector Also called an XLR, this large, barrel-shaped, locking three-pin connector has been a standard for carrying balanced audio for generations.

Capture card Capture cards are designed to process video, converting it to digital form for recording on a computer's hard disk.

Capturing Digitizing

CCD A CCD, or charge coupled device, is a silicon chip that converts light to electricity. A camera's lens focuses light onto the CCD(s), which reacts by producing signals that are converted to video information. When it comes to CCDs, three are better than one and always, the bigger, the better.

Chromakey When chromakeying, the screen image is examined for areas of predetermined color, usually green or blue. Those areas are then cut from the frame allowing other images to show through. Chromakey is the method used to put weather people in front of electronic weather maps.

Chroma Chroma is color level, often quantified as saturation.

Clearscan Some camera shutters allow fine adjustment through the frequency range matching standard refresh rates of CRT computer monitors. The result is shutter speeds can be found that eliminate the phenomenon of hum bars, the pesky thick black or white scanning bars often seen when one points a camera at a CRT computer monitor.

Close-up See *Framing*.

Codec Shortened from compress/decompress, a software algorithm applied to video to squeeze it into less storage space or down pipes with smaller diameters (see *Bandwidth*).

Color bars See *Bars and Tone*.

Color depth Color depth, usually expressed as 8-, 16-, 32-, or 64-bit; the number of bits per pixel, used to define colors. The deeper, the better.

Color temperature Color temperature is a reference cameras use to understand how to display white. Once white is established, called white balancing, the rest of the color spectrum falls into place. Color temperature is expressed on the Kelvin temperature scale. Common values range from 3,200°K for the more golden indoor, incandescent sources and 5,600°K for the bluer light of the sun. Further left and right, the very red light of a candle would fall closer to 2,600°K and the very blue color in outdoor shadows closer to 6,200°K.

Component Component video is divided into three color channels, each combined with the appropriate luminance information. Component transmission requires three wires and reduces loss typically suffered in composite video transmission with all color information combined on one wire.

Composite Video Composite video uses a transmission scheme where both luminance and color information are combined and transmitted on a single wire.

Compression Video files are often compressed using various codecs to make them smaller and more manageable. Every time video is compressed and then decompressed, there is both a loss in quality and the introduction of artifacts. Highly compressed codecs are called "lossy." Lightly compressed codecs approach "lossless." One advantage of the DV format is, though the video compression ratio is nearly 5:1, it's compressed in the camera and generally dealt with in the compressed form.

Continuity Continuity speaks to believability. Say someone is standing in one shot. Then, when we cut to the next shot, that same person is sitting—the laws of physics have been violated. No one can sit "instantaneously." The continuity is broken if the meal is finished in one shot, then just starting in the next, or if the woman was wearing a red dress in one shot and a blue dress in the next. All these edits that break continuity are called jump cuts and should be avoided unless intentional.

Contrast Contrast is the difference between the luminance values of the brightest and darkest areas of an image.

Cookie Cookies are used to add patterns or simply break up light thrown on a surface. Sometimes, cookies are made to look like Venetian blinds or window mullions but just as often the cookie is cut into a random pattern. The cookie, also known as a cuculoris, is named for early Hollywood cinematographer George "Cookie" Cuculoris. See also *Gobo and Breakup*.

Cover The term cover refers to the video shown during narration. Usually the term denotes nonspecific shots as opposed to scenes that are carefully designed to appear during specific lines of narration. Cover is often used to hide a talking head. See *B-roll*.

Crane shot A shot in which the camera is raised or lowered vertically, usually while the camera is mounted on a crane.

Crawl When text information is displayed in a crawl, the letters begin appearing from the right side of the screen and travel across the screen horizontally. News departments use the crawl to display bulletins during regular programming. The crawl has taken on the connotation of "special" information

Crosscutting Editing between two simultaneous or otherwise related actions is called crosscutting. For instance, we've all seen crosscutting between the Canadian Mountie trying to untie Nell from the train tracks and the approaching train.

C-stands C-stand is short for Century Stand, a common articulated stand used for setting lighting instruments, cutters, flags, and rigs.

Cube tap An AC adapter that turns a single outlet into three outlets.

Cut The cut is the simplest of transitions and involves the direct replacement of one image by another. Traditionally, a cut implies continuity and chronology. Simple cuts don't stand out when they join expected images or follow a simple narrative. Cuts used to join odd or discontinuous images can have a jarring or surreal effect. Quick cuts can be used to relate images in a montage. Very quick cuts, a frame or two in length, of slightly varied images is animation.

Cutaway A cutaway is a shot inserted into the main camera shot or shot sequence. A cutaway can be used to show a simultaneous action, a reaction, or to focus attention on something. Typical cutaways might be the shot of the clock as the tech tries to defuse the bomb or the shot of the person listening to the supposedly private conversation. Cutaways are also widely used to cover potential jump cuts. In an interview situation, if portions of the speaker's remarks are cut out you'll have a jump cut unless you insert a shot, often of a person listening.

Cutters A variety of commercially available cloth screens stretched over wire frames, designed to be inserted into the knuckles of C-stands, used to reduce light by throwing shadows or partial shadows. See *flags*.

Cutting the frame For visual interest a director will call for action between the main action and the camera. That action, a person walking by, a car passing, and the like, is said to cut the frame.

Cyc Called either a Cyc (pronounced like psych), Cyclorama, or sometimes a "sweep," studios often finish one or two walls with a big radius instead of a square corner where the walls meet the floor. When well lit, a sweep can give the impression of going to infinity.

Data rate The data rate indicates the quantity of digital information passing a point in a given amount of time, usually measured in megabytes per second. Data rate is especially important in video production because a specific amount of data per second is required to produce a full-motion, full-speed moving picture.

dB dB or decibel is the unit of loudness.

Depth of field Though the camera may be focused on an object 4 feet (1.2 m) in front of the lens, objects between 2 feet (0.6 m) and 6 feet (1.8 m) from the lens might appear to be in focus as well. This range of acceptable focus is called the depth of field.

Digital video DV or digital video is a generic term indicating the image is recorded as digital information. There are several formats that include DV in their name like DVCPRO, DVCAM, DVCPRO25, and DVCPRO50. Digital video formats are popular for many reasons including the fact that they hold up better through editing and image manipulation than their analog brethren.

Digital Information recorded and expressed as a series of ones and zeros. See *Analog* for a discussion of digital versus analog video signal processing.

Digital8 A DV format that records on 8mm or Hi8 tapes.

Digitize To digitize is to capture video footage in digital form within a nonlinear editing computer. *See Capture and Redigitize.*

Dissolve A dissolve is a transition where one video image blends with and then becomes a second video image. In a standard narrative sense, a dissolve usually indicates a passage of time, a change in location or both. By traveling only halfway through a dissolve, creating a half-dissolve, two images can be combined on-screen and in the viewer's mind. A dissolve is also called a mix, a mix dissolve, a cross fade, or more rarely, a lap dissolve.

Dolly A wheeled camera platform, often run on track, allowing smooth horizontal camera movement. High-end dollies offer some, but relatively limited, up and down movement.

Dollying Moving a camera toward, away from, or with a subject, mostly in a single plane.

Down convert Dubbing content from a higher quality format to a lower quality format. For example, dubbing high definition to any other format.

DPI Dots per inch is a measurement of resolution in the print world. Television monitors and, therefore, television images are limited to 72 DPI.

Drop frame There is a discrepancy between the nominal 30 frames per second we expect in video and the actual frame rate of 29.97 frames per second. The result is an extra 108 frames, or 3.6 seconds every hour. In the world of broadcast TV, where everything runs by the clock, those extra seconds are troublesome. Drop frame time code eliminates the discrepancy by dropping frame *numbers,* not actual frames.

DTV DTV, or digital television, refers to standard definition (SD) or high definition (HD) TV signals broadcast as digital information.

Dub A copy made of a video program is a dub. An exact digital copy is called a clone.

Duration Duration is a length of time measured in frames of video. Durations are used to express shot lengths and transition.

ENG ENG is an acronym for electronic news gathering. The term became popular at the time when some news was still being shot on film. "ENG style" has come to refer to a "run and gun," limited take, lower budget style of production shooting.

EFP EFP is short for electronic field production. This term rose from the need to differentiate between film production and videotape production.

Establishing shot Usually a wide shot used to orient the viewers and introduce a location.

EXT, INT Abbreviations used in a script to specify exterior and interior locations.

Eye light An eye light is a tiny light set to add a sparkle to someone's eyes.

Eye lines Follow someone's gaze and you're following their eye line. For continuity's sake, if people are looking at each other or the same thing, their eyelines should match.

Eyebrow A small, metal square on a gooseneck used right at the lens to keep light from shining directly into the lens and causing lens flare. Also called a French flag.

Fade A fade-in or a fade-up is simply a dissolve from black to a shot or graphic. A fade-out is the opposite, a dissolve from a shot or graphic to black. A quick fade-out followed by a quick fade-in is called a "dip" to black.

Field A video image is made up of 30 frames per second and each frame is made up of two fields—two entire scans of the screen filling in every other horizontal line. The alternating horizontal lines of the two field level scans are combined or interlaced to form a single frame. In the PAL standard, it's 25 frames per second and 50 fields.

Fill Either a lighting instrument or a bounce card used to add extra light where needed.

FireWire (IEEE 1394) FireWire is a data transmission protocol with sufficient throughput to allow compressed video, audio, and machine control commands, in digital form, to travel simultaneously. FireWire, developed by Apple, is also called IEEE 1394, a numbered standard of the Institute for Electronic and Electrical Engineers.

Flag A device, sometimes a metal sheet, sometimes dark cloth or screen stretched over a metal frame, used to block unwanted light throw.

Flare Lens flares are usually round, often rainbow colored artifacts created by light bouncing among elements within the lens itself.

Flash Frame A flash frame, or simply a flash, is an extraneous frame of video at an edit point.

Flashback Defying chronology by jumping back to an earlier point in time, often to fill in elements of a character's back-story.

Flats Scenery pieces, usually walls.

Focus Rotating a lens' focus ring for maximum sharpness and clarity.

Foldover An indication of overexposure in some camera viewfinders where the brightest, whitest areas of the screen reverse to black at some preset plateau, say 110 percent.

Frame rate The number of frames per second (fps) recorded and/or played back. The three most common frame rates are 30 fps in NTSC (the North American television standard), 25 fps in PAL (the European television standard), and 24 fps for film worldwide. Note that although NTSC is nominally 30 fps and PAL is 25 fps, they are actually 29.97 fps and 24.98 fps respectively. *See also Drop frame, Time code, Field.*

Framing Framing refers to the position of your screen elements within a frame of video; as in "she's almost out of the frame" or "I don't like that framing." Frames are described by a series of designations starting with the extreme close-up (ECU), then the close-up (CU), extreme tight shot (ETS), tight shot (TS), medium shot (MS), medium wide shot (MWS), wide shot (WS), and finally the extreme wide shot (EWS). See chapter 4/On Location/Rolling Tape/Framing for a complete discussion of camera framing and examples.

Freeze frame A still image created by designating a single frame (usually including both fields) and repeating it for as long as needed.

French flag See *Eyebrow.*

f-stop See *Aperture.*

Full sound Full sound is sound at full volume. Narration is always full sound unless manipulated for effect. Sometimes the natural sound is brought full as a method of pacing or transitioning.

Gaffer's tape Though easily ripped when necessary, this strong cloth-backed adhesive tape adheres firmly, yet releases leaving little glue residue or damage. Gaffer's tape is as indispensable to production as duct tape is to home and auto repair. Duct tape is not gaffer's tape, it just looks like gaffer's tape.

Gain Gain is the level of amplification expressed in dB.

Generation loss Due to the nature of analog signal processing, there is often information lost every time video is dubbed or edited. That loss is called generation loss. There is little generation loss associated with digital signal processing. See *Analog*.

Glass Lens, as in "That new lens sure is crisp. What a great piece of glass!"

Gobo Gobo is short for go-between, referring to a flat metal pattern placed between the lamp and the lens of a lighting instrument. Gobos are commercially cut in the shape of logos, Venetian blinds, sunbursts, skylines, etc. See also *Breakup* and *Cookie*.

Gofer You know, "Hey you, go fer coffee."

GUI GUI (pronounced "gooey") stands for graphical user interface, the face a software product presents to the user. The friendliness of the GUI is often a good measure of the software.

HDTV High-definition television, a loose term referring to a group of digital high-resolution television standards, usually with a 16:9 screen ratio as opposed to the older 4:3 convention.

Head room Head room is the amount of space between the subject of your picture and the top of the frame. Head room should be adjusted with regard to the safe action area.

Head A tripod consists of legs and head, the actual device to which the camera attaches. The head does the actual panning and tilting.

Heat Electrical power, as in "Let's get some heat on this stinger."

Holding air Holding air means establishing a frame with the intention of allowing the action to enter the empty frame. A director might "hold air" allowing the murderer's knife to rise into the frame.

Iris The adjustable opening regulating the amount of light allowed into a camera. See *Aperture*.

JBOD JBOD is short for just a bunch of disks. Unlike a RAID array, a JBOD does not have a striping scheme, making the drives interdependent.

J-K-L J-K-L refers to the common keyboard control convention where the J key plays the source in reverse, the K key stops the source, and the L key plays the source forward.

Jump Cut A jump cut is any edit that defies continuity. When constructing a narrative, where continuity is important, jump cuts are a bad thing. When creating eye candy, such as in music videos, jump cuts are merely another acceptable technique. See *Continuity*.

Key light The key light is the primary light source in a scene. Most other lights (the fill light, the back light, etc) are set in relation to the key light. The key light need not be a lighting instrument but can be the Sun, the sunlight through a window, or spill light from the street.

Key As a verb, to cut a hole in a picture, usually to fill with another source. A weather forecaster is keyed over his weather maps. As a noun, the result of keying, as in "Nice key!" There are several types of keys, all based on criteria used to cut the hole (color, brightness, a matte, etc).

Keyframes Keyframes are cusps; points in the timeline where values such as opacity, size, or speed change. Keyframing allows the application of an effect to vary over time.

Lavalier Lavaliers are the most common microphone used for recording dialogue in the field. Often as small as a match head, lavalieres can be either hard wired or wireless and are usually held in place by a tie-clasp or tie-pin type mic clip.

LCD LCD, or liquid crystal display, is the lightweight flat-screen device we see both as fold-out camera viewfinders and in the form of full-size desktop flat-screen displays.

Lead room Lead room is the space allowed in front of a subject in order for the framing to appear natural. The frame should lead the subject left if they are looking screen left and right if they are looking screen right. Lead room is also called nose room.

Leatherman A combination tool often carried by grips, gaffers, and gofers on set. Gerber is another popular brand.

Lens shade Also called a lens hood, this inverted cone is attached to the front of a lens to help shade the forward element and cut down on lens flare.

Lensing Lensing is another expression for shooting.

Letterbox A term invented to describe the formatting method of showing a 16:9 picture on a 4:3 screen by adding a black masking band at the top and bottom. Nowadays, it is also common to see black bars added to the left and right sides of a 4:3 picture being shown on a 16:9 screen. This is known as poster framing.

Limbo A lighting style where everything but the subject of the shot is allowed to fall off into darkness.

Live shot A live shot is a remote transmission broadcast as it happens.

Live-to-tape Anything recorded in real time, as if it were being broadcast live.

Looping Looping is repeating a short video or audio clip to produce a continuous clip longer than the original short clip.

Lower third Lower third refers to the lower third of the screen where name, title, and location information is traditionally displayed.

Luminance key When luminance keying, the screen image is examined for luminance values either above or below a predetermined level. Those areas are then cut from the frame allowing other images to show through.

Luminance Luminance refers to the brightness of an image.

Mammal on a stick A shotgun microphone mounted on a fishpole, covered with a good deal of fake fur.

Masking Just as when painting, when you might use masking tape to keep paint off an area, an electronic mask defines an area either to be affected or an area to be left alone. See also *Matte*.

Master The actual tape containing your finished, edited product is your master.

Match edit Matches are used to maintain continuity or connect two shots. Match-on-action is a technique used mostly to maintain continuity but can be equally effective to connect two different people or objects performing roughly the same action. If in the first shot of a sequence a woman is getting ready to stand up, then the next shot should complete the motion to avoid a jump cut. If the match-on-action is not properly timed, the edit looks bad. Match-on-action can also be used to draw a connection or as a transitional device within a story. Three common matches used as transitional devices are the match-on-shape, match-on-object, and the match-on-color.

Matte A mask, often an active, changing mask referred to as a traveling matte. For instance, if you intended to replace the football a player was carrying with a liter bottle of Pepsi, a traveling matte would have to be created to cut the football out of the player's hand.

Medium shot (MS) See *Framing*.

Mic Microphone (pronounced "mike").

Mixer A device allowing a number of individual sound source outputs to be electronically combined at appropriate gain levels into a single output.

Monitor As a verb, to pay close attention to the quality of an audio or video signal. As a noun, monitor refers to the screens you watch in order to pay close attention to the quality of an audio or video signal. This may seem like a minor point, but what you own at home is a television set; it has a tuner and a speaker. What you see in a professional setting, with its very high quality picture and no speaker, is a monitor. Large, studio-quality speakers are referred to as audio monitors.

MOS In news, candid comments gathered from the arbitrary man-on-the-street. In film production MOS means "without sound." Why MOS and not WOS? Well, there are two prevailing explanations. The most logical, MOS is an arcane reference to a long-passed system where the sound recordist regulated system voltage and, therefore, camera speed (which is why we still hear "Speed!" to indicate the camera is rolling). When the sound motors were run on silent shots simply to regulate camera speed it was noted on the film reel by writing motor only synch or MOS. The explanation I prefer is the German director (some say Fritz Lang) indicating a shot would be silent by declaring, "Ve'll shoot mitout sound!" or MOS.

MPEG MPEG stands for Motion Picture Experts Group. They are responsible for several widely accepted video codecs.

NARR Narrator

Natural sound Natural sound is the actual sound recorded at the same time as the video. Natural sound is often called nat sound, SOT (short for sound on tape), or simply nat.

Needle drop The term needle drop refers to music or sound effect tracks pulled from a record library.

Neutral density filter A filter that reduces overall light entering the lens without affecting color.

NLE NLE, or nonlinear editing, is a generic term applied to computer-based video edit systems where clips of video and audio are positioned as desired, usually by cutting-and-pasting or dragging-and-dropping along a representative timeline.

NTSC NTSC is the predominant North American video standard of 525 scan lines, presented at 29.97 frames per second, 59.94 interlaced fields per second.

Omnidirectional mic A microphone that has a circular, non-directional pick-up pattern.

Overdriven Overdriven means being fed a signal at a higher level than the system was designed to accept. Mics, mixers, recorders, and wireless receivers are the usual victims of this electronic assault.

Overscan Overscan represents an estimate of the portion of a video signal (approximately 10 percent) that won't be seen due to the physical frame around the edges of most television sets. This estimate is often represented by a lined overlay in viewfinders and monitors demarking "safe action." The presumption is that anything happening within safe action will be seen on most television sets. Overscan is sometimes called "home scan." Underscan is a setting available on many professional monitors that shrinks the image by a little more than 10 percent so that the image can be seen all the way to the edges (as it would be seen if projected).

Over-the-shoulder Over-the-shoulder is a common convention in shot/reverse shot situations where the back of one person's head and one shoulder is included in the front shot of the person to whom they're talking.

PAL PAL (phase alternate line) is the original European video standard of 625 lines, presented at 25 frames per second, 50 interlaced fields.

Pan The left and right swivel of a camera around a vertical axis is called a pan, as in "Pan left!" Pan is also used as an indication of whether a stereo source is directed more to one channel than the other. In "center" position the left and right channels are fed equally.

Pixel A television image is made up of hundreds of thousands of tiny dots, each with a luminance and color value. Any one of those dots is referred to as a pixel or picture element.

PD PD is short for producer/director. See also *WD* and *Preditor.*

Playhead In the world of nonlinear editing, the playhead is essentially the cursor when scrubbing a timeline. In some NLEs, it's called the current time indicator, or CTI.

Plot points Points within the arc of a script upon which the plot turns. For instance, when Rick receives the letters of transit in Casablanca, that is a plot point. When he recognizes Elsa in his club, that is another plot point.

Plug-ins Most nonlinear editing, effects, and paint software accept specially written subprograms designed to perform specific functions. For example, various companies have written plug-ins designed to alter video to give it the look of film.

Pop When a mic is placed too close and/or directly in front of a speaker's mouth, certain consonants can overdrive the mic element yielding an undesirable popping sound. This can happen on B's and K's but more often you'll hear people pop their P's.

Potting down "Potting it down" is the same thing as "turning it down," a reference to adjusting a variable electronic resistor called a potentiometer.

POV POV means point of view and implies actions are perceived from one person's frame of reference. A camera shot can be from the POV of a character or even the audience. A script can also be described as being from one person's POV.

Preditor Preditor is short for producer/editor. With the proliferation of desktop edit systems, a more and more common job description. See also *PD* and *WD.*

Presence Presence describes the degree to which audio sounds natural. When dialogue is dubbed in a studio, it lacks the presence of dialogue recorded on location. This is corrected by adding ambience or buzz track.

Prosumer A contraction of "professional" and "consumer," prosumer is used to describe equipment that, often to the surprise of manufacturers, serves both the high-end consumer market and the low-end production market.

Push-push A button that when pushed once engages a setting and when pushed again returns to the original setting is called push-push. The button on the end of a retractable ballpoint pen is a push-push.

QuickTime One of the most common standardized software wrappers for various video codecs, developed by Apple and widely used by video editing, compression, and effects software.

Rack focus Turning the focus ring on a lens to shift emphasis from one object in the frame to another is called a rack focus shot.

RAID RAID stands for redundant array of inexpensive disks. The real utility in RAID arrays comes in how they are striped. Some use teamwork to allow their disks to be accessed faster. Others are configured to compensate if another disk fails by rebuilding the data from redundant files stored elsewhere in the RAID.

Rasterizing Rasterizing is the process of squeezing all variables out of an image, often a paint image, and flattening it into a simple bitmap image.

RCA connector A very common two-conductor, unbalanced connector often used on consumer and prosumer A/V equipment. There are often red and white plugs for the stereo audio channels and a yellow plug for video.

Reaction A reaction shot might be a shot of the person listening to the on-camera speaker or a shot of the crowd as the aerialist hangs by a wire, swinging precariously above the stage.

Real time Real time is true to the clock. Digitizing footage is usually done in real time; a minute of footage takes a minute to digitize. In the context of effects and editing programs, any effect added to the video that can play back instantaneously, without waiting to render, is considered real time (often abbreviated RT).

Rendering Rendering is the internal number crunching a computer must do to display an image the operator has specified. Special effects, or depending on how slow a system might be, simple effects will often require rendering. Real-time effects are effects that can be processed instantaneously and don't require rendering.

Resolution The ability of a system (cameras, monitors, recorders, etc) to express fine detail is called resolution.

RF RF is short for radio frequency. Wireless mics, because they transmit and receive on radio frequencies, are often called RF mics. RF, referring to stray radio frequency transmissions, is often named as the culprit in many situations where electronic systems suffer interference. The resulting interference is called "noise." See *Wireless mic.*

Rim light A light set to draw edges on a subject.

RS 422 A machine control protocol common on older Beta, 1", ¾", and professional grade VHS decks, available still on most DV decks.

Run and gun A term often used by news and documentary shooters indicating a tight shooting schedule.

Rundown The rundown, broken into timed segments indicating the position of commercial breaks, stories, and so on, is an outline of a production.

Running time The running time is the program length to a designated point. See *TRT.*

Safe action Even considering the variability of overscan on home sets, action confined to the safe action area should "get home." There is often a marking for safe action in camera (especially professional camera) viewfinders. Since the safe action area is a "worst case" limit, you are reasonably safe in pushing the limit slightly.

Safe title The safe title area is even further inside the safe action area. If you limit your on-screen text information to the safe title area, even on the most misaligned TV sets, the viewer will be able to read it. Again, as a "worst case" limit, you are safe in pushing the limit slightly.

Safety The extra "good take" you roll, just in case something went wrong with the take you liked best, is your safety. An extra copy of your finished master program is your safety master.

Saturation Saturation is the difference between a dark red and a pastel pink. Saturation can be thought of as the strength or deepness of a color.

Scene Loose subdivisions within a script. A scene's limits might be defined by plot point, location, characters, or subject.

Screen direction Perceived direction of movement or action relative to the TV screen is screen direction. Screen direction is critical in chase and action scenes. Screen direction is intimately related to the 180° rule.

Scrim A wire screen placed on a light to cut down its brightness.

Scrolling Rolling credits from the bottom of the screen upward.

Scrubbing In nonlinear editing, viewing your sequence or clips at a variable rate by dragging your cursor, or playhead, along the scrubber bar or timeline.

SCSI SCSI stands for Small Computer System Interface and is often chosen to connect storage drives and computers because of the high throughput and sustained data transfer rates.

Set jacks Triangular supports clamped to the rear side of flats to keep them standing.

Shock mount A shock mount is a mic mount where rubber (sometimes rubber bands) or foam are used to isolate a microphone from handling noise and vibration.

Shooting ratio The ratio of raw footage acquired to footage actually used in the final edit. Thirty hours of footage acquired for a one hour show is a 30:1 shooting ratio.

Shot bags Originally filled with lead shot, now more often filled with sand, shot bags are used to add stability by weighing down light stands or other rigs on a set.

Shot reverse shot Shot reverse shot is a convention employed when shooting two people in a conversational orientation. One shot is over the shoulder of speaker B looking at speaker A. The shot over the shoulder of speaker A looking at speaker B is called the reverse shot. See *180° rule, Over the shoulder*.

Shotgun microphone A shotgun mic, named for its long barrel, is unidirectional and excludes most sound outside of its narrow pattern.

Shutter Like the mechanical shutters on film cameras, the electronic shutters on digital cameras limit to fractions of a second the amount of time light will be gathered. Fast shutter settings reduce the amount of light available and require the iris to be opened to compensate. See also *Clearscan*.

Slate The slate is a screen full of information at the beginning of a production listing the title, client, producer, production house, length, airdates, engineer, and any other information that would assist in identifying people, product, or contents of the videotape. Slate can also refer to the traditional clap board used to record scene and reel information on film shoots.

SMPTE Society of Motion Picture and Television Engineers.

Sound bites Selected cuts from longer interview clips are called soundbites. It's often said of good communicators that they have the ability to speak in soundbites.

Sound blankets Quilted blankets, like the ones movers use to cushion furniture, spread around a set, on floors or very close walls, to deaden reflected sound. They're also called furniture pads or furni pads.

Sound under When an audio source is potted down so as not to interfere with other full sound audio, it is referred to as sound under. Sound under implies that the audio was at full volume before being potted down.

Special effects Sometimes noted as SFX, FX, or SPFX, film special effects are almost always used to simulate some scene, action, or situation impossible (or too expensive) to create in reality. Just about every frame of *Star Wars I* and *II* are special effect shots. Special effects has also come to denote digital effects such as explosions and kaleidoscopes created in paint, visual effects, or video editing software, often with the help of plug-ins.

Spike To mark with tape or chalk to establish position, as in, "Spike the location of that chair then get it out of my way."

Spill Unintentional illumination is called spill light.

Split-field bars SMPTE developed this standard set of bars for ease of machine set-up. Bright white, plus critical levels of black are represented. Additionally, each bar contains blocks of opposite color value for luminance matching.

Spot A commercial.

Spray the area Rather than going in with a script, often documentary and news shooters enter a situation and shoot what they see or spray the area.

Sticks A tripod and head together is often called a "set of sticks."

Stinger An electrical extension cord.

Storyboard The storyboard is a series of illustrations depicting the visual progression of a story.

Streaming video Streaming video is played as it downloads over an Internet connection.

Strike "Strike the set!" is a command issued at the end of a shoot indicating it's safe to begin breaking down the set and putting away equipment.

Super Type, graphics, or logos superimposed over video. See *Lower thirds, Titles*.

S-video A video signal better than composite but not as good as component.

Talent Talent refers to the people who appear on camera or as voice-only narrators.

Talking head A talking head is a person either speaking to an interviewer or directly to the camera. The shot is usually a fairly tight head and shoulders shot with little else going on in the frame. Talking heads are considered visually dull and beg cover. But then, that all depends on what the talking heads are saying. See *B-roll, Cover*.

Throughline Characters in stories will have an emotional and experiential arc, for example changing from someone who often surrenders to someone who stands and fights. This progression of the character is called the throughline. Since most films and videos are shot out of order, it's important for actors to have a clear understanding of their character's throughline.

Tilt The angling up and down of a camera around a horizontal axis is called a tilt as in "Tilt up!"

Time code Time code is a system by which each frame of video is electronically assigned a unique and individual number that can be read and reacted to by the camera and edit computer. See *Drop frame.*

Timeline A timeline is a specially purposed window in most video editing programs where a graphic representation of edit sequences (video and audio sources arranged over time) is displayed. See *Sequence.*

Titles Text and graphics on screen, usually at the beginning and end. See *Supers.*

Transition A transition is a change from one on-screen image to another. The cut, the dissolve, and the wipe are three kinds of transitions. Transitions have meanings that aid in visual storytelling.

TRT TRT, or total running time, is the program length from beginning to end.

Trucking Moving the camera horizontally left or right, usually while the camera is mounted on a wheeled pedestal. Also called "tracking."

Underscan Underscan is a setting available on many professional monitors and viewfinders that shrinks the screen image enough to allow the true electronic edges of the image to be seen and inspected. See *Overscan.*

Updub Dubbing content from a lower quality format to a higher quality format, for instance, dubbing from any other format to high definition. Also called up-rezzing. Updubbing is also used to refer to redigitizing footage at a higher resolution.

Vertical interval The "bit between the bottom of one image and the top of the next" on video or TV screens if you allow the picture to "roll"—lose vertical hold. Technically, it's the time when the electron beam that is scanning to form the image is turned off so it can fly back to the top of the screen. Signals imposed into the vertical interval is often used for Vertical Interval Timecode (VITC, often pronounced "vit-see"), test signals and teletext or closed captioning.

Videographer A term, coined in the 1970s to distinguish between cinematographers who shoot film and those who shoot video.

Voice-over Voice-over, often noted as VO, is the narration, announce, or interview sound played over cover video.

VTR Videotape recorder.

Waveform monitor Mimicking standalone waveform monitors, most NLE programs offer digital waveform monitors that allow composite video to be graphically displayed for adjustment against luminance standards.

WD WD is short for writer/director. See also *PD* and *Preditor.*

White balance A white balance is an internal reference cameras need to properly display white light. White is established by pointing the camera at a pure white surface and holding down the white balance button. Many camcorders do this automatically. Once the camera understands white, the rest of the color spectrum falls into place. It is common to change the look of a shot by changing the white balance, fooling the camera into thinking another color is actually white. For example, white balance on pale, pale green and the overall color spectrum will shift toward red.

Wide shot See *Framing.*

Wild sound Sound, often dialogue or comments, recorded without accompanying video.

Wind screen A wind screen is a mic cover, aurally transparent, designed to reduce wind noise. A wind screen is usually made of low-density foam but can be made of cloth or fake fur. See *Mammal on a Stick.*

Wipe A wipe is a transitional device in which one screen image is progressively replaced by another. The method of replacement is called the wipe pattern. Wipes can be as simple as a vertical dividing line progressing across the screen or as complicated as a 3-D explosion. Wipes are different from cuts and dissolves in that most, other than the classic clock wipe, don't really have traditional meanings. They do suggest a major, but rarely somber, change in scene or storyline.

Wireless mic A microphone system that offers total mobility by relying on a radio frequency connection between the mic and the camera rather than wires.

Wrangler Someone assigned to handling the more unruly camera subjects. Most commonly, this term refers to animal wranglers but there are child wranglers as well.

Wrap A command marking the end of a shoot. Most often heard as, "That's a wrap!"

XLR See *Canon connector.*

Zebra pattern An optional indication of exposure available in some camera viewfinders, where areas brighter than a preset value are overlaid with dark, diagonal lines. Zebra patterns are typically set at either 75 or 80 percent, the recommended brightness of skin tones. Some prefer the zebra set at 100 percent.

Zoom lens A zoom lens is an adjustable lens with a variable focal length.

Zoom ratio Zoom ratio is the ratio of the longest focal length of a zoom lens to the shortest focal length.

Zoom Zooming takes advantage of the adjustable nature of the zoom lens to narrow or widen the camera's field of vision. A shot fully narrowed, or zoomed in, is considered telephoto.

PHOTO CREDITS:

About the Author

In a career spanning 25 years, Pete May has served as photographer, editor, producer, director, and writer on scores of television projects for the broadcast, corporate, and home video markets, including more than 50 award-winning travel, industrial, and documentary programs. He is recognized internationally as a leading authority in his field. Pete lives in Milwaukee, Wisconsin and enjoys hearing from readers at www.petemay.com.

Acknowledgments

Matt Allard
Mary Archer
The Astrodudes
Alicia Aubrey
Dave Ball
Rebecca Banks
Seth Banks
Lisa Bisciglia
Steve Boettcher
Rochelle Bourgault
Jan Brethauer—Jennifer's
    Talent Agency
Portia Cobb
Molly Collins
David Crause
Gordon Crimmins
Kurt Dalziel
Kurt Dennisen
Colleen Devlin
Pete Dickert
Bob Donnelly
Haley Dresang
Joel Dresang
Maxine Fleckner Ducey
Chip Duncan
Jon Duxbury
Anne Haas Dyson
Lisa Edgar
Genyne Edwards
Bill Elliot
Kristin Ellison
Jeff Enders
Alice Eubank
Farah Ewing
Steve Ewing
Bill Finn
Maddy Fischer

Robb Fischer
Vicki Fischer
Janet Fitch
Tess Gallun
Kenny Garman
Bob Gessert
Lisa Gildehaus
Ira Glass
Deb Glick
Gay Gluth
Regina Grenier
Athleen Haas
Dorinda Hartmann
Cora Hawks
Brent Hazelton
Eileen Healy
Kathryn Henry
Max Hoezl
Elizabeth Kay Hoylman
John Hoylman
Jerry Hsu
Bob Huck
Patrick Jarvis
Matt Johnson
Evan Jones
Nelson Jones
Hillary Jones
Tom Kertscher
Ellen Koehl
Jason Koehl
Taylor Jade Koehl
Dave Kuhnen
Bob Landaas
Larry Lauffer
Jim Lavold
Kathleen Lawler
Bill Leinenkugel

Dick Leinenkugel
Jake Leinenkugel
John Leinenkugel
Beth Logan
Jim Logan
Mader Communications
    Group
John Mader
Mark Maiman
Mainly Editing
Barry Mainwood
Julie Mainwood
Mary May
Peter May Sr.
John McCullough
Dan McGuire
Harry Milke
Jeff Mikula
Brad Milsap
Doug Misner
Dan Mooney
Kathy Morales
Kristy Mulkern
Dave Murphy
Lucy Navas-Watson
Mike Nichols
Northwestern Mutual Financial
    Network
Willie, Megan, and Jay Olsen
Mary Ann Onorato
Steve Pantaleo
Sofia Paredes
Dan Poh
Jill Prescott
Brad Pruitt
Otto Rammer
John Rankin

Carol Rathe—Arlene Wilson
    Talent Agency
Guy Repa
Joette Rockow
Carol Rockow
Amy Rohan
Bradd Romant
Mike Roth
Barry Sattler
Keith Schmitz
Paul Sendry
Jimmy Sammarco
Diane Smith
Jenna Smith
Rick Smith
James Steinbach
Scott Stueckle
tabula rasa
Susan Templin
Paul Tepper
Stephanie Theisen
Marcia Thurnbauer
Deanna Tillisch
David Toy
USAV
Versant Communications
Brent Vitale
Sarah Vowell
Keri Walker
Peter Wejksnora
Donna Weller
Pat Westman
John Wilson
Karl Winkler
Charlie White
Denise White
Dave Zale